A DREAM DEFAULTED

A DREAM DEFAULTED

The Student Loan Crisis Among Black Borrowers

JASON N. HOULE
FENABA R. ADDO

Harvard Education Press
Cambridge, MA

Paperback ISBN: 978-1-68253-756-5

Library of Congress Cataloging-in-Publication Data is on file.

Published by Harvard Education Press,
an imprint of the Harvard Education Publishing Group
Harvard Education Press
8 Story Street
Cambridge, MA 02138

Cover Design: Ciano Design
Cover Image: Vectorig/DigitalVision Vectors via Getty Images

The typefaces in this book are Minion Pro and Myriad Pro.

CONTENTS

Foreword / vii

Introduction: Missing Race in the Student Debt Debate / 1

1 The Racialization of Student Debt / 13

2 Off to College, Into the Red / 29

3 Progressing Through College: No Room for Error / 45

4 Life After College: "It Just Seems Like You're Going to Pay Forever" / 67

5 The Hidden Costs of Debt Repayment / 85

6 Student Debt and the Reproduction of the (Fragile) Black Middle Class / 107

7 Upstream and Downstream Solutions / 123

Afterword: The COVID-19 Pandemic / 143

Methodological Appendix / 147

Notes / 157

Acknowledgments / 181

About the Authors / 183

Index / 185

FOREWORD

Our nation remains in the midst of concurrent crises—a public health crisis and an economic crisis disproportionately ravaging our Black communities and threatening the livelihoods of Black workers and families. The COVID-19 pandemic has laid bare many of our nation's deeply entrenched inequities and disparities—including the ways in which our student loan debt crisis has disparately impacted the financial resiliency of the Black community and hindered our ability to build wealth and prosper. In this book, Jason Houle and Fenaba Addo treat the student loan crisis as what it is: a racial justice issue. They show how the rise in student loans has been racialized and highlight the voices of Black borrowers who have been so deeply impacted by this system.

In this ongoing moment of national reckoning, we must remain unapologetic in our efforts to dismantle policies and systems that perpetuate and exacerbate racial inequities in our country and build the foundation for a just and equitable future. Addressing the student loan debt crisis as the racial and economic justice issue that it is, is critical to this goal.

For too long, the narrative surrounding student loan debt has ignored the ways in which our predominately debt-based system of financing a higher education has reinforced the racial wealth gap and exacerbated racial inequality. Due to systemic racism, generations of policy violence like redlining and employment discrimination, Black families have been locked out of wealth-building opportunities. As a result of the uneven and lingering financial impact of the Great Recession, when Black families saw their net worth cut in half, many of us are still struggling to fully recover. Failed policies that have resulted in the chronic underfunding of our Historically Black Colleges and Universities, community colleges, and state public universities have contributed to skyrocketing college costs and pushed a higher education further out of reach for far too many.

The culmination of these systemic failures has driven Black and low-income families to borrow more often and at higher levels simply for the chance to earn the same degree as their white counterparts. Due to ongoing discrimination in the workplace and persistent race and gender pay gaps, Black borrowers are more likely to face challenges repaying these debts and default at higher rates than their white peers, as Houle and Addo convincingly show in this book. It is time to confront this crisis head on.

Over the course of the pandemic, the federal government has recognized the economic burden of student debt and provided relief to millions through a historic moratorium on student loan payments. The payment pause has provided millions of borrowers and their families with an extra layer of financial protection that has helped them cover health-care costs, childcare, and keep food on the table as the pandemic persists.

But it is clear that this crisis requires bold and sweeping action to provide permanent relief to the forty-five million federal student loan borrowers—disproportionately Black and brown individuals—who continue to find themselves crushed under the weight of this debt. Thankfully, within the Higher Education Act, Congress granted the President of the United States, through the Secretary of Education, the authority to make broad-based student debt cancellation a reality.

Earlier this year, along with Senators Elizabeth Warren (D-MA) and Senate Majority Leader Chuck Schumer (D-NY), I reintroduced H.Res. 100, legislation outlining a pathway for President Biden to unilaterally cancel $50,000 in federal student loan debt. We know that student debt cancellation, by executive action, is one of the most effective ways to provide sweeping relief to millions of families while helping to reduce the racial wealth gap and lay the groundwork for an equitable and just long-term recovery. In this moment, our communities deserve and demand bold action. They deserve and demand a more just and equitable future. Student debt cancellation is core to these demands, and we are closer than ever to getting this done.

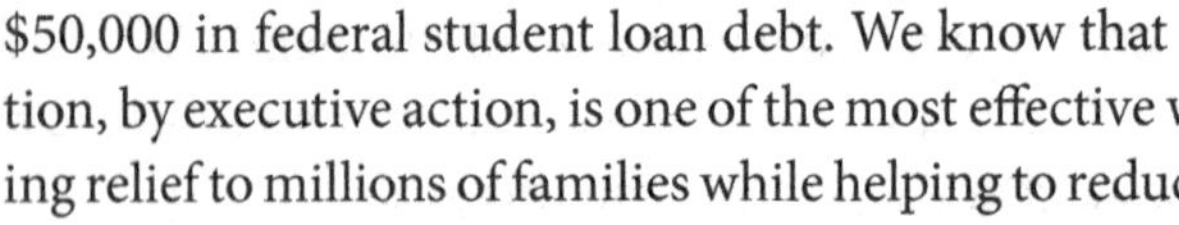

Ayanna Pressley
Member of Congress

INTRODUCTION

Missing Race in the Student Debt Debate

When we think about student debt in the United States, we often reflect on the stories we hear in the media. In November 2015, the *New York Times* published a story on student loan debt that focused on the plight of Liz Kelley, a college graduate, mother of four, and high school teacher who owed a whopping $410,000 in federal student loans.[1] In 2017, *USA Today* profiled Melissa Cefalu and her husband, Andrew, two white-collar professionals saddled with $365,000 in debt.[2] One year later, they profiled Jodi Meyers, whose $60,000 in student debt kept her dreams of homeownership on hold.[3] The *Chicago Sun Times* highlighted Tiela Halpin, who said she "expects to die" before repaying her $80,000 debt, as well as Amanda Spizzirri, a four-year college graduate with $90,000 in debt who is struggling to repay her loans while working as a barista and a server.[4]

Such stories, while powerful, newsworthy, and indicative of real economic pain, are outliers. They misrepresent the burden of debt and its implications for both current and former college students in this country. Student loan experts would be quick to point out the various ways that these cherry-picked examples of young people are not representative of, or indicative of, a student loan debt crisis.

First, they would note that these large student debt figures are not representative of the average borrower—very few students have debt burdens this high. In 2018, 56 percent of borrowers held less than $20,000 (or 35 percent held less than $10,000), while 33 percent of the outstanding federal education loan debt was held by 6 percent of borrowers owing more than $100,000.[5] They would also note that those who do have six-figure debt loads have little difficulty paying it off. We know, for example, that people with $100,000 or more in student debt tend to be doctors, lawyers, and other professionals who accumulated debt in graduate school, but their lucrative occupations make it relatively easy for them to pay down that debt. In fact, those who default on their loans are far more likely to have relatively small amounts of debt—think $1,000 or $2,000—than large amounts of debt.[6] They might also note that all the people profiled in the preceding paragraphs are four-year college graduates (or more), who tend to struggle less with debt than those who do not complete college. But what policy wonks and scholars might fail to recognize is that the young adults profiled here are all white Americans.

In sensationalizing the problem of student debt, the media have, not surprisingly, made the face of student debt a white one. Jen, a Black woman profiled by BuzzFeed, has a story that more accurately reflects the empirical and racial reality of student loan debt in the United States.[7] Jen has $50,000 in debt and is now on an income-based repayment plan after struggling to repay her loans. Jen's $50,000 in outstanding student loan debt is higher than the national average, but research shows that Black borrowers are more deeply indebted than their white counterparts.[8]

In addition to *accumulating* more debt, Jen, like many other Black borrowers, struggled to *repay* her debt and defaulted on her student loans.[9] Racial disparities in student loan default are, to be frank, massive. Black college graduates are more than five times as likely to default on their loans in the decade following graduation than white college graduates.[10] Judith Scott-Clayton, an economist and financial aid expert, calls these high default rates a "crisis" among Black college students—a correct assessment in our opinion. These stark racial disparities in student loan debt accumulation and repayment make it clear that race and racial inequality are central to understanding student loan debt in the United States. Any discussion of student debt that fails to consider race is missing a crucial piece of the puzzle. The problem, however, is that too much of the public discussion about student loan debt has failed to recognize this point.

Among scholars and policy makers, there are differing opinions on whether student loan debt constitutes a crisis. Some argue that it is self-evident that student loan debt is a crisis and that a generation of young people (and their parents) are drowning in a sea of student debt.[11] They see a debt *accumulation* crisis, driven by a real crisis of college costs. Others argue there is not a student loan *accumulation* crisis, but a student debt *repayment* crisis, given that almost 20 percent of federal loan borrowers are in default.[12] Then there are those who argue that rising student debt is no crisis at all—that the typical debtor does not devote much more of their income to student loan payments today than they did a few decades ago and that the economic value (or wage-surplus) of a college degree remains as high as ever.[13] They might argue that we do not have a debt crisis, but a completion crisis, as the risks of failing to complete a college degree are high, and completion rates have stagnated even in the face of a growing college-going population. Still others might say that student loan debt is a terrific, and rational, investment: for the debt you might accrue for the price of a (very expensive) car, you get a lifetime of social and economic benefits that come with a college degree. So, is student debt a crisis, or is it not? In the end, the answer depends on whom you ask and whom you believe. But we argue that these are not mutually exclusive issues. Depending on your evidence, the case could be made for an *accumulation crisis*, a *repayment crisis*, a *college completion crisis*, or *no crisis at all*. All of these positions hold some kernel of truth. Our question is, then, for *whom* do we see evidence of a crisis, and for *whom* do we not?

Our answer is that student loans are a crisis for Black borrowers. To the extent that student loan debt does all the things that we fear it does—that it holds back a talented generation of young people socially and economically, that it creates a drag on the economy, that it makes college less effective at promoting upward mobility—it does so in a way that reproduces and exacerbates the stark racial divides in this country.

This is the story we tell in this book: that the student debt crisis, though it may not be a crisis for all, is a crisis for Black borrowers. We focus on Black borrowers not because other groups of color do not struggle with debt, but because these are the borrowers for whom the crisis is most dire. For example, Black-white disparities in debt accumulation and repayment are substantially larger than the disparities among other groups of color, including Asian American and Latinx borrowers.[14] And, the typical Black family has less wealth than Asian American, Latinx, and White families.

In this book, we argue that racial disparities in student debt both reflect and contribute to the persistence of racial economic inequality among the current generation of college-going young adults. Racial disparities in student debt are not only a product of centuries of systematic racism and exclusion, but this debt holds back the next generation of young adults and helps to reproduce these long-standing racial inequalities. Broadly, we contend that in an era of rising college costs and declining support for higher education, Black young adults start their careers deep in the red, take on far more financial risks and obligations, and reap fewer rewards from their education than white college-goers. These racial disparities grow across the early life course and contribute to the fragility of the next generation of the Black middle class. Considering these trends, we argue that student debt is a new mechanism by which racial, social, and economic inequalities are reproduced across generations.

SOCIAL INEQUALITY AND THE ROOTS OF RISING STUDENT DEBT

From 2003 to 2019 outstanding student loan debt in the aggregate increased by more than 500 percent and passed the $1 trillion mark, as shown in figure I.1. According to the Federal Reserve Bank of New York, as of 2018 aggregate outstanding student loan debt is at $1.5 trillion and counting and has surpassed credit card debt ($0.85 trillion) and auto loan debt ($1.28 trillion) on the household balance sheet. Only mortgage debt is higher. These aggregate student loan figures partially reflect a growing college population: as more people go to college, more people borrow, and thus aggregate debt increases. However, even among those who are attending colleges, average debt balances are on the rise. From 1996 to 2016, the percentage of graduating seniors who borrowed while in college increased from 58 percent to 69 percent.[15] During the same time, the average inflation-adjusted average debt load of four-year college graduates with debt increased by over 50 percent, from $19,900 to $30,000. Similar increases can be observed among two-year college graduates and those who do not complete college.

In addition to growing balances, student debt has been getting harder to repay. Default rates have been rising steadily over the last two decades. Judith Scott-Clayton shows that, twelve years after college entry, 10 percent of the cohort that started college in 1996 had defaulted on a federal student loan. For those who started in 2004, the default rate was nearly 20 percent. And she projects that nearly 40 percent of these borrowers will default on their loans by 2023.[16] Default rates capture extreme distress: only borrowers who have failed to make a payment for 270 days are in default. But even those who are able to make their payments struggle to pay down their debt. Recent estimates show that less than half (47 percent) of borrowers in repayment have paid at least one dollar toward their principal five years into repayment, suggesting that millions of borrowers are not making much

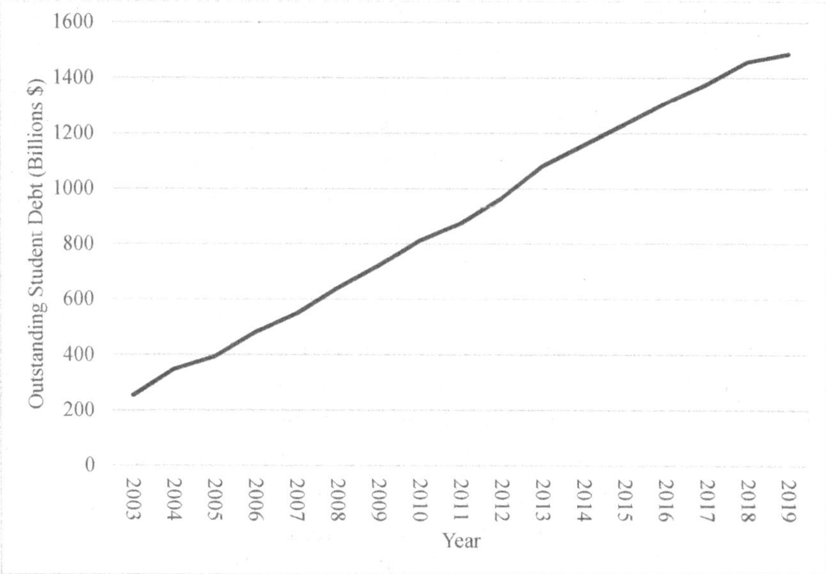

FIGURE I.1 Aggregate outstanding student loan debt in the United States

Source: Federal Reserve Bank of New York, www.newyorkfed.org/microeconomics/topics/student-debt

progress toward paying down their debts, even if they are not defaulting on their loans.[17] The numbers suggest, then, that student debt is on the rise and is getting harder to repay. But what explains these trends?

Some politicians and pundits have pointed to individual fiscal irresponsibility as a key driver of rising student loan debt. In 2012, Congresswoman Virginia Foxx (R-NC), former chair of the House Committee on Higher Education, famously stated:

> *I went through school, I worked my way through, it took me seven years, I never borrowed a dime of money. I have very little tolerance for people who tell me that they graduate with $200,000 of debt or even $80,000 of debt because there's no reason for that. We live in an opportunity society and people are forgetting that. I remind folks all the time that the Declaration of Independence says "life, liberty, and the pursuit of happiness." You don't have it dumped in your lap.*

Congresswoman Foxx's comments underscore a favorite talking point of some pundits: if you find yourself in debt, it is a result of your own poor financial decision-making and lack of hard work. Media stories, too, have picked up on this theme, blaming rising debt on college students' flagrant spending habits. Media coverage in the *New York Post* and *Forbes*, for example, used questionable evidence to argue that college students are squandering their student loan checks on spring break trips, booze, and drugs.[18] This narrative would have us believe that rising student debt can be reduced to bad character and poor decision-making.

This narrative is obviously false and needlessly stigmatizes student loan debtors. For instance, in a recent study we found that measures related to financial decision-making, such as financial literacy and risk preferences, have no correlation with student loan debt accumulation or repayment.[19] This story is not about millennials being irresponsible misanthropes. Rather, it is about students having no choice but to borrow money, and a lot of it, in pursuit of a college degree.

As the late sociologist C. Wright Mills would point out, Foxx's narrative misconstrues a *social problem* as an *individual trouble.* Why was Congresswoman Foxx able to attend University of North Carolina–Chapel Hill and graduate debt-free, while the median UNC graduate leaves school with $16,661 in debt today?[20] She may have worked hard and was careful with her money, but that does not explain why she was able to avoid accruing debt. Congresswoman Foxx went to a public university at a time when public universities were truly public. High state and federal appropriations allowed institutions like UNC to keep their costs low. In 1968, when Rep. Foxx was in college, annual in-state tuition at UNC–Chapel Hill was $2,193 in today's dollars. In 2018, in-state tuition was more than four times higher ($9,018).[21] But tuition is not the only cost that has increased since Rep. Foxx's college days. The cost of living, including room and board (or housing more generally), books, and other miscellaneous costs necessary for any college student, has increased even more rapidly. In 1968, the suggested room, board, and miscellaneous costs at UNC were $5,617 in today's dollars—about one-third of what the average UNC student should expect to spend today while going to college to simply eat, purchase their textbooks, and eke out a living. It comes as no surprise, then, that Rep. Foxx was able to graduate from college debt-free while working only part-time. In 1968, you would have to work only twenty hours per week at a minimum wage job to keep up with the costs of tuition and the costs of living, plus some additional expenses. A student today would need to work the equivalent of more than *two* full-time minimum wage jobs to keep up with these costs and graduate debt-free.

To compound the problem, the minimum wage, adjusted for inflation, has barely moved in decades. This phenomenon is not unique to UNC–Chapel Hill: college costs (tuition and living expenses) have risen dramatically across the country, at private and public colleges, at two-year and four-year institutions, over the last several decades. According to the National Center for Education Statistics, in the last four decades, these college costs (adjusted for inflation) increased by over 165 percent at four-year public colleges and nearly 200 percent at four-year private colleges. At two-year public institutions—community colleges—the cost has doubled.[22]

It is clear from the scholarly evidence that rising student debt is not the result of individual failings, but structural failings. What are some of these structural failings? The simplest answer is that student debt is the result of a perfect storm of several key factors: (1) rising college costs, including both tuition and costs of living; (2) falling (or stalled) student aid in the context of stagnant family incomes; and (3) a changing landscape of higher education.[23] In short, college costs have been increasingly privatized. State, local, and federal appropriations for higher education have failed to keep pace with the growth of postsecondary institutions and populations. As a result, colleges, especially public colleges (the vast majority of students attend public institutions), have become more reliant on tuition to cover their operating costs. At the same time, federal, state, and institutional aid has not kept pace with rising costs, and students and families have been left to foot the bill. Not surprisingly, students and families have turned to student loans to bridge the gap between familial resources and the rising costs of college. In fact, student loans are now one of the most prevalent forms of financial aid (if it can be called that) for college students.[24]

This simple narrative is not wrong, but it misses wide variation in how students and their families experience and pay for college, as well as what happens once students leave college. It fails to recognize the role that racial and economic inequality play in the college experience, how much debt is accrued, and how easy it is to repay that debt after college.

Rising college costs have made it more difficult for the average family to pay for college, but this pressure has hit those with the least resources the hardest. In the last forty years, median family incomes have changed very little, with most income gains over this period accruing to the top 1 percent (or more accurately, .01 percent) of earners.[25] To make matters worse, most federal and institutional aid considers familial income, but not familial wealth, despite vast inequalities in wealth (and thus the ability to pay for college) at similar income levels. Thus, Black families are hit especially hard given the racial wealth gap: on average, white families have thirteen times greater wealth than Black families.[26] In short, families have been asked to do more with less: to help cover the rising costs of college, despite not seeing equivalent gains in their economic status.

Changes in the landscape of higher education—both in the number and type of institutions—are also an important part of this story. Students of color and Black students in particular have made important gains in college enrollment over the past several decades. But just as access to postsecondary institutions has increased throughout the course of the twentieth century, these institutions have become more stratified and segregated in ways that may exacerbate, rather than ameliorate, inequality.[27] Wealthy, elite institutions—such as private colleges and public flagship universities—have been able to weather the cuts to higher education thanks in part to a strong pool of wealthy alumni donors and large endowments. These are the schools that primarily serve white and more affluent students. Schools that primarily serve students of color and other disadvantaged students—including regional colleges, branch campuses, and minority serving institutions (MSIs)—have been the hardest hit by cuts to higher education. First-generation, low-income, students of color, and especially Black students are more likely to attend these underfunded colleges and universities, which often have fewer financial and social resources to support students.[28]

What emerges from this picture is that it is difficult to understand student debt unless we recognize the importance of social inequality for debt *accumulation* and *repayment*. In our early research, we found that youth from socially and economically disadvantaged backgrounds—low-income and first-generation, as well as students from single-parent households—accumulate substantially more student debt in their pursuit of a college degree than their more advantaged counterparts. The reason, in part, is that their parents simply cannot contribute financially to college in the way that families of students in more advantaged families can.[29] Importantly, we find that these social inequalities in debt are largest at more expensive institutions, suggesting that rising costs have led socially disadvantaged populations to borrow more. As these costs have risen, inequalities in debt accrual have emerged and widened over time.

Inequality also shapes students' ability to repay debt. Not only do socially disadvantaged students need to borrow more to go to college, but they are also far more likely to attend underresourced schools that may provide fewer opportunities in the labor market and have high dropout rates. Four-year college graduates, who are far more likely to be white, and from middle- or upper-class backgrounds, tend to have relatively low unemployment rates and high wages, and thus have little difficulty paying down their debt. In the decade after leaving college, only 5.6 percent of four-year college graduates have defaulted on their student debt, compared to 14 percent of two-year college graduates and 24 percent of those who left college without a degree.[30]

When we take this research together, it becomes clear that to understand rising debt, we need to take into account the importance of social inequality as it unfolds over time and across individuals' lives as they age: how inequalities in students' social background (their parents' generation) lead to inequalities in debt; how what happens in college matters for how much debt students take on and how easy it will be for them to repay for debt; and how their social and economic success (or lack thereof) after college matters for debt repayment. This is a process that unfolds over time: across generations as parents (and grandparents) pass on wealth and resources to their adult children; and within generations as students enter and advance through college, borrow money to realize that possibility, and later transition out of college and into adulthood.

Much of the discussion that surrounds student debt and inequality focuses on social class: how parents' income and other resources shape how families pay for college, or how first-generation students fare in college. While these factors are important, there has been less discussion on the importance of race and the experience of Black students. These discussions fail to account for the fact that many of the social and economic disadvantages described here are faced by Black students more so than white students. Black students are also disproportionately enrolled in postsecondary institutions that are at best underfunded and at worst predatory, and they face racial discrimination, racism, and other hardships that shape their debt accumulation and repayment both during and after college.

Focusing on race and racism reveals important lessons that have been hidden from discussions on student loan debt. For example, previously we noted that four-year college graduates have little difficulty repaying their student debts and have substantially lower default rates than noncompleters. This statistic suggests a rather simple solution to the student debt problem: increase college graduation rates, and debt will be easily repaid. But what this solution misses is that a four-year degree does not provide the same protections for borrowers of color, and especially Black students. The same data that show low default rates among four-year college graduates also reveal a gaping racial gap: only 4 percent of white college graduates default on their loans, compared to an astonishing 21 percent of Black college graduates.[31] A college degree is not paying off for Black borrowers in the same way that it does for white borrowers. The student debt crisis cannot be solved by higher education reform alone.

The central argument of this book is that rising student debt is racialized, and is both a consequence of racial inequality and a cause of a new, emerging form of inequality among the next generation of young adults. Drawing from a decade of our research, we contend that racial disparities in debt are large and increase across the early adult life course and that racial disparities in student debt are contributing to Black-white wealth inequality among a recent cohort of college-going young adults.[32] We assert that racial disparities in debt accrual and repayment reflect existing and historical processes of racialized economic hardship and discrimination that accumulate across the life course for recent cohorts of young adults to create inequalities in debt and debt burdens. If we want to understand how and why Black students become more deeply indebted and have more difficulty repaying debt, we need to look beyond what college people choose to attend and their major choice. We need to understand the broader social context: how racist policies and practices from this nation's foundation contribute to this process and how these long-standing racial inequalities influence how and why people take on debt and continue to shape indebtedness long after people leave college.

To make this case, we bring together new and existing qualitative and quantitative data on race and student debt. For this book, we interviewed nearly fifty Black student loan borrowers all of whom attended four-year colleges and universities. We intentionally limit our focus to this group because it is precisely the group for whom debt repayment is often thought of as a nonissue, and these borrowers represent a "best-case scenario" of the student debt crisis among Black Americans. A four-year college degree is one of the few reliable launching pads to the American middle class, and so our interview respondents provide a glimpse into the social origins of the fragility of the Black middle class, as well as a case study of how a college degree does not provide the same benefits for Black Americans as it does for white Americans. We weave these stories together with over a decade of largely quantitative academic research on the causes and consequences of student loan debt, including much of our own published and unpublished research. If our quantitative research provides convincing evidence of the student loan debt crisis among Black Americans, then our qualitative interviews give us a look into the lives of these borrowers and allow them a chance to tell their stories in their own words. We describe these data sources further in the Methodological Appendix.

The book is organized as follows. In chapter 1, we summarize what we know—and what we don't know—about Black-white disparities in student debt accumulation and repayment, introduce our interview respondents, and make the case that the student debt crisis is racialized. The remaining chapters follow respondents over time as they enter college and accumulate debt, leave college, and enter adulthood. Chapters 2 and 3 focus on *debt accumulation*: how and why Black students accumulate more debt in their pursuit of a college education than their white peers. Chapter 2 begins with the acceptance to college and focuses on how students and their families navigate the transition to college and fund the first year. Here, we ask how long-standing racial inequalities in parents' wealth, education, and income exacerbate Black students' need to borrow for college and complicate their transition to college. Chapter 3 centers on how students progress through college, and how the hardships they experience and the types of colleges they attend leave Black students with no choice but to borrow, and keep borrowing, to stay in school.

We then turn to *debt repayment*. Chapter 4 tells the story of Black young adults after they leave college and start repaying their student loans. This chapter documents the trials and tribulations as they try to both find their economic footing and navigate a complex student loan repayment system. Many turn to income-driven repayment (IDR) plans to help them balance their loans and their living expenses, only to find that IDR is either not accessible or does not offer the relief it was designed to provide. In chapter 5, we consider the consequences of student debt for economic, psychological, and social well-being and show how student loan debt has made the transition to adulthood more fragile and precarious for Black youth. Chapter 6 explores the consequences of rising student loan debt for intergenerational inequality. We focus specifically on the racial wealth gap—which is rooted in historical processes of racial discrimination and exclusion—and has increased in the wake of the Great Recession.[33] Here we argue that while higher education is often thought of as an "engine of upward mobility" and a ticket to the middle class, the student debt crisis has made the fragile Black middle class ever more fragile. Black youth are taking on student debt to achieve upward mobility and gain access to the middle class, but rising student debt has made these young adults economically insecure, effectively reproducing long-standing wealth inequalities by race.

In the concluding chapter we ask, "What can be done?" Here, we consider solutions to this multifaceted problem and argue that policy solutions must look beyond debt reduction and financial literacy and consider broader patterns of racial inequality and racial discrimination both inside and outside of institutions of higher education.

While we do not deny that going to college could be a key pathway to upward mobility—and perhaps one of the few pathways to mobility that remain in the twenty-first century—the benefits of college disproportionately accrue to white people, and the costs of college disproportionately burden Black people. In the end, education is not a panacea for racial inequality. To paraphrase stratification economists and scholars Darrick Hamilton and William ("Sandy") Darity, "higher education has not, and will not, solve the problem of racial inequality."[34] We add that in an era when students and their families are expected to cover a growing portion of rising college costs and go deep into the red to get through college, it might make matters worse.

1

The Racialization of Student Debt

In 2018, Stacey Abrams was the first Black woman to run as a major party candidate for governor of Georgia. Abrams made waves in the polls, running a tight race with Republican Brian Kemp, a white man. Her campaign was a surprise for a Democratic candidate in a deep red state. Like in any hard-fought political campaign, Abrams was subject to criticisms by the opposition. Chief among these criticisms was that her high student loan debt should disqualify her from political office after her financial disclosures were made public revealing that she had over $100,000 in student loan debt. Abrams wrote an op-ed defending herself, saying that "I am in debt, but I am not alone. Debt is a millstone that weighs down more than three-quarters of Americans. It can determine whether we are able to run for office, to launch a business, to quit a job we hate. But it should not—and cannot—be a disqualification for ambition."[1] But the damage was done, and the rebuke was swift. Abrams was accused of being "bad with money" and "unfit for office." Abrams's mostly white and wealthy detractors argued that her debt was evidence that she could not manage a budget, and that electing her would mean financial disaster for the state of Georgia. Abrams's detractors framed her debt as a reflection of her bad character. Ultimately, Abrams fell short in her bid for the governorship.

Abrams's experiences with debt, and the criticisms she received for it, are not uncommon among Black borrowers. Her experiences reflect two broader realities common among Black borrowers: (1) that Black college-goers often need to take on more student debt due to racialized economic inequality and have more trouble repaying debt for the same reason; (2) Black people are often subject to a racist double standard in that they are judged to be morally or culturally inferior because of their debts.

Many Black borrowers need to borrow, and borrow more, to go to college, which is in large part a function of historical and contemporary processes of racial inequality and discrimination. Abrams, for example, grew up in a poor family and racked up student debt because she could not rely on her parents to help pay for her college or expenses. She also took on debt to support her family while she was in school. As she notes, "Paying the bills for two households has taken its toll. Nearly twenty years after graduating, I am still paying down student loans, and am on a payment plan to settle my debt to the IRS."[2] Abrams's story of debt is not unlike that of many Black Americans: it is a story of intergenerational racial wealth inequality, of providing help to underresourced family members and kin, of being a first-generation college student.[3] As we show in this book, these factors are essential for understanding racial disparities in student loan debt accumulation, as well as debt repayment and its consequences.

Abrams was also subject to a racist double standard for her debts, with her opponents arguing that her debts showed that she was irresponsible and unfit to lead. The reality is that Abrams's debts are not uncommon among those in the political elite. Writing in the *New York Times*, Michelle Goldberg pointed out that Brian Kemp had faced little scrutiny for failing to repay a $500,000 business loan and was more deeply in debt than Abrams.[4] It is also not uncommon for law students to accumulate six-figure debt loads.[5] Given that many politicians are former lawyers, Abrams's debt is not unique among lawmakers. How she was judged for it and the consequences it had on her career, however, were different. As Goldberg writes, "It says something about the racial and class politics of owing money that Republicans nevertheless feel safe attacking Abrams for *her* debt."[6] The price Abrams paid for her debt is considerably steeper than the price paid by her white counterparts.

Abrams's case is but one example of how student debt has been racialized. We use the term *racialization* to refer to the social processes that both create and then maintain racial inequality. As sociologist Eduardo Bonilla-Silva writes, "racialization forms a real structure . . . racialized groups are hierarchically ordered and 'social relations' and 'practices' emerge that fit the position of the groups in the racial regime."[7] When we argue that student debt is racialized, what we mean is that racial disparities in student debt are both a result of historical and contemporary racial inequality and discrimination embedded in the structure of society, and also in effect justify, and reproduce, racial inequality. Abrams borrowed because she had no choice but to borrow, and then her debt was used in the court of public opinion to "prove" that she was irresponsible. Her debt became a *millstone* that weighed her down, complicating and perhaps costing her the governor's office.

The critique against Abrams is a common argument against Black people by white people in modern society. Bonilla-Silva notes that racism by whites in the post–civil rights (post-1960s) era is based on an ideology that nonwhite people are "culturally inferior" and that contemporary racial inequality is the result of these cultural failings (e.g., that Black people are lazy, criminal, or from broken families).[8] This ideology is racist, Bonilla-Silva argues, because it ignores historical, systemic, and structural injustices, while providing a *cultural* justification for racial inequalities that are in fact rooted in *structural conditions*. The critique of Abrams aligns with Bonilla-Silva's explanation: Abrams's debt is due to her bad decisions, while Kemp is doing what any good businessman would do. Case in point: Donald Trump is lauded (by some) as a brilliant businessman despite his multiple bankruptcies and history with failing to repay debts. Abrams was not extended that privilege. Trump was able to ascend to the nation's highest political office despite his debt, while Abrams's debt may have lost her the election. These two realities—that Black college-goers need to borrow more as a result of racial inequality, but then that debt is used as evidence for their moral or cultural failings, therefore reinforcing inequality—comprise our broader claim about the "racialization" of student debt in the United States. For interested readers, Louise Seamster's #blackdebtwhitedebt Twitter hashtag provides a wealth of examples of this racist double standard.[9]

Abrams is a successful author, politician, and activist, but her struggles with student debt are not uncommon among Black college-goers. We interviewed nearly fifty Black borrowers who attended four-year colleges and universities and heard stories about their debt accumulation and repayment that, while varied, all shared some striking similarities: nearly everyone we talked to felt they had no choice but to borrow to fund their college education; all of them went to college with *best-laid plans*—a clear plan for their course of study and how they would fund their college degree, but this was not enough to protect them from taking on excessive debts; and for too many, their debt feels like a *millstone that weighs them down* after they leave college. These are some of their stories.

Jourdin was a first-generation college student who did everything she could to save money when selecting a college. Even though she applied to fifteen colleges, she stayed close to home and chose the cheapest college—a regional public college in her home state—to qualify for in-state tuition. Her goal was to avoid taking on too much debt and not be a financial burden on her family. But when her dad lost his job, the family struggled to make tuition payments, and her *best-laid plans* went out the window. She took on $30,000 in private and federal student loans, and her parents took on thousands more in Parent Loan for Undergraduate Student (PLUS) loans. Since college, Jourdin has struggled to repay her debt, and her loan balance increased to $40,000 after she lost her job and put her loans in deferment. She moved back in with her mom to save money while she tries to repay her debt, but she's still not sure how or when she will be able to pay off her loans.

On the other side of the country, Georgia, who described her family as "middle class," went into her first year at a private liberal arts college secure in the knowledge that between financial aid and her parents' contribution, she would not have to worry about paying for college and could put all of her energy into her studies. But by the end of her college career, her financial aid dried up, her parents lost their jobs, and she was juggling four part-time jobs to afford her rent and tuition bill. She left undergraduate study with $20,000 in debt. Ever the planner, she said she's developed a "stress culture" around saving money, has trouble sleeping at night, and is constantly worried about how she will afford to pay down her debt.

Anthony was raised by his single mother, and around the time he was applying to colleges, she began showing early signs of a severe debilitating mental illness—a condition that would worsen while Anthony was at college. He went to college from 2003 to 2006 at a public flagship in his home state so he could stay close to home, but he had trouble juggling college, a full-time job, and what he described as a chaotic home life. After taking on $40,000 in debt in his first three years of college, he decided to leave before finishing his degree. Fast forward to today, and Anthony has deferred and defaulted on his loans, and now has a balance of over $70,000. He is currently enrolled in an online bachelor's degree program but has not yet finished his degree. When we asked him how he feels about his current situation, he said he doesn't have any regrets. "I'm never going to feel bad about doing what I need to do to put myself on a level playing field."

In the southern US, Danielle was a first-generation college student from a low-income family. Her family didn't know very much about paying for college, but a counselor told them that they shouldn't be scared away by the high sticker price of private colleges: Pell Grants and other financial aid should make college virtually free. So she applied, and got into a private Historically Black College (HBCU) in the south. But when she got her financial aid letter, she was surprised that it classified loans as a form of financial aid. On the recommendation of the financial aid letter, her family took out

$10,000 per year to pay for college. Balancing work and classes during her college career, she took six years to complete her degree. Today, she works as a representative at a call center and lives at home to care for her mother, who recently fell ill, and her younger sibling who suffers from a developmental disorder. After defaulting on her debt and struggling to make payments, her $40,000 in debt has ballooned to $68,000. Unlike Anthony, Danielle has regrets, and feels as though she went to college and into debt for nothing. "The company I work at now, my girlfriend works there with me, and she just got her high school diploma. So, it's like it hasn't done anything for me. . . . If I had a redo, I definitely wouldn't do it." She paused. "Unless I had a scholarship or went to a school that was free. Now, if I could do it without the loans and without all of that, yeah, I would do it all over again."

Lucy, a US-born child of African immigrants, attended a prestigious college in the northeast and left school with $50,000 in student loan debt. She feels as though she somehow slipped through the cracks: she was told that her college had enough financial aid to ensure that students did not fall into too much debt, but she didn't learn of these programs until it was too late. Since she has left college, her life has revolved around debt. She has tried to balance the need to find a job that allows her to pay down her debt, while also pursuing her career passions. She is currently enrolled in a master's degree program, taking on another $50,000 in debt in pursuit of that degree. She says she can't win. She feels as though she has to stay in school to get ahead, but the longer she stays in school, the more debt she accumulates. So why go?

WHY GO TO COLLEGE? "BECAUSE THERE IS NO OTHER OPTION"

> *You have to invest in your education because there is no other option.*
>
> —Debra

From a young age, many of our respondents were socialized to believe that going to college was the only option. Naomi recalled conversations with her parents that left no doubt that she would be attending college. "[My parents would tell me] 'You're going to go to school. You're going to get good grades. Don't bring home Ds, Cs, and Fs. And you're going to go to college because we went to college.' It was a very normal thing." One of the messages that our respondents emphasized was just how important it is to get a college degree. In her book *Lower Ed*, Tressie McMillan Cottom writes about the significance of the *education gospel* in the Black community, "a belief that pursuing education is 'personally edifying, collectively beneficial, and a worthwhile investment no matter the cost.'"[10] These Black young adults pursue and aspire to higher education to not only better themselves but also to gain access to secure professional jobs that they hope will buy financial stability for them, their families, and their communities. In so doing, Black students and their families are responding to several signals. One signal is that postsecondary education is an "engine of upward mobility" in US society, one that will gain them access to financial resources and allow them to live comfortably. The second signal is that due to racial disparities in the labor market, the need for a college credential is imperative, outweighing all potential costs.[11] While a college education may not level the playing field, they are in fact betting on its ability to be a mechanism for catching up, rather than dragging them further behind. This thinking highlights the inherent fear of the known alternative. Black Americans trail far behind white Americans in almost all socioeconomic indicators. This has been the case since the end of the Civil War and American chattel slavery, through Jim Crow, civil rights, and equal employment opportunity legislation, to the present. In short, the *education gospel* is rooted in structural realities of racial inequality and discrimination.

It is therefore unsurprising, yet not widely known, that Black students are more likely to attend and complete college than their white counterparts, after accounting for racial differences in socioeconomic background and college preparation.[12] Black students are, in fact, behaving quite rationally in their pursuit of postsecondary education, in part because they are keenly aware of the racial discrimination that they will need to overcome in the labor market and other arenas to succeed. Khadija said that her parents were insistent that she go to college because it would open doors that were not available to them. "It offers opportunities that allow one to be financially stable," she said. "I also think there's a bit of—if they had the opportunity, that's what they would have done. So I think they always had in their mind that our children are going to take advantage of the opportunities that are here." These parents' mantras are in line with reports that show 79 percent of Black parents believe it is extremely or very important for their children to earn a college degree.[13]

A belief in the power of a college degree—the education gospel—was near universal among our respondents. Calee was no exception. "I heard it pretty often that the way to make it was to go to college," she said. "I think coming from a life that I had come from, it was like you've got to do what you've got to do to get the degree. And everybody takes out [debt to do it]. That was my understanding at the time." Calee's path to college was one paved in social mobility dreams and individual and familial advancement, no matter the cost. But for these young people, access to college has come at a steep price, as they take on enormous risk and exorbitant student debts in the hopes that a college degree can bring them comfort, security, and upward mobility. In this sense, they're on the front lines of a new form of racialized economic inequality.

These are just a few of the stories of Black student borrowers that we feature in the book. Everyone we interviewed is part of a new generation of Black young adults who are attending college at higher rates than their parents' generation.[14] Like many Black young adults, they are committed to higher education and are part of a society that has bought into the *education gospel*: they believe in the power of higher education for bettering their future and communities.[15] And so they go.

RACIAL DISPARITIES IN DEBT ACCUMULATION AND REPAYMENT: LARGE AND GROWING

Racial disparities in student debt and the racialization of student debt did not happen overnight. In the 1980s and '90s, few Black families held any student debt and were about as likely to have student debt as whites.[16] Recent data from the Survey of Consumer Finances shows the emergence of a racial debt disparity. In 2001, 15 percent of Black households held student loan debt, compared to around 10 percent of white households. By 2013, this disparity had tripled, with 32 percent of Black households holding student debt and only 18 percent of white households reporting student debt.[17] These racial disparities in student debt are substantially larger than racial disparities in credit card, mortgage, and automobile debt.

In the aggregate, these growing disparities reflect increasing access to college among Black Americans. It makes sense that the racial debt gap may be increasing in the aggregate if more Black people are attending college and thus need to borrow. But growing college attendance is not the only reason. If we zoom in on what is happening only among those who go to college, we also find evidence for a growing racial debt gap. In our analysis of two longitudinal datasets that follow two cohorts (or more colloquially, "generations") of people who hit their mid twenties in the mid-1980s and the mid-2000s, we find clear generational differences in student debt among college-goers.[18] In the 1980s, 16 percent of Black college-goers reported having any student debt, compared to 18 percent of white college-going young adults. A negligible difference. Fast forward to the mid-2000s, and 44 percent of white college-going young adults reported having student loan debt, compared to 52 percent of Black young adults.[19]

Part of these growing disparities are because Black young people are gaining access to college at a time when the cost burden is being shifted to students and their families. Black postsecondary enrollment has increased markedly over the past several decades.[20] For this reason, many Black college-goers are the first in their family to go to college; they are first-generation college students. Anthony is one of these students. One of the things he said frustrates him is that his mom and his grandmother did not understand what it meant to finance college. They never went to college, and so they don't know much about how to navigate financial aid. "I think for a lot of African Americans, we don't have much guidance when it comes from transitioning to high school or college because, it's not all of us, but there's a good majority of us that don't have family members that go to college," he said. "So we're trying to figure it all out—trying to figure it out on our own once we get there." Trying to figure it all out without the financial support, wealth, and knowledge of higher education often leads to more debt. But rising debt among Black Americans is not just a story of first-generation college-going. It cannot be understood without also recognizing structural racism.

Historically, Black Americans—people like Anthony's parents and grandparents—have been locked out of predominantly white colleges and universities due to explicit discriminatory practices. But while these explicit exclusionary practices may have declined, they were replaced by other—more subtle—practices that create difficulty and risk among more recent college-goers. At the historical moment when people of color were finally gaining access to college, public support for higher education declined, raising costs and shortchanging these new students. How this happened is a question of scholarly debate: some argue that states could no longer support colleges and universities as the number of students grew; it is much easier for a tax base to fund colleges if the student body is relatively small. But others argue that the intentions were more insidious: a long line of research shows that the (white) public and policy makers are less likely to support public spending on social goods like higher education and welfare if it may benefit "others" who are seen as unworthy, especially people of color.[21] Perhaps the most famous example here is Ronald Reagan's cuts to higher education. As governor of California in the 1960s, Reagan spearheaded funding cuts to the University of California system and helped create the tuition-based system that we know today. Many scholars argue that Reagan's cuts were at least partially in response to student unrest and protest that were centered around the Vietnam War and the civil rights movement. In public speeches and private correspondence, Reagan condemned the largely nonwhite protesters as "filthy" and "trash" and claimed that instituting tuition would make students value their education instead of protest.[22] Later, as president, Reagan continued his campaign to cut higher education and other socially funded programs, often invoking racist stereotypes of "bums" and "welfare queens" when selling his plans to the public.[23]

Whether these cuts were intentionally or unintentionally made in response to a growing nonwhite student body, the consequences are all the same: college became harder to afford, and racial disparities in debt emerged, and climbed, as a result. Sociologists Louise Seamster and Raphaël Charron-Chénier call this large and growing debt gap an example of "predatory inclusion."[24] That is, over the past several decades, Black youth have gained greater access to postsecondary institutions, but they have made these gains on exploitative or unequal terms—terms that thrust Black youth deep into the red relative to whites.

Racial Disparities in Debt Accumulation

Black youth like Jourdin, Anthony, and Danielle may have greater access to college than their parents, but they need to take on more debt to attend. How much more debt? The most recent estimates show that racial disparities in debt have been climbing for decades and are now at an all-time high. Judith Scott-Clayton and Jing Li find that among students who graduated with a four-year degree in 2008—at the height of the recession—Black borrowers left school with around $7,400 more in debt than whites.[25] Brandon Jackson and John Reynolds, using similar data, found that racial debt disparities were prevalent both among college graduates and those who dropped out of four-year institutions.[26] They found that Black students were both significantly more likely to borrow, and reported around $5,000–$10,000 more in debt than whites, regardless of whether or not they graduate or later default on their loans. Other scholars have found that Black-white disparities in debt are present among those who attend community colleges, for-profit colleges, public schools, and private schools.[27] That these racial disparities in debt are detectable among graduates, dropouts, and two-year and four-year college attendees suggests that racial disparities in debt cannot be reduced to a story of college completion or college choice. What happens in college is part of the story, but not all of the story. Something else is going on.

When we began researching this issue around a decade ago, we wanted to understand more behind these shocking numbers: why are Black students going deeper into debt than white students? What are the consequences? And what can be done about it? In our earliest research on this question, we analyzed data from the Bureau of Labor Statistics' National Longitudinal Study of Youth, 1997 Cohort (NLSY97)—an ongoing nationally representative longitudinal data collection effort that follows a cohort of young adults from around their teens through their mid-thirties. Unlike more specialized data that follow only college graduates, these data allowed us to track a range of college-goers from a variety of social backgrounds—including those who left college without a degree, like Anthony. At the time, our goal was to understand what led Black young adults to *accumulate* more debt than their white counterparts. What we found was that, by age twenty-five, Black college-going young adults reported nearly double the amount of debt as their white counterparts.[28] Put in dollar values, if the average white debtor owed $22,000, we would expect a comparable Black young adult to owe $43,516, as demonstrated in figure 1.1.[29] If you're wondering just how large these gaps are or how important race is for understanding student debt relative to other factors, for comparison, the Black-white disparity in debt is substantially larger than gender differences, differences by social class (parents' education and income), and about as large as differences in debt between those who attend for-profit colleges and those who do not.

But what explains these vast racial disparities in debt accumulation? Critics who accused Stacey Abrams of being unfit for office might argue that racial debt disparities can be explained by bad decision-making—a claim that we argue is rooted in racist cultural tropes. Instead, we found that racial disparities in student loan debt *accumulation* were more strongly explained by racial differences in family socioeconomic background and parental wealth, familial financial contributions to college, and attendance at underfunded and predatory colleges. As we show in figure 1.1, these factors explain the majority of the Black-white disparity in student debt at age twenty-five. And just as importantly, we found no support for the racist critiques of Stacey Abrams and other Black borrowers. In our analysis of the

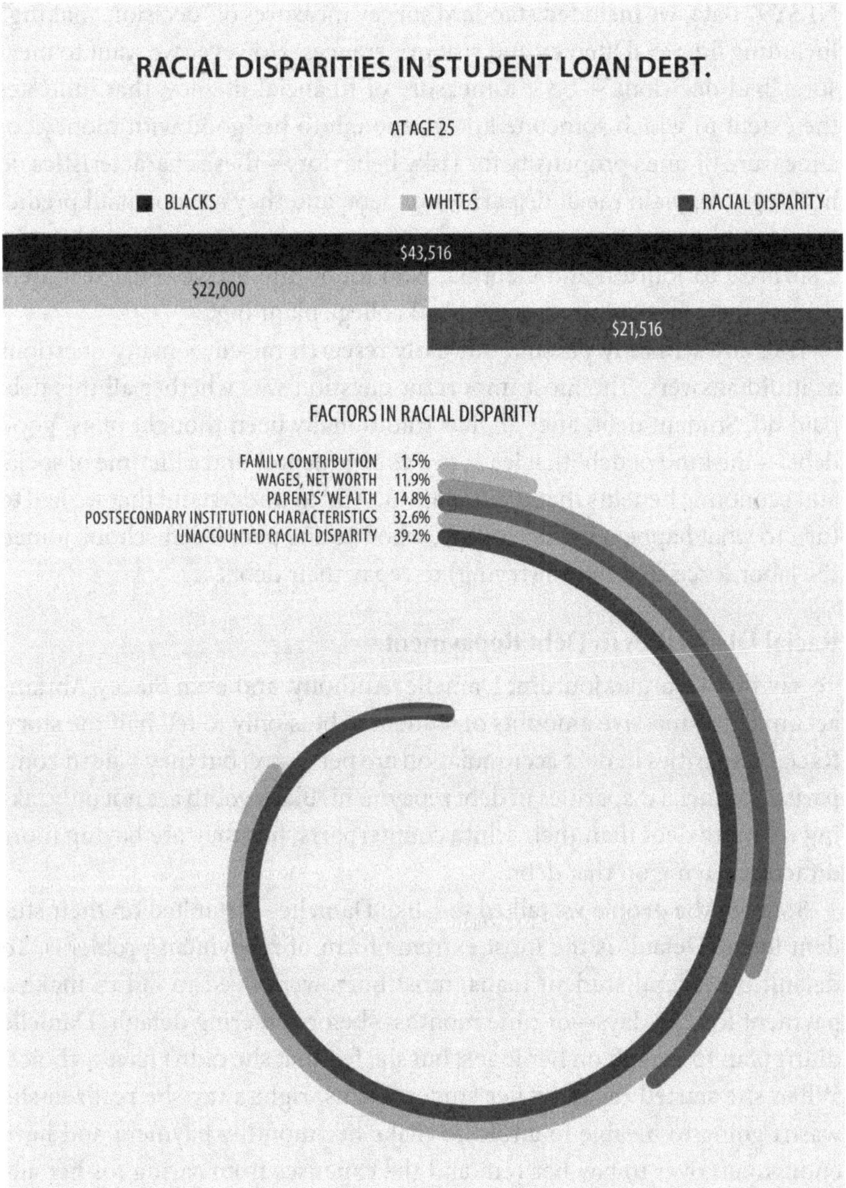

FIGURE 1.1 Black-white disparities in student debt at age twenty-five

Source: National Longitudinal Study of Youth, 1997 Cohort; Image courtesy Jeffrey Himpele, VizE Lab for Ethnographic Data Visualization

NLSY97 data, we included standard survey measures of "decision-making," including financial literacy and risk preferences. However we want to measure "bad decisions"—be it a measure of financial literacy, that indicates the extent to which someone knows enough to be "good with money," or a measure of one's propensity for risky behaviors—these characteristics do nothing to explain racial disparities in debt, and they are not at all predictive of student debt accumulation.[30] Of course, these results would not be a surprise to Jourdin and Georgia, who found themselves buried in debt despite their meticulous financial and college planning.

Like any scholarly pursuit, our early research raised as many questions as it did answers. The most important question was whether all this debt paid off. Student debt, after all, has traditionally been thought of as "good debt"—the kind of debt that leads to a college degree and a lifetime of social and economic benefits that accompany it. And to understand that we had to turn to what happened after college, when young people left school, joined the labor force, and began (trying) to repay their debts.

Racial Disparities in Debt Repayment

To say that Georgia, Jourdin, Danielle, Anthony, and even Stacey Abrams accumulated massive amounts of student debt is only to tell half the story. Racial disparities in debt accumulation are pervasive, but they pale in comparison to racial disparities in debt repayment. Black youth are not only taking on more debt than their white counterparts, but they are having more difficulty paying off that debt.

Some of the people we talked to—like Danielle—defaulted on their student loans. Default is the most extreme form of repayment problems. To default on federal student loans, most borrowers need to fail to make a payment for 270 days—or nine months—before entering default. Danielle didn't plan to default on her loans, but she felt that she didn't have a choice. When she started repaying her student loans, right away she realized she wasn't going to be able to afford to make her monthly payment and have enough left over to pay her rent and the expenses from caring for her ailing mother and young brother. So, she filled out the paperwork to get on an income-based repayment plan that would lower her monthly payment, and she waited. And waited. "I've been dealing with this paperwork for some months now. And I'm not understanding what's going on with it, why they aren't receiving things that I'm sending over to them. It's just been a real hassle this past year," she said. "I feel like I'm kind of on my own because I don't know exactly who to talk to." Danielle went into default while waiting for her income-based repayment, and as a result her balance has continued to grow, and she says her credit has been ruined.

Scholars and policy makers rely on aggregated default rates to understand the most extreme repayment problems. Racial disparities in student loan default—usually the best available measure of debt *repayment* that we have—are stark, and they have gotten worse over time. Scott-Clayton finds that among students who began at a four-year college in 1996, 7.4 percent of white people defaulted on their loans, compared to 23.4 percent of Black people—a three-fold difference.[31] Among those who began college in 2004, 12.4 percent of white people defaulted on their debt twelve years later, compared to 37.5 percent of Black people. In other words, racial disparities in default have existed since at least the 1990s—long before the massive rise in student debt—and over the course of the past decade, default rates among Black college-goers have increased by over 60 percent.[32] While those who do not graduate from college have the highest risk of default, even among college graduates we see stark racial disparities: over 20 percent of Black college graduates (one in five) defaulted on their loans within twelve years, compared to only 4 percent of white college graduates. The investment in a four-year college degree appears to be paying off for white borrowers, but not for Black borrowers.

Race is central to understanding student loan default in the United States. In their review of the literature, Jacob Gross and colleagues bring up two important points regarding the size and scope of racial disparities in student loan default.[33] First, race is a stronger predictor of default than almost any other factor, and race explains almost as much variation in default rates (20 percent) as degree completion (26 percent). Second, racial disparities in debt cannot be reduced to the types of colleges that Black and white students attend. Racial disparities in default persist even after adjusting for the type of college people attend and are present at almost every type of institution—two-year, four-year, public, and private. In other words, telling students they should make different choices about where they go to college will not solve this problem.

The data on racial disparities in default rates show a repayment crisis among Black borrowers. But default rates don't tell the whole story. Most borrowers—and most Black borrowers—do not default on their student loans, but that doesn't mean they can easily repay their debts. Lucy has never defaulted on her loans, but she feels as though she's constantly scrambling to keep up with her payments. When Lucy entered repayment, she was shocked at how much she owed and the monthly payment. "It was something ridiculous, like $900 a month and I was like 'Oh my goodness, I can't afford this, this is crazy.' Honestly, because I don't have any discretionary income, I really just pay the minimum." When we talked to her, Lucy had just gotten off the phone with her loan servicers because she was three days behind on her payments, and she was worried that one day she might miss a payment. "So it just feels like my debt is this heavy, oppressive force that's always with me." Lucy never defaulted on her loans, but her student debt has loomed large over her life. She said that her inability to find a job that paid her enough to keep up with her debts is one of the factors that led her to graduate school—which ultimately led her to take on more debt.

Loan defaults are indicators of extreme distress, but they are only the tip of the iceberg of the debt repayment crisis. Recent estimates show that less than half (47 percent) of borrowers in repayment have paid at least one dollar toward their principal five years into repayment, even though only a small minority of these borrowers will ever enter default.[34] This means that the majority of young adults are carrying debt well into their postcollege years that they are unable to pay down, or are accumulating debt through interest and fees. Our quantitative research suggests that repayment struggles vary dramatically by race.[35] Using data from the NLSY97, we tracked trajectories of debt accumulation and repayment beginning when individuals enrolled in college, until (in some cases) around fifteen years after they left college. What we found was astounding: on college exit, Black college-goers reported 85 percent more debt than their white counterparts, and this disparity more than doubled in the decade after they left college. Put differently, Black young adults have more debt a decade after they leave college than white people do when they leave college and before they start repaying their debts. The takeaway here is that Black youth start their young adult careers with more debt than whites, and this disparity grows over time, in large part because Black youth have a harder time repaying their debts.

As with any shocking finding, it would be easy to wonder whether these results are accurate. But other research teams—who use different data and methods—are coming to the same conclusion. A recent study by Judith Scott-Clayton and Jing Li tracks four-year college graduates—like Lucy—for about five years after they graduate and finds that while Black-white disparities in debt at graduation are large and pervasive, this disparity more than *triples* in the years following graduation.[36] Scott-Clayton and Li show that the Black-white debt disparity at graduation—around $7,400—balloons to nearly $25,000 just four years after graduation. They also find that nearly half of Black college graduates owe more than they did when they graduated, compared to only 17 percent of whites. Some of the reason, Scott-Clayton and Li contend, is that Black college graduates like Lucy are going on to graduate school and taking on more debt in the process. But some of it also reflects that white college graduates are having an easier time paying down their debts, while many Black college graduates are struggling to repay their debts, and watching their balances climb rather than fall, in the years after leaving college. Where there is smoke, there is fire.

Race matters for student debt, and it has only come to matter more over time. The racialization of debt that has increased *across* generations is also increasing *within generations*: the alarming racial disparities in student debt that have emerged over the last several decades only get larger as young people leave college and get older. The questions that remain, then, are Why do we see these massive racial disparities in debt, why do they seem to increase over time, and what are the consequences—for financial well-being, for upward mobility, and for racial economic inequality? To answer these questions, it is necessary to track individuals before they enter school and start accumulating debt; through college when they take on debt; and after college when they enter the labor force, start families, "transition into adulthood," and begin repaying that debt. In other words, it is necessary to take the long view, or a life course approach—and track people as they age, enter, and leave different social roles, and engage with different social institutions—to understand racial disparities in student loan debt.[37]

These are the questions that we have tried to answer in our quantitative research. In a 2019 paper published in the journal *Sociology of Race and Ethnicity*, we found that racial disparities in debt accumulation were in part a function of racial differences in family background and college experiences: Black students accumulate more debt in part because their families have less wealth and are not able to contribute financially to defray costs, and they attend underfunded colleges and universities. Racial disparities in debt repayment, on the other hand, were more strongly associated with young adults' economic and social well-being in the transition to adulthood, especially their employment history. We also found compelling evidence that racial disparities in student debt—themselves a result of the sedimentation of centuries of racial, social, and economic inequality in the US—contributed to the racial wealth gap among the latest generation of young adults. If we could snap our fingers and make Black and white student debt equal, the racial wealth gap among college-going adults would be reduced by nearly 25 percent.[38]

Our quantitative research suggests that racial disparities in student debt are pervasive and consequential, and that it is Black borrowers who struggle the most financially among college-goers in the twenty-first century. But the numbers, however shocking, tell only part of the story. The quantitative data can tell us what is happening but tell us little about the how or the why. Borrowers like Jourdin, Georgia, Anthony, Danielle, Lucy, and even Stacey Abrams help us understand the experiences, frustration, tragedies, and occasional successes, of student loan debt among Black Americans. Their stories are those of historical legacies and contemporary processes of structural racism and the racial wealth gap. Stories of the extraordinary risks that are taken on by Black young adults in pursuit of a degree; of colleges and universities that at best do not offer enough support and at worst are predatory; of young adults who leave college with high hopes, only to face a grim choice between paying their student debts and pursuing their dreams. These are the stories of the myth of racial progress betrayed by *predatory inclusion*, and how the racialization of student debt has led college to reproduce—rather than alleviate—social and economic inequalities by race. These stories reveal that solutions to the student debt crisis that are rooted in deficit frameworks—including financial literacy—are doomed to fail because the problem is a failure of social institutions and systems, not a failure of individuals. Racial disparities in student debt reflect and refract historical inequalities and injustices that date back centuries in the US, and the solutions must also be systemic.

2

Off to College, Into the Red

When Danielle received her acceptance to a private Historically Black College (HBCU) in the South, she was elated. Her parents were proud and hopeful when hearing the news; Danielle would be the first in her family to attend college and had an opportunity nobody else in her family had ever had.

Across the country, Naomi received her acceptance letter to a large public flagship university in the Midwest. A child of college graduates, whose siblings had all attended college, there was no question that she would go to college. For both Danielle and Naomi, the acceptance letter was a joyous moment and brought a profound sense of pride. But what comes next? The obvious answer is: college. The less obvious answer? How to pay for it.

Danielle and Naomi were accepted to college at a time when higher education has become more expensive, more difficult to navigate, and has put the onus on families and students to figure out how to pay for it. Rising costs have made students like Danielle and Naomi more reliant than ever on their family's social and financial resources to pay for and successfully transition to college. At the time the acceptance letter came, they had no idea just how much their family would struggle to pull together the money, manage unexpected expenses, and navigate a complex financial aid system to get them to college.

In a higher education system where students and their families are increasingly reliant on their own economic and social resources to get to and pay for college, Black students like Danielle—a first-generation college student from a low-income background—are at an extreme disadvantage and go deep into debt because of that disadvantage. On average, Black families have lower incomes, less liquid financial assets, and less familiarity and experience navigating the bureaucracy of college and financial aid than their white counterparts.[1] But even "middle class" Black students—those with college-educated parents with stable jobs and high incomes, like Naomi—struggle to pay for college and fall into debt. Naomi's family represents what social scientists have referred to as the *fragile Black middle class*; due to a legacy of slavery and racism, these "middle-class" families have little intergenerational wealth to draw from to pay for college or weather financial adversity.[2]

In this chapter we tell this story: college is a fragile entryway to the fragile Black middle class. After overcoming hurdles to get to college, Black students go to college in socially and economically vulnerable positions and have little room for error as they navigate the transition to college. These social forces conspire to make it harder for students like Danielle, Naomi, and their families to savor that moment of joy that comes with the acceptance letter. Instead, it plunges students and families into a complicated system that is expensive and difficult to navigate, creating frustration, burnout, and broken dreams. And it fuels vast disparities in debt by race.

"TAKE THE LOANS AND GO OR JUST NOT GO AT ALL:" STUDENT DEBT ACCUMULATION AND THE RACIAL WEALTH GAP

Most schools send the acceptance letter and financial aid package separately, and in that order. It is as if they both know and want students and their families, cloaked in excitement, to start envisioning their college life or their child's future at that school. By the time the financial aid package arrives, for many it becomes a question of *How do we make this happen?* rather than *Will it happen?* For many, this was the first moment when they realized that if they wanted to go to college, they would have no choice but to borrow.

When Danielle was accepted to a private liberal arts HBCU in the South, she did not worry much about how she would pay for school. She would be the first member of her family to attend college, and given her family's limited income, she knew that she would be eligible for a Pell Grant. She hoped that the grant would be enough to cover her tuition, room, and board, but she admits, "I really didn't understand much about college and the payment because no one in my family had gone to college prior to me going." But she sorted through the necessary paperwork on her own, filled out her Free Application for Federal Student Aid (FAFSA), submitted it online, and waited. When she got her financial aid letter, Danielle received a Pell Grant that covered a portion of the costs, along with a recommendation that she and her parents borrow around $10,000 for the year in student loans to make up the difference. As she puts it: "I really didn't know until I got the letter back with the financial obligations and stuff. And then when I got my letter back from FAFSA, and then it had the loans on there. And then I was just pretty much just stuck with the decision like, 'Take the loans and go or just not go at all.' So I just went with the loans."

Similarly, Naomi thought she would be able to afford college after receiving a full tuition scholarship to a major public flagship university in the Midwest, thinking that the patchwork of scholarships, federal aid, and other institutional aid would cover the remaining costs associated with room and board: "But I also thought—I was under the impression, by way of my family as well as my school, if you were smart enough and you get a good enough grade that the school will pay for you to be there. I really didn't understand fully. I didn't even know there was a separate cost of tuition and then room and board." After discussing the circumstances with her parents, Naomi took out a $9,000 loan in her first year to make up the difference between her scholarship, aid, and the cost of room and board.

Daniel, who attended a private MSI in the southeastern United States, admitted being flabbergasted when he first sat down with the financial aid officers at his school to work out how much he owed. Daniel received a prestigious $10,000 merit scholarship that required him to live on campus. At the time, he thought this scholarship would be enough: "So I got to the [financial aid] office, and Mom and Dad and I were just going through the motions, and we realized that, 'Hey, maybe we don't have enough to cover the expenses.' We thought everything was taken care of, because I got tons of scholarships, and I worked really hard. But that $45,000 number [the total cost of attendance in his first year] was just really daunting to me." Daniel was embarassed when he and his family couldn't come up with the money to pay for his first semester, and his account was put on hold as he came up several thousand dollars short on his bill. "I was eighteen at the time—so getting that email and going and finding out that I can't enroll in classes just really rocked the world—rocked my world and Mom's world as well. The financial aid officer just put this [loan] option in front of us and at that point, we had no choice." As Jourdin put it, "It wasn't really a conversation. It was just like, 'Well, you need to go to school. And you need to pay for it. And this is how you can do it if you don't have the money yourself.'"

The prospect of borrowing substantial sums of money—even $5,000 or $10,000—can be frightening for students who grew up in precarious financial situations. Hillary borrowed $5,000 in her first year at college, in addition to some financial aid, and anticipated that she would need to borrow that same $5,000 every year in order to graduate. "I remember being very scared about taking loans, but I do know my number wasn't so huge, and my parents were like, 'You have to take loans, and you're going to take it in your name,' because we heard too many stories of some people's parents basically paying all the kid's portion of the loans," she said. "So I took about $5,000 in loans or a little bit more than that because I know by the time I graduated in 2004, I had something around like $22,000 in loans. I just remember being scared about it. It seemed like a big number to me at that time, given that we didn't have much money." The financial aid officer assured Hillary that it was perfectly normal to borrow money to go to college. At the time she was in college, $22,000 was right around the average debt level for four-year undergraduates.[3] She took the advice . . . and the loans.

Like millions of other prospective students, Danielle, Daniel, and Hillary had no choice but to borrow if they were to go to college. Their surprise, confusion, and resignation to borrow are broadly representative of the experience that many Black students have when it comes time to pay for the first year.

Part of this surprise and confusion might stem from the socioeconomic, or social class, background of Black college-goers, who are more likely to be both low-income and first-generation college students than their white counterparts. Our quantitative research shows that low-income and first-generation college students are both more likely to borrow and take on more debt than their more socioeconomically advantaged counterparts.[4] Families with higher incomes, for example, are better able to financially prepare for college, anticipate the costs, and save for the eventual expenses that left Daniel and his family flabbergasted.[5] Having college-educated parents who have a level of comfort with college finances and an understanding of the system—what sociologists refer to as *cultural capital*—is similarly beneficial for students, and is associated with lower debt loads.[6] It might be easy to look at the data and conclude that it's all about class, not race.

Socioeconomic disadvantage by income and education is a convenient but insufficient explanation for racial disparities in debt. Naomi and others we interviewed had parents with college degrees and came from "middle-class" backgrounds, but they still had no choice to borrow substantially more than their white, middle-class peers. For these Black families, high incomes and college educations are not enough to overcome the vast, historic racial wealth disparities that make paying the high costs of college more difficult for Black families and drive racial disparities in student debt.

"Not Rich, but Also Not Poor"

When we asked our respondents to reflect on their family's financial resources when they were growing up, most, like many Americans, said they grew up "middle class." But Nathan paused when describing his social class background, before landing on "lower middle class." "We're not like . . . my mom is not wealthy, but she's not poor either, if that makes any sense," he said. "It's not paycheck to paycheck, but we don't have a lot of active money. I don't know how to describe our situation. I guess I'll say lower middle class."

Lack of "active money" or emergency savings, or not having the ability to save means that households tend to rely on earned income and steady employment for financial security and day-to-day expenses. This also means they are one job loss or unexpected expense away from financial ruin. Georgia, like Nathan, said that she grew up "lower middle class," but she was keenly aware just how fragile, precarious, and illusory her family's class status was. "My parents both graduated from undergraduate and graduate schools, so they both have graduate degrees . . . generally speaking, always had food on the table, always had a home over our head," she said. For many social scientists, her family's high education and comfortable lifestyle would be enough to classify Georgia as solidly middle class. But, she added, "the amount of debt that they had had an effect on our lives financially. We almost lost our home at one point because of debt and my parents' credit. Again, another categorization of not quite feeling middle class."

Similar to Naomi, Georgia and Nathan come from families that have all the traditional trappings of what many consider to be "middle class"—they had good, decent-paying jobs and college educations. But their families had little wealth (few assets, little savings, and high debts) that they could fall back on, making their middle-class status precarious and fragile. They are part of the fragile Black middle class, characterized by low levels of familial wealth and high rates of downward mobility out of the middle class.[7] While income, employment, and educational attainment may signal class status, access to wealth is what really defines it. Middle class stability is unattainable with wealth fragility.

Present-day racial wealth inequality reflects both historical legacies of government policies that extracted wealth from Black communities and current systems that exploit and continue to disadvantage wealth-building opportunities. And racial wealth disparities have grown, not shrunk, in the twenty-first century.[8] As of 2019, the median net wealth (total assets minus total debts) of white households was $188,200, compared with $22,400 for

Black households, or seven times as much wealth. We find similar disparities in parents' wealth among NLSY97 respondents who attended college, as we show in table 2.1. These wealth disparities make the Black middle class tenuous, and college increasingly unaffordable for Black students, who are disproportionately more likely to be wealth poor.[9]

Even more so than income or education, familial wealth is an important resource that drives racial disparities in student debt accumulation.[10] Most obviously, wealthy (white) families can tap into their savings or investment assets to help pay for college, and give money to their children for their education.[11] As we show in table 2.1, white families have substantially more financial assets (savings) than Black families, and on average contributed almost $12,000 to their children over the course of a college career, whereas Black parents contributed approximately $4,200. This is not to say that Black parents do not financially support their children; in fact, research indicates

TABLE 2.1 Racial disparities in parents' wealth among NLSY97 college-goers

	Respondent race	
	White	**Black**
	(N = 3258)	(N = 1244)
Parents' wealth (assets-debts)		
Mean net worth	174,871	48,494
Median net worth	101,376	9,497
% with Negative net worth	7%	16%
Parents' wealth by asset type		
Financial assets	31,001	6,363
% Home owners	74%	46%
Home equity (among owners)	98,202	41,517
Retirement accounts	48,211	13,280
Other assets	11,231	4,092
Parents' financial contributions		
Percent with college savings account	11%	6%
CSA amount among holders	40,786	27,068
Financial transfers to children in college	11,679	4,217

Source: National Longitudinal Study of Youth, 1997 Cohort

that despite having fewer resources Black families are more likely to provide financial support for higher education, even if their lack of wealth limits their ability to contribute as much as they would like to.[12]

Outside of savings and investment assets, it has become more common for families to tap into their home equity to help pay for college, which has important implications for racial disparities in debt. Home ownership and housing equity are typically the most valuable assets that families own, and are major drivers of the racial wealth gap.[13] White families are more likely to own homes than Black families, have greater home equity, and are more likely to see their homes appreciate in value over the life of their mortgage—trends that are evident among the parents of NLSY97 respondents.[14] This is true even among the wealthiest Black and white families. At the top of the wealth distribution, wealthy white families have higher levels of home equity and other liquid assets that can more easily be transferred to their children. This, in effect, means that white families can more easily liquidate their wealth—including their home equity—to help pay for college and protect their children from taking on debt. Not only are there vast racial wealth disparities, but white families are better positioned to use that wealth to invest in their children's education.

To illustrate this point, consider the central finding from one of our early analyses of student loan debt, published in the journal *Race and Social Problems*. Here, we asked whether parental wealth was associated with lower debt loads for young adult college-goers. Not surprisingly, it was: young adults from wealthy families left college with very little debt when compared to those from less wealthy families. But further investigation revealed a stark difference by race. Parental wealth was strongly associated with reduced debt loads among white young adults, but wealth had almost no effect on student debt among Black young adults.[15] Not only are white families wealthier than Black families, but they can more easily use that wealth to reduce their children's debt, which further fuels racial disparities in student debt.

Another, less obvious reason as to why racial wealth inequality drives racial disparities in debt is that that wealth is largely invisible on the FAFSA. For the most part, federal financial aid decisions are primarily based on household income rather than wealth. Applicants are asked to report assets, but they are not verified; this creates a disincentive to report savings, while increasing the likelihood of misreporting or nonreports. And, some assets—like home equity—are not reported on the FAFSA.[16] Not only does the typical white household have more wealth than the typical Black household, but Black households are much more likely to be income rich and wealth poor. How does this impact financial aid packages? Black and white households with similar incomes may have the same expected family contribution (or EFC), but the typical Black family will have significantly less resources to draw from to meet that need. This scenario creates a "middle income squeeze" among some middle-class Black students and their families: they make too much to qualify for most need-based financial aid, but too little to truly afford the rising costs of college, leading to higher debt burdens among students from middle-income families in comparison to their high- and low-income counterparts.[17]

That this middle-income squeeze disproportionately impacts Black families was not lost on many of our respondents. Corinne recalls her conversations about paying for college with her parents when she was in high school: "My parents were like, 'Listen, our income is very high, so you're not going to get financial aid. So you either get a full scholarship, or you're going to be taking out loans. We live in New York. Cost of living is high. They don't take any of that stuff into account.'" Lucy, too, conveys how being in this financial predicament stressed her out during her first year at an elite college in the Northeast. "I remember feeling very annoyed, and I felt kind of like I fell through the cracks, in a sense. Because it's like, okay. Well, my family is not poor enough to qualify for [most need-based scholarships]. But apparently, they make enough that they think I should be taking out all of this debt. It just didn't make any sense to me. So I found myself feeling really upset." This is one of the many ways that Black students like Lucy, Corinne, and their families—even though they come from "middle-class" backgrounds—find themselves struggling to afford college.

All Hands on Deck: Making a Way Out of No (Financial) Way

For many Black families who lack substantial financial resources and have college-bound children, figuring out how to pay for college can be a years-long process that requires "all hands on deck." Many of our respondents said their parents exhausted many different avenues to increase their knowledge about the process, how much it costs, and how to pay for it. Parents enlisted help and drew from the resources of their extended family and nonfamily social networks—what sociologists refer to as *social capital*. For a lucky few, these resources were enough to make college happen. Others put their hopes on scholarships that are difficult to attain but came with the promise of a free ride to college. When these resources were not enough, parents and grandparents stepped in, taking on debt to prevent students from taking it on themselves.

Many of the people we talked to credited their extended family—aunts, uncles, grandparents—with providing them a financial boost when they got to college. Daniel acknowledged his aunt for helping him pay for unforeseen expenses in college when his parents could not help. "Mom and Dad were just always there," he said. "But my aunt committed to what she called the *Aunt Scholarship*. She paid for my books every semester as long as I kept my GPA at a certain level. That was out of the kindness of her heart, which was a super-duper big help." Others received substantial financial help from their grandparents, including Charity, whose grandparents paid for her rent during her first semester in college when her financial aid and student loans were not enough to cover her living expenses in the city where she went to college. For Agnes, it was truly all hands on deck—parents, aunts, uncles, siblings, and grandparents. "Freshman year, everybody helped in terms of extra money that I needed. [I was] still broke, but if I needed something, I could ask. [But] that changed [after freshman year]."

Informal financial support from extended family is more common among Black families than white families, and it both reflects and can exacerbate racial wealth disparities.[18] For cash-strapped families, getting help from extended family members is a necessary strategy to pay for college, but it comes at a cost. Financial transfers sap grandparents, aunts, and uncles of their financial resources, diminishing their wealth.[19] For Daniel, Agnes, Charity, and others, this means that the money they counted on in the first year of college may not be available to them as they progress through college—a theme we return to in chapter 3.

Parents also sought out programs and schools that would provide them with additional resources for college. "I would say my mother was very proactive about making sure I had resources like college prep resources," said Elise, who attended an elite private college on the West Coast. "I was in a program where I got free SAT prep, college counseling, just the application process counseling. So I had someone reviewing my essays for free. And then they did a bit of financial counseling too. And it became clear then, at least for my mom, that it would be far less expensive to go to [an elite private university] where they had financial aid, an abundance of financial aid, versus a state school. So it was definitely trying my best to get into there to a top university because they have more resources." This social capital proved to be beneficial to Elise, helped her get accepted to a selective elite college, and allowed her to take advantage of her institution's generous financial aid packages. Elise was one of the few people we talked to who graduated debt-free, only acquiring loans once in graduate school. She credits her mom's diligence for her success. "I think her thing was being smart on the front end so you didn't have to really pay for college, which works in her favor. So, yeah, I think she understands that life works best when you put it that way."

After exhausting the resources from their networks, parents and students put their hopes into scholarships. Nearly everyone we interviewed recalled their parents telling them that they would need to apply for, and win, scholarships if they wanted to go to college. Corinne's family put it bluntly: "You either get a full scholarship, or you're going to be taking out loans." Many parents bet on their children's academic achievements and sports participation to pay off in the form of scholarships to help cover the costs of attendance. Little do they know that the deck is stacked against them. Despite rises in scholarship (merit-based) aid in recent years, the funds are overwhelmingly awarded to white students from socioeconomically advantaged backgrounds, making it unlikely that Black students will be able to count on scholarships to pay for college.[20] Even those who did win scholarships were surprised to learn that even large scholarships cover only a small portion of their college costs—like Daniel and his parents when they were sitting in his school's financial aid office. According to higher education scholar Derek Price, the shift to merit aid has redirected aid to those with the least financial need and increased the costs and debt burdens for students with the most financial need.[21] With no other options, many Black students have no choice but to borrow to enroll in college. But parents have one card left to play to protect their children from burdensome debts: take it on themselves.

Kellyanne feels grateful, and more than a little guilty, that her mom took on so much debt for her to attend college. "She told me she did not want me to have to take on all that debt. So she was going to take that on for me. And so that was about it. I was really grateful. But I also knew that was kind of ridiculous about how much debt I haven't taken on in the name of my education." By the end of her college career at a regional college in the South, Kellyanne said she had around $42,000 in student debt to pay back—a high number, but not uncommon for Black students. In that same time, Kellyanne's mother had racked up nearly $100,000 in Parent Loan for Undergraduate Student (PLUS) loans to help cover tuition, room and board, and other expenses not covered by Kellyanne's financial aid or loans. Unlike federal undergraduate loans, PLUS loans have no loan limits, which means that parents can go deeper into debt than their children. Alexandra has a similar story from when she was at college. "[During my college career] I took out like $20,000. And then the loans that my parents took out—I don't know the exact number, but I think it was closer to maybe $80,000 or $90,000."

Black parents are a hidden face of the student debt crisis. Decades of research—including our own—demonstrates how Black students take on substantially more debt than their white counterparts to go to college, but far less attention is paid to the parents of these students, who themselves go deep into debt to fund their children's college. In a study published by the New America Foundation, Rachel Fishman writes that PLUS loan borrowing tends to "fly under the radar," in part because it makes up a small proportion of total student borrowing, and because there is so little data on PLUS borrowing.[22] But the available data are shocking. Adam Looney and Vivien Lee at the Brookings Institution found that the average amount owed among PLUS borrowers has more than doubled in recent years, from around $17,000 in 2004 to $38,000 in 2014, and repayment rates have plummeted. Some of this increase has been driven by a rise in parents who hold six-figure debts—like Kellyanne's mom—who now make up almost 10 percent of PLUS borrowers.[23]

Black parents have been disproportionately burdened by the growth in PLUS loans and are more likely than white parents to borrow to pay for their children's education.[24] Fishman's study found that Black parents—especially those with low to moderate income—were far more likely to borrow than their white counterparts.[25] In other words, Black families are in a vicious intergenerational cycle: because financial aid underestimates their financial need and fails to consider their lack of wealth, they go deeply into debt to send their children to college—which further diminishes their wealth. Sofia thinks about this a lot.

Sofia is thankful that her parents took out loans to help her pay for college, but these days she finds herself worrying about how that debt is going to affect them moving forward. "There's no sugarcoating it. I think [the debt is] the main reason why they're not going to be retiring as early as they would like to. They're approaching their sixties, and they'd [like to retire by sixty-five]. But that's impossible. It's not going to happen unless they won the lottery. Retirement without any savings or very minimal savings is not possible for them." She paused. "For me, my goal is to be able to help them pay that back. They don't expect it but, for me, I'm hoping that, because where I'm hoping to go with my career, I can pay them back."

PLUS loans represent a Faustian bargain for Black parents: if you want to send your child to college, you have to take the financial hit. The necessity of PLUS loans for Black families was never made more clear than in 2011, when the Department of Education tightened the credit eligibility for PLUS loan borrowers. Overnight, Black parents were unable to pay their children's tuition bills. Olympia remembers that year vividly. "I remember when the Obama administration had created more strict requirements on Parent PLUS loans. And I think my mom had got denied at first. We were like, 'Oh, we need this money. What's going on?' And we were kind of freaking out. And it ended up getting fixed in the end, but I think that was one of the scariest moments where we were kind of unsure if I would be able to finish. Because if that loan didn't go through to pay for whatever it needed to pay for—and my parents didn't really have at that time extra money to just pay out of pocket. I mean they just had a mortgage. They had car payments. And I think we had a lot of financial strain at that point in my college career. So if it wasn't for Parent PLUS loans, I probably wouldn't have finished, or I would have had to take out a private loan."

THE FAILURE OF FINANCIAL AID

Sofia, Olympia, Danielle, Naomi, Daniel, and others we talked to went into college thinking that they would receive sufficient financial aid to help pay for college. But they were quickly disabused of that notion after receiving their financial aid packages, and had to rely on help from family, student loans, and parent loans to make up the difference. Some argue that Pell Grants, when used in concert with other forms of financial aid, are more than adequate to provide access to college—that students should not be scared away by the high "sticker price" of college because it does not reflect the "net price" that students and their families actually pay. The truth is that Black students pay the price of a financial aid system that is inadequate for students of color.

Higher education scholars have long argued that the methodology used by FAFSA to calculate need and distribute financial aid is deeply flawed. Among other things, FAFSA provides students with an expected family contribution, or what students and their families are expected to pay toward college costs. As we discussed previously, one reason the EFC is flawed is that it relies heavily on income and fails to address the vast racial disparities in wealth that affect Black families' ability to pay. Sara Goldrick-Rab, a higher education policy scholar at Temple University and the director of the HOPE Lab, argues that the EFC is flawed in other ways, in that it assumes that families are able to help their children pay for college at all.[26] For many Black students, the opposite is true: their expected family contribution is that they are expected to contribute to their family. For some, this means that student loans are used to help out family: "I stayed at home the first two years of college," said Anthony, who attended a large public flagship university in the South. "But you can say it went to room and board because I had to help my mom with the mortgage. So a good chunk [of my loans] went to that." Kirsten adds, "In terms of people borrowing money from me, like I said, my family is always—every time I get my reimbursement check, I always give about $2,000 at least to my family to help them kind of supplement what they've helped me. . . . But there's back and forth. I've sort of always been getting money and receiving money but also giving it back to people who've given me."

The EFC also assumes that colleges are willing and able to meet 100 percent of a student's need, but only a few select wealthy colleges are able to do so.[27] Beyond federal need-based aid, students have become more reliant on the aid provided by colleges and universities—like the scholarship that Naomi received. As colleges and universities become more tuition-reliant, they have transitioned to a "high-cost, high-aid" model—where high "sticker prices" are offset by generous financial aid packages for the students who need them most. The idea is that wealthy students will pay close to the full sticker price, while more disdavantaged students will pay a much lower, more affordable price. The problem is that this approach doesn't seem to work: low-income students still pay more at institutions with higher sticker prices, in part because colleges and universities are using the revenue to invest in merit-based rather than need-based aid, which is generally more accessible to white students from affluent backgrounds.[28] William Elliott and Terri Friedline argue that these changes in financial aid policy have shifted the burden of college costs onto students of color, and especially Black students. Recent research by economists confirms this shift and finds that financial aid in the United States is "suboptimal," and not as based on financial need as it should be.[29] In fact, the majority (56 percent) of Black students have "unmet need" after all sources of financial aid are taken into account, compared to only 40 percent of their white peers.[30]

The upshot is that need-based aid is broadly inadequate for students of color to be able to afford college without taking significant amounts of debt. In a landscape where the costs associated with college are high and rising, this means financial aid is a high-stakes game: if you miss a deadline or mess up a form, the financial consequences loom large. Were financial aid a simple process, this might not be a concern. But simple it is not.

The financial aid system in the United States is notorious for being a complex, byzantine system that is difficult for anyone to figure out, but especially for Black students who often navigate this system alone. After getting accepted to an elite private liberal arts college on the East Coast, Hillary, the child of African immigrants, was tasked with filling out the FAFSA on her own. "It was stressful, because . . . I had to fill out the FAFSA by myself. So I remember being like, 'Parents are supposed to fill this out.' And they're like, 'No, you're going to college, you need to fill this out,'" Hillary said. "So I remember feeling that as a high school kid, 'Am I going to mess up this government form that I have to submit?' So that was stressful. I'm still stressed from that."

Heather had difficulty navigating the financial aid office at her East Coast private college, saying, "I think it was overall a pretty frustrating experience dealing with financial aid and the bursar's office this year. 'Cause they're treated as two separate entities; they're not all in the same space. So having to go from talking to financial aid to renegotiate my aid, and having to go back to the bursar's office and saying, 'Oh, I need to fix this number.' Or, 'I need to take out this loan instead of this one.' And trying to navigate interest rates or a payment plan or things like that was super confusing and could get really really frustrating at times. And I think that's a failure on [the institution's] part. The majority of students here have parents with a lot of financial resources, but for everybody else, it's not necessarily the case. So then you're found—or you have to do a lot of it yourself. Which can get pretty difficult and time-consuming, and frustrating."

Kathleen echoed similar frustrations while attending a private HBCU on the East Coast. "I went to financial aid every day sometimes and tried to get information from them. They also weren't very helpful. They don't give you other options unless you ask. There might be scholarships available, but unless you ask, you'll never know. There might [be] grants available that I probably could've gotten, but also that information wasn't offered to me," she said. "It kind of felt like I had to figure it out by any means necessary. It's just kind of like you're on a crunch or a deadline to have these loans covered, have the balance covered. And say they say your balance has to be covered by October 16th, you're just on the crunch trying to find the money and you're kind of just signing away anything that's given to you, which might not be the best option in the end."

More than just frustration and confusion, missing a deadline or failing to file the correct paperwork can have dire financial consequences for students and their families. Virgil experienced this when his college plans changed. After being accepted to a small public university in Tennessee, he had to move back home, so he applied and was accepted to a regional branch campus in his home state. As Virgil said, "I ended up applying to go to [the regional branch campus] and not being able to get any loans or Pell Grants or anything because of some miscommunication that happened with the other school that I was going to go to. And so I wasn't able to get any help my first semester, so my grandfather ended up having to pay for my first semester on his credit card." While Virgil later sorted out the paperwork and was able to receive Pell Grants and student loans in later years, this initial confusion was costly.

The confusion created by the financial aid system costs more than money: it costs opportunities. Naomi felt as though she was never able to participate in normal college life, in part because she didn't have the money, but also because she didn't realize that money was available to her. "I think there are certain things that I avoided that I would've wanted to do. I remember my first summer. After freshman year, I got a[n] internship, and I was very excited. But I would have to take out loan money to support me, not knowing that I could ask for grant money or apply for grant money from the university." Naomi didn't take the internship. "Most of the assistance at my school, I didn't know about."

Students can also face costly administrative delays when cobbling together scholarships and other forms of aid to help pay for college. For Lucy, these administrative delays forced her to pay her tuition on a credit card. "When registering for classes, I had to take out a cash advance on my credit card because the scholarship that I had applied for was late, or it was processed late, right? And so I wasn't able to enroll. So I have to run around, take out this cash advance, and then pay it towards my tuition so that I could enroll."

Financial aid is broken. Not only does it provide insufficient aid, but that aid is difficult for many students to access, especially for students who have exhausted their family resources. Economists like Susan Dynarski argue that the complexity of the financial aid system undermines the redistributive goals of the system and disproportionately burdens students with the most need.[31] The financial aid system is in fact so complex that approximately 20 percent of students who are eligible for aid fail to apply for the FAFSA.[32] Dynarski argues that simplifying or eliminating the FAFSA—for example, by reducing it to a one-page application, or using tax information collected by the IRS to determine aid eligibility—would increase uptake in aid.[33] Studies show that even simple nudges, like having a financial expert at a tax preparation service help students fill out their FAFSA, increase the likelihood that students complete the form and the amount of aid they receive.[34] Others advocate for the creation of a negative EFC to reflect the fact that many students will not be able to rely on family contributions and in fact may need to help their families financially while in college.[35] Simplifying financial aid and getting students more aid might even reduce debt. When students are given more financial aid, perhaps unsurprisingly, they accumulate less debt and are more likely to graduate college.[36] Ultimately, that is the goal: to graduate college, which means that these challenges don't end in the first year. Black students face additonal obstacles and accumulate more debt in the years that follow in their quest to graduate from college.

3

Progressing Through College: No Room for Error

After finishing her first year at a private liberal arts college in the Northeast, Georgia had a plan: she looked at her aid packages and scholarships she took out in her first year and calculated that if she got that same package every year, she would need to borrow only a few thousand dollars per year to finish school. She felt comfortable; her parents had solidly middle-class jobs and were able to contribute financially, and she had enough money to focus on her studies. In fact, in her first year, her aid package was so generous that she got a refund check that she was able to use toward living expenses and books. But then a perfect storm hit. In her second year, her aid was less generous. Tuition increased. Some of the scholarships she had in her first year expired, and she was not able to reapply. Then, her dad lost his job, and her parents were no longer able to contribute, even though their expected family contribution (EFC) remained as high as it was in her first year. Georgia started working four jobs on and off campus to make up the difference and borrowed more than she would have liked to help defray costs. She kept up this schedule for the next three years. "I was tired most of my senior year," she said. "I was always exhausted, but I don't think I ever really thought about dropping anything because it needed to happen." By the time she graduated, Georgia accumulated substantially more debt than she had planned, and was over $25,000 in debt.

In some ways, Georgia was luckier than most: she managed to graduate college, even if she took on more debt than she had planned. But many others who face this "perfect storm" are not so lucky. Black students drop out of college at a much higher rate than white students, and many cite debt and financial struggles as a key reason for doing so.[1] Those who are able to persist and make it to graduation often take longer to graduate and take on more debt in the process. And sometimes, these individuals have no choice but to take on high-cost, risky private loans in order to do so.[2] Getting through college requires them to juggle a host of competing priorities: work, school, and paying for college. There is no room for error as they navigate this gauntlet.

These students do this all without the institutional safety nets enjoyed by their white peers. The defunding of higher education has hit students of color, and Black students specifically, harder than their white counterparts. The defunding of higher education has come at a time when the racial diversity of the undergraduate student body has increased: Black Americans are attending college in higher numbers and at higher rates than they were twenty years ago.[3] But while colleges and universities are (publicly, at least) seeking to diversify their student body, this diversity has come without funding. It is an irony that is not lost on Black college-goers. In turn, most Black students are attending colleges that, at best, lack the resources to support them financially and socially and are, at worst, predatory. At the same time, many of these students face dire challenges in college: caring for sick family members, watching parents lose their jobs, dealing with their own health problems—all challenges that are created from a legacy of racism and discrimination that lands squarely on their shoulders and threatens to knock them off-balance.

BAIT AND SWITCH

Georgia's experience with volatile aid packages from year to year was common among our interview respondents, and common among Black students more generally. Many schools provide generous financial aid packages in the first year to entice students to enroll, but those packages are often front-loaded in the first year—a practice referred to as "bait and switch pricing."[4] In a recent study that documents the pathways to financing college that students take as they progress through college, Janice McCabe and Brandon Jackson find that first-generation, low-income, and Black students often have to shoulder the burden of paying for college themselves later in their career, after early sources of funding—financial aid, scholarships, and parents' financing—dried up.[5]

Linda had a similar experience. "I had a few scholarships, and most of those scholarships I didn't realize were just for my first year. And so you live and you learn," she said. "So I also did work-study. And then we took out just a few loans, but it was very little. So my first year we took out less than $5,000 to kind of make ends meet or whatnot. Even my sophomore [year] wasn't so bad. By my junior year, most of the scholarship had dried up. Junior year kind of snuck up on me, and I had to pay for it, and we didn't really have a way, not realizing that I hadn't taken out the maximum for my student loans and so that was how I was able to pay for a required class. And here's the thing, had I not taken it then, it would have pushed me back a year from graduating."

For other respondents, the confusion and administrative burden they experienced at college entry continued in later years. Sarah had to borrow more in her third year of college, due to what she said was an error in her financial aid forms. Sarah's mom was normally in charge of filling out financial aid forms, but Sarah's father, who was less familiar with financial aid than her mother, filled out the forms that year. Sarah explained, "I'm pretty sure the third year my parents may have messed up on the form . . . there was a much larger [expected] family contribution during that year though our finances didn't change in any way. . . . And I would see the bill because I had access to stuff and it was $10,000 or something. I'm just like, 'This doesn't make any sense.' They didn't get any sort of super increase in wages or anything; it was just I think some sort of weird mix-up that happened, but then by the next year it was all sorted out, and I had everything back that I needed."

In addition to inconsistent aid packages, the price of college can also change from year to year. On average, tuition increases by about 8 percent per year.[6] Over the course of a four-year college career, students can anticipate that tuition could increase by one-third, on average, not including increases in rent or room and board. As Naomi put it, "The tuition goes up every year. And then sometimes, usually, you get a really nice aid package your first year. And then that dries up in second, third, and fourth year. So usually, people need to borrow more as they go through college."

And borrow more they do. Federal student loan limits increase by about $1,000 per year, meaning that students are able to borrow more the longer they are enrolled in college.[7] In our own research using NLSY97 data, we find that for each additional year of college attended, student debt increases by approximately 63 percent, net of family background characteristics.[8] As student debt-related financial pressures mounted, these students did what anyone would do in their situation: they got a job. Or in Georgia's case, four jobs.

MAKING ENDS MEET: PART-TIME JOBS AND SIDE HUSTLES

Nearly all of the people we interviewed reported working to pay for college through a combination of off-campus, on-campus, and work-study jobs. While studying as a full-time student, Georgia juggled a work-study job, an internship, and two nannying jobs on the side so that she could send money home to help out her parents and pay for her living expenses. Naomi worked three on-campus jobs. Sofia used money from her teaching assistant job to send money to her parents, aunt, and grandmother in South Africa every month—a practice she continues to this day, three years after leaving college. Jacqueline worked as a resident assistant so that she could defray housing costs. Anthony worked at the local hospital. Calee worked at a hotel.

Like most college students, our interview respondents worked during college, but working to survive is different from the kinds of work that most college students do. Studies show that the vast majority (around 80 percent) of students work while in college, but the nature of that work varies by race and class background.[9] Low-income and first-generation students, who are disproportionately students of color, are more likely to work more than fifteen hours per week, and these long hours increase the risk of dropout.[10] These same students are more likely to be in jobs that help them pay for college, while privileged students are more likely to be employed in jobs that help them advance their career, such as internships.[11] Black students are working hard to pay the bills and experience greater risks and fewer rewards for their employment while in college.

This begs the question: if students are working to pay for college, does their work help them avoid debt? Perhaps, but research on student debt and time use in college paints a different picture. In a study conducted by Natasha Quadlin and Daniel Rudel, the researchers found that students who take on debt in college spend more time working than those who do not.[12] While it is possible that working helps students avoid taking on more debt, this finding suggests that students are not substituting debt for work. Instead, it suggests that students who are financially strapped need to both work *and* take on debt to pay for college. Calee described trying to make ends meet in college this way: "I had got the disbursement back from my loan. I was trying to work in the hotel. And I felt like I still didn't have enough money to be able to afford food on the weekends."

Many of these part-time jobs that students relied on were precarious and irregular. Virgil was juggling four jobs to pay for living expenses and tuition.

But then, "At one point I lost three of the four jobs that I was working, which made it even more difficult. So I ended up from that point taking out more of the loans just so that I can have money to, I guess, to survive because the twenty hours that they were paying me a week weren't always guaranteed," said Virgil. "It just didn't make ends meet."

Student workers like Virgil, Georgia, and Calee are exhausting themselves, doing everything they can to keep their financial heads above the water, all while borrowing to help make ends meet. They are balancing work, school, family, and doing their best to hold it all together. But it does not take much for it all to come crashing down.

"A SPRITZ OF WATER ON THE FIRE": PRECARITY, LOSS, AND DESPAIR COME TO COLLEGE

Jourdin did everything that financial aid experts and college counselors tell students to do. She applied to several schools. She picked the cheaper, in-state school that provided the best aid package. She applied for scholarships. She talked about paying for college with her family, and her parents were prepared to help her out. Her parents had saved enough money—around $25,000—to help send her to college. "So the first two years—actually, maybe a year and a half, my parents had built up enough money to help me out, a contingency," said Jourdin. "But then, life kind of happened for my family. And when I went into school in 2011, and my mom actually lost her job. And then around that two-year time, sophomore going in junior [year], my dad lost his job, as well. And then the money kind of ran out."

Jourdin's experience of "best-laid plans" is one that is common among our interview respondents. No amount of financial literacy, planning, or efforts to save money could prepare her for her family's financial collapse. Georgia also thought that she would be protected by what she thought of as her family's "middle-class" status while she was in college. But then her family lost their house.

Parental job loss, downward social class mobility, a sick family member—these were common challenges faced by our study respondents, and for many it was also their breaking point: when all of the balls they were juggling came crashing down and when their best-laid plans crumbled. Georgia and Jourdin started borrowing more after their parents lost their jobs and homes, and could no longer financially contribute to college. They both started sending home what little money they could to help out with the family. College—the classes, their social lives—took a backseat, and they plunged deeper into the red.

It would be easy for people, especially white people, to see Georgia's and Jourdin's stories and say that any student can face family tragedy while in college. That it is just part of growing up. But the risks of exposure to these life-altering events are starkly unequal by race. Black college students are far more likely to see their parents and their extended family lose their jobs or lose the family home than their white counterparts.[13] And they face these circumstances under more duress and economic strain.

The fragility of the Black middle class is characterized by economic precarity and the lack of a safety net (wealth) to buffer unexpected shocks, leading young people to take on more debt when they get to college. This fragility follows them as they progress through college. Derek put it this way, when his parents went through a divorce after he got to college and then filed for bankruptcy: "I was probably upset with my parents back when I was in my earlier twenties because I didn't feel like I got enough help. Looking back on it [now], I don't think they had the resources. They were barely helping themselves anymore. So I don't blame them for that, just poor timing."

Many of our interview respondents also found themselves coping with and caring for sick family members. For Naomi, everything changed when her father's mental health problems spiraled out of control. "By my senior year, my family finances had changed completely. That was the year my dad stopped working completely. He has mental health issues. My family was losing our home, so I ended up with three different jobs." Jacqueline's parents had always struggled to pay the bills because her younger brother was born with a severe medical condition that drained the family's savings, and balancing a sick child with a kid in college proved to be too much. Anthony's mother was diagnosed with a debilitating mental illness, and her symptoms worsened right around the time he went off to college. Racial disparities in health and illness are well-documented, pervasive, the end result of stress that accumulates from centuries of racism, racial discrimination, and unequal social conditions and access to medical care.[14] Sociologist Debra Umberson and colleagues show that by the age of thirty, Black young adults are substantially more likely to have a close family member experience a severe illness, or die, relative to whites.[15] Umberson describes these losses as "life course flashpoints in a racist society" that sap Black young adults like Naomi, Jacqueline, and Anthony, of social and financial support at a time in their life when they need it most.[16]

When Naomi's father lost his job and they lost their family home, she told herself that she had to rely on herself to make it through college because her family would no longer be able to help her. After taking on three part-time jobs in her senior year, Naomi hoped that she could focus on her studies long enough to graduate: "But I knew I had to have them because I didn't have anybody to call for money. So at that point, I don't know if I took out more loans. I just know I worked hard." Naomi barely made enough money at her jobs to pay her tuition and rent, but her sister was able to help where Naomi could not. Her sister moved back home, helped with the bills, and got their mother into a new apartment after they lost the house. Naomi wanted to do more but felt like she could only watch from afar. "I wish I was in a position to help my mother and help pay part of her mortgage or something. But no, that's not my situation." For Naomi, having a family in crisis meant relying on herself and living with the guilt of not being able to do more.

Some were able to do more to support their families financially, but this support came at a cost. Sofia and Anthony both worked several jobs and took out the maximum amount of student loans to help their families cover expenses. Sofia recounted how difficult it was to juggle all of her finances: "So once the rent's gone, and then you have—you send money home to your family, and then you need to buy food. And then, you have to pay for the metro, and then by the time that's all said and done, [there's only a little left]." Georgia gave when she could, usually when she went home to help out her sister, and lent money to her parents to help them get by. "Things for my sister, for example, if she needed something for school or had a project at school or something like that. Sometimes they needed it to pay for something that came up or something came up so they needed more money. Like if a medical bill came up, they might ask me for money for groceries or something like that. Or if I was home for the holidays and I went grocery shopping, I paid for it out of my pocket and then they'll pay me back later."

Despite working multiple jobs, taking out loans, and doing everything in their power to help their families, many felt as though their efforts were not enough. Anthony had a falling out with his mother as her mental illness symptoms worsened. He moved out and found his own place, but he kept sending money home to help out with the mortgage. When he looks back on his falling out with his mother, he blames himself. "I guess I was a little selfish, but [when I was eighteen], the money I got was like, 'This is my money.' At that time, you're not thinking about mortgages." Sofia called the money she sent home "a spritz of water I can put on that fire," and she agonized over who should get the little money she was able to send back home. "It was a bit stressful trying to manage who's going to get what, and having it not kind of—end up kind of feeling political in a sense of, 'Well, I gave more to Grandma this time than my parents.' And they always say they're fine. They're happy with whatever I'm able to give them. But internally, it feels like, 'I wish I could be giving more.'"

For others, like Jourdin, only one answer remained to make it all work: the private loan market.

PRIVATE LOAN BLUES: TURNING TO THE LENDER OF LAST RESORT

After her parents lost their jobs, Jourdin was at a crossroads. Should she leave college to go home and help the family? Or should she stay and finish? Jourdin said she never wavered; she had to finish. The real question was how could she manage to complete her studies, pay her tuition and expenses, and help out her family. But the timing could not have been worse. Right before Jourdin's dad lost his job, she had declined federal loans for the semester because she thought she would not need them. "So it was just like, I have to do what I have to do to stay in school. When my parents told me that they had ran out [of money], I had already declined my federal. And it was too late to go back and accept. That's how I ended up getting [private loans from] Sallie Mae. So I just kind of made the decision to continue on." Jourdin borrowed a private loan from Sallie Mae for around $11,000, at 12 percent APR, which allowed her to make meet her financial needs for the year.

When disaster strikes, or when need is dire, many students find they don't have enough to cover tuition, room and board, and other living expenses, even after taking out the maximum federal student loans. For these borrowers, the only option is to take out private student loans, which often have less favorable terms and fewer protections than federal student loans. This is what happened to Malik. After he struggled with a mental illness diagnosis, Malik decided to move off campus. "The following year, I took out private loans because I was living off-campus and working a little part-time job, but it wasn't nearly enough money to pay for my rent, not even close, so I took out more for that. And so that was at this juncture a mistake, very clearly, a mistake. And that's about all I can say." Malik regrets taking out his private loans, remembers that "the interest rate was exorbitantly high," and that he took out somewhere between $10,000 and $20,000.

Private loans make up only a small portion (around 8 percent) of the total amount of outstanding student loans in the United States.[17] Compared to federal student loans, comparatively little data are available on the private loan market. But from the data we do have, we know that private loan use has grown in lockstep with the cost of going to college over the last several decades.[18] Erin Dillon and Kevin Carey note in their research that private loans "barely existed" in 1993, but by 2008, nearly 15 percent of undergraduates were taking out private loans.[19] In the decade that followed, private loan originations grew by more than 75 percent.[20] As private loans grew, so too did racial disparities. Although evidence is sparse, Dillon and Carey's research shows that private loan use is substantially higher among Black undergraduates than white undergraduates, with about one in five (22 percent) Black students borrowing private loans. Twenty percent of the people we interviewed for this book took out private loans at some point during college.

Even those who avoid the private student debt market often take on debt from private lenders in the form of credit cards to help them pay for school. Recall Virgil, whose grandfather put his first semester tuition on his credit card. Anthony got into some trouble with credit card debt in college when he was trying to stay afloat financially, take classes, and send money back home to cover his sick mother's mortgage payment. For this reason, data on private loans may underestimate racial disparities in financial need and participation in private lending markets in college.

One reason we lack data on private student loan use is they are just that—private. Sallie Mae, a student loan lender, and many major banks and credit card companies issue private loans, and they are not beholden to the federal student loan rules and regulations. This means that they can offer variable, rather than fixed, interest rates, charge higher interest rates than the federal government, and offer loans that are not necessarily eligible for income-based repayment or loan forgiveness.[21] These loans vary widely in their interest rates, but nearly all of them have substantially higher interest rates than federal loans. Some have interest rates of 17 percent or even 20 percent that resemble high interest credit cards. A $10,000 loan at a 17 percent interest rate can get out of hand quickly. At these interest rates, a consumer could rack up $1,700 in interest after the first year and nearly $2,000 in year two. When you consider that students sometimes borrow several thousands of dollars that are repaid over a five- or ten-year period, it is easy to see how private student loans are harder to repay than federal loans. Jacqueline, who took on private loans when federal loans were not enough to cover her expenses, isn't quite sure how much she borrowed. "I don't remember exactly. I think it was just a few thousand. But what I borrowed compared to what I owe is a whole 'nother story."

Because the private loan market lacks the regulation of the federal student loan market, there is greater opportunity for discrimination against Black borrowers. Private loans are known for having high interest rates, but Black students are charged substantially higher interest rates and fees for these loans than their white peers. A recent report by the Student Borrower Protection Center shows evidence that lenders such as Wells Fargo and Upstart (an online lending platform) charged higher interest rates and greater origination fees for those attending HBCUs and two-year institutions—the kinds of schools that disproportionately serve a Black student populace.[22] Senate Democrats have asked the Consumer Financial Protection Bureau to investigate, but so far, no action has been taken.[23]

Private loans are another example of what Louise Seamster and Raphaël Charron-Chénier call "predatory inclusion"—a form of educational "reverse redlining" that allows Black students access to college, but at a higher price than their white counterparts.[24] Historically, Black people in the United States have been denied access to credit, shutting them out of education, homeownership, and full participation in US society. This exclusion and marginalization created enduring racial inequalities in wealth and residential segregation that continue to this day.[25] But over the past several decades, while access to credit has expanded, it has also been deregulated, giving private lenders a great deal of power in setting terms and interest rates. This process has created a two-tiered lending market: one for "prime" borrowers, deemed creditworthy, and one for "subprime" borrowers, who are deemed less creditworthy.[26] For Black borrowers, inclusion in these new credit markets has come at a cost, and historical issues of fair access to credit now revolve around access to *fair* credit.[27] This educational redlining, or predatory inclusion, is but another chapter in a long, sordid history of marginalization and discrimination of Black people in the United States.

"I GIVE UP:" THE TOLL OF DEBT AND FINANCIAL STRAIN ON COLLEGE PERSISTENCE

From their first day at college to their last, Black students are managing multiple demands that detract from their studies: navigating the bureaucracy of financial aid; stitching together scholarships and grants; juggling work, family, and school as they try to make ends meet; supporting their families through crisis; and all the while accumulating debt. Anthony was trying to balance the demands of working full-time, attending classes, and earning enough money to help his mother with her mortgage. But when he and his mother had a falling out, and he decided to move into his own place, he couldn't keep up with classes anymore. "Working and school, one of them had to go, and it wasn't going to be my job or place. That's when school kind of took a backseat." Anthony dropped out of school. While he would come back to school a few years later to pursue a degree online, he has yet to graduate.

Black college students in the United States have a 66 percent higher chance of leaving a four-year college without a degree than their white counterparts. The majority of Black four-year college students (60 percent) leave college without a degree, compared to only 36 percent of whites.[28] Many Black students, though not all, drop out or stop out due to the financial pressures in the face of high college costs, and some scholars argue that racial differences in financial strain account for the majority of the Black-white gap in college graduation.[29] In a recent report from the Federal Reserve Bank of New York, Rajashri Chakrabarti and colleagues provide some of the most compelling causal evidence to date on college costs and college dropout. Specifically, they found that increases in the costs of college have caused higher dropout rates among credit-constrained undergraduate students, confirming that many Black students are leaving school because of their financial sitaution.[30]

When we asked Anthony whether his financial situation factored into his decision to leave college, he said: "Heavily, because I was taking a full course load, twelve to fifteen credits, and working forty hours. And for me, I just didn't have the time to dedicate to school because I had to work because I lived on my own when I was nineteen. So for me, I needed to make more money in order to pay bills, credit cards. I had credit cards at the time too. So yeah, it influenced it heavily, my decision to leave." Calee, who worked at a hotel to try to make ends meet, described her decision to leave college in similar terms: "Well, I think I wasn't sure, necessarily, that I was ready for school at the time. It was just really, really difficult for me to manage even being a university student, meeting my basic needs. It was just a very bad financial situation."

Anthony and Calee say their financial situations led them to leave college, and that student debt was part of their decision. Scholars have started to ask whether taking on student debt helps or hinders students as they progress through college: on the one hand, student debt provides students with the money they need to afford and persist in college. On the other, the specter of debt repayment looms large, and many students may decide to leave college as financial pressures mount. So, which is it? In a 2012 study, sociologists Rachel Dwyer, Laura McCloud, and Randy Hodson suggested that the answer to this question is: both.[31] Using data from the NLSY97, they found that the relationship between student debt and college dropout is curvilinear: that is, at lower levels of student debt—up to around $10,000—taking on student debt seemed to increase the rate of graduating from college. But beyond that point, the relationship turned negative: students who took out more debt were less likely to graduate college. This inverted U-shaped association was starker for students from lower- and middle-income backgrounds, who were more likely to drop out as their debt climbed. Other research confirms Dwyer and colleagues' findings, and shows that student debt increases the risk of dropout for Black and low-income students more so than for other students.[32] For example, 69 percent of Black students who drop out cite student debt as a primary reason for not completing their degree, compared to 43 percent of white students.[33] Dwyer and colleagues refer to student debt as a "double-edged sword"—on the one hand, a necessary financial resource that helps students make it through college, but on the other hand, a stressful financial burden that will need to be repaid.[34] Debt is a resource, until it isn't.

Melody put her decision to leave college this way: "[Student debt is] always on my mind. Like up until this point, I'm trying to figure out, okay, how can I pay this all? Because it's going to come back. After, like I can't really continue with an education, like continue with life until I figure out how to pay these debts off." Derek said it more succinctly: "[I] decided to stop wasting my time and money." Our respondents felt they had no choice but to leave college, given their overall financial situation and their student debt. The problem is that leaving college with debt but no degree is a recipe for disaster when it comes time for young people like Derek, Anthony, and Calee to repay those debts.

While dropping out represents an extreme risk, even those who manage to persist in college face challenges that increase both their time to graduation and their debt accumulation. Malik started college at a four-year private institution in the Midwest but transferred to a local community college after struggling with mental health problems and finances. Following that, he transferred to a four-year public institution to finish his undergraduate degree. In total, Malik took seven years and three institutions to complete his degree—considerably longer than he had expected. "So the transfer process, you'll lose credits here and there. Get some lost time. In addition, I had to do some soul searching from time to time like, 'Am I cut out for this? Is this really going to be something in which I can succeed?' And so those are real questions which I had to ask myself and I'm still asking myself in some way or another."

Similarly, Alyssa got her degree in five-and-a-half years—longer than she expected—because she lost her scholarship at a four-year public regional school and had to transfer to another school in the same state. "My freshman year, I was on two scholarships. And after my first semester, I was placed on academic warning because my GPA was so low. So as a result, I lost my scholarship, which meant that we had take out more loans on top of the loans we already took out for me to keep going to [that college]. And so I transferred to [another college in] my third year, and I think that's what set me back. There was a couple of classes I had to retake or that I couldn't transfer. So even though both schools are under the same [state] system, my credit didn't transfer."

These barriers to graduating "on time" were common in our sample and among Black college students more generally. Among those who complete a four-year degree, Black students take a median sixty-four months (5.3 years) to complete their degree, as compared to fifty-two (4.3 years) for whites.[35] Black students are also more likely to transfer colleges and experience a "reverse transfer" (moving from a four-year to a two-year institution) than whites, which can increase the time to degree completion.[36] In our analysis of NLSY97 data, we find that students who spend an additional year in college, and who transfer across colleges, accumulate significantly more student debt.[37] Alyssa and Malik both recalled that transferring schools increased their time to degree and the amount of debt they accumulated. Still others reported taking longer to graduate than they expected, even if they stayed at the same school for their entire college career. This extra time to graduate was mostly because they were juggling work, family, and challenges that led them to reduce their courseload.

Despite these challenges, many Black students, including Sofia, manage to graduate "on time," as they define it. But they do so under immense pressure. "I was pretty much on track," recalled Sofia. "I knew I wanted to graduate with my class. I was okay with choosing my major on time and everything like that. But I think, also, because I knew I couldn't afford a fifth year, it just had to be done in a four-year time span. There just wasn't any other option to spend more time to keep paying the amount that we're paying." For Sofia, student debt was a resource that helped her finish college; she called student debt "a motivator," but she did so under immense financial pressure, knowing that one wrong move could be the difference between success and failure. While Sofia's grace under pressure is laudable, it raises questions as to why we should expect Black students to walk a tightrope to make it through college and what can be done to help relieve this pressure.

RICH COLLEGE, POOR COLLEGE, PREDATORY COLLEGE: THE RACIALIZED DEFUNDING OF HIGHER EDUCATION

Many of the people we talked to faced challenges in college, but some fared better than others. Some experienced less financial strain and fewer work obligations, were more protected from financially ruinous life events, and ultimately accumulated less debt as they progressed through college. Family resources are one reason why. But postsecondary institutions also play an important role.

In an era when higher education has been defunded by state and federal governments, need-based aid has flagged, and costs are rising, postsecondary institutions are one of the few remaining safety nets for students. For some, it is the only source they can draw from for social and financial support. But many of these institutions are ill-equipped and lack the resources to help students. Others—such as for-profit colleges—actively profit from the harm they do to students. Previously, we argued that state and federal governments have abdicated their responsibility to students and left them at risk of accumulating a great deal of student debt in the pursuit of a degree. State and federal governments have done the same to institutions of higher education and have effectively privatized risk: defunding public universities, leaving them with few resources to support their student bodies, and opening the door for predatory institutions to gain a foothold to further exploit Black students.

The defunding of higher education—and its impact on postsecondary institutions—is racialized in both its causes and consequences. Cuts to higher education, while stark, have been deeply uneven across institutions. The institutions that have suffered the worst cuts are also institutions that serve Black students. Two-year institutions, nonflagship or regional four-year public colleges, HBCUs, and other MSIs have been doing more with less for decades, and these institutions have experienced greater declines in appropriations than other colleges that primarily serve white students.[38] Again, the irony here is that the institutions which serve the populations with the greatest need—first-generation, low-income, and students of color—face the deepest cuts.

Consider, for example, Historically Black Colleges and Universities. Many HBCUs were founded shortly after the Emancipation Proclamation to educate Black Americans in response to racist laws that segregated Black and white Americans and shut Black students out of predominantly white institutions. Today, HBCUs represent only 2.3 percent of all postsecondary institutions in the US, yet they enroll 10 percent of all Black students and produce nearly 20 percent of all Black graduates. Both public and private HBCUs complete their mission with considerably fewer resources than white institutions. Public HBCUs have historically been funded by (mostly white) state legislatures and have received less in state appropriations than comparable white institutions. These public HBCUs experience deeper cuts in recessionary periods, despite serving a population with greater financial need.[39] When you look at the data, it is difficult not to conclude that states are intentionally starving Black institutions. Private HBCUs are also a victim of the racial wealth gap: private schools rely on a wealthy donor base to build their endowments, but alumni from private HBCUs are less wealthy than white graduates from private institutions.[40] HBCUs are just one example. Other schools that primarily serve Black students—including regional colleges and branch campuses—are historically underfunded and are often in a position where they must do more with less to support their students.[41]

The consequences of the racialized defunding of higher education extend beyond those institutions directly affected by the cuts. For-profit universities have experienced a rapid surge in growth since the 1990s, increasing in lockstep alongside cuts to higher education. These institutions are notorious for leaving their students buried in debt and preying on disadvantaged populations. Students who attend for-profits are both more likely to borrow and accumulate thousands more in student debt (approximately $15,000 more than those at public institutions).[42] They are also more likely to leave college with debt but no degree, and are more likely to default on their loans than those who attend public institutions.[43] For-profit colleges enroll only a small percentage of all college-going students (less than 10 percent), but they have a knack for attracting vulnerable populations: for-profit enrollees are disproportionately individuals from low-income backgrounds and people of color. Sixteen percent of Black college-goers attend for-profit institutions, compared to only 7 percent of whites.[44] Tressie McMillan Cottom's *Lower Ed* remains the definitive source on understanding how for-profits operate, and why Black Americans, and overwhelmingly Black women, come to enroll in for-profit colleges.[45] But one thing is clear: these institutions thrive because public institutions have been starved. For-profit colleges have filled the void left by the defunding of public colleges—the logical conclusion of what happens when we replace public goods with a blind faith in private markets.[46] In a recent study with our colleagues, we draw a direct line between defunding of higher education and the rise of for-profits, and show that, within states, declines in state appropriations are associated with a rise in for-profit enrollment.[47] We find that this process is accelerated in states with a higher proportion of Black residents, suggesting yet another way that the racialized defunding of higher education has contributed to vast racial disparities in student debt.

The racialized defunding of higher education—and the lack of resources available for institutions that serve Black students—is partially responsible for racial disparities in student debt accumulation. In our 2016 study, we found that the underfunding of institutions of higher education and the rise of for-profit schools were key factors in explaining racial disparities in student debt accumulation. As we showed in figure 1.1, about one-third of the Black-white student debt disparity is explained by racial differences in the types of colleges young adults attend. We found that a key part of that story is that Black young adults are more likely to attend for-profit schools and underfunded schools that provide less generous financial support. Importantly, we found little evidence that attending HBCUs was associated with increased debt, net of funding shortfalls.[48]

In a higher education landscape of underfunded and predatory institutions, only the richest institutions—and institutions that make explicit choices to support their students—can provide sufficient aid to their students. A small handful of elite colleges—whose high sticker prices might scare off some students—employ need-blind admissions and offer generous aid packages that cover the cost of college for those whose families make less than some income threshold. Stanford, Northwestern, Rice, Vanderbilt, Washington University in St. Louis, and the Ivy League schools are some of the few colleges and universities that have endowments that allow them to offer grants to low- and middle-income students that cover the cost of tuition and (in some cases) room, board, and expenses. This financial support is a lifeline for many students. College persistence is higher at these institutions, in part because high-achieving students who are more likely to graduate college attend these institutions, but also in part due to the institutional support students receive that allows them to persist in college.

Elise attended one of these institutions and is one of the few respondents in our sample who graduated debt-free. Elise's parents, who divorced shortly before she went to college, made less than $75,000 per year, and she therefore qualified for free tuition, room, and board from her institution. After cobbling together some other aid and a modest contribution from her father, she was able to achieve some financial security more easily than some of our other respondents. In addition to the grant from her institution, Elise said, "I had also received a $5,000 scholarship for a program that I had done in high school. And so I didn't have a student contribution. And then I also received a Pell Grant because of my mom's income. And then on top of that, my dad was a noncustodial parent. So whatever of my contribution that was left over, it was manageable for him given his income. So I didn't have to pay for any fees from [my institution]. I did work. I worked at the library. I did some research assistant jobs throughout my time there, but it was never [like] I needed it to get through certain payments or to make it through the school year. Also [the college] guaranteed housing all four years. I never had to live off-campus or have any of those kind of expenses." Elise admitted that she did extensive research prior to applying and that, "It became clear, then, . . . that it would be far less expensive to go to [this university] where they had financial aid, an abundance of financial aid, versus a state school. So I was definitely trying my best to get into there, to a top university, because they have more resources."

Elise faced similar challenges as some of our other respondents: her parents got a divorce, she worked in college, and yet her institution helped buffer this stress. Elise graduated on time and credits her institution's financial aid policies and the financial support she got in college for helping her meet that goal.

While elite colleges may be in the best position to support Black students financially, many institutions have had success in doing more with less. Kirsten attended a four-year public state school in college but received a full scholarship from a prestigious program—part of her college's efforts to promote and retain students of color. Between her scholarship, financial aid, and on-campus job, she was able to avoid taking on any debt, even though her parents were unable to contribute financially. Kirsten's institution shares similarities with Georgia State University, a school that has made headlines for leading the US in college graduation rates among Black students.[49] Georgia State has increased its student diversity in recent years, has increasingly accepted students from the bottom and middle of the income distribution, and has been heralded as an "engine of upward mobility" based on data from Raj Chetty's Equality of Opportunity Project.[50] Institutions like Georgia State have accomplished these changes by implementing a series of programs to provide a safety net for students of color, including microgrants to cover fees, expenses, and late charges, and a robust system of advising and mentorship. The message here is rather simple: Black students do better and accumulate less debt at institutions that can support them financially and socially.

Michelle benefited both from attending an elite institution with generous aid policies and receiving financial support from a program that supports the education of students of color. After Michelle's mother lost her job, they both worried about how they would afford college. But, like Elise, Michelle attended an elite, predominantly white college—this one in the Northeast—that provided full tuition and room and board to students whose parents made less than $100,000 per year. After her mom lost her job, her family fell below the income threshold and qualified for grant aid, which Michelle found ironic: "It seems like she actually had to lose her job in order for us to afford college, which seems, like, very odd and backwards in my opinion." Like Kirsten, she also benefitted from the support of a program targeted toward students of color—in her case the Mellon Mays Program—which provided her with a stipend to defray expenses. Michelle credits the Mellon Mays Program for her success in college: "One of the purposes of the stipend for Mellon Mays is so that students of color don't have to—or underrepresented students—don't have to focus on working. They can focus on studying their research interests or focusing on their coursework because they know that students of color [disproportionately] have to work, in addition to their studies." This combination of a generous, need-based aid policy from her institution and financial and social support from Mellon Mays helped Michelle graduate on time and without debt.

Student success—particularly for students who have a great deal of financial need—is increasingly dependent on an institution's resources and what that insitution does with these resources. Elite institutions and institutions with targeted programs can provide a safety net for students like Michelle and help minimize the financial challenges faced by so many Black students.

But at elite institutions, which are predominantly white and wealthy, it is far too easy for Black students to slip through the cracks.

Lucy attended the same elite college in the Northeast as Michelle, but her experiences were quite different. Lucy's parents were not able to help her pay for college, and she either did not know about or did not access the institution's need-based grant aid. Lucy primarily financed her education with loans, taking out several thousand a year. "When I entered my senior year, I had a conversation with the financial aid counselor, and she said, 'Hey, the average student loan debt amount from this college is twenty-something thousand, and you're like two times that.' And I was like, 'What the heck?'"

By the end of her college career, Lucy was buried in debt. And yet, Michelle—who came from a similar income bracket and went to the same college at roughly the same time—was not. What explains their disparate experiences? For one, Michelle's parents were college-educated and had a good understanding of higher education in the US. They also knew how to find and look for financial aid, which was critical. Michelle's mother was the one who told her about the institutional policies, and she had heard about Mellon Mays from friends who had previously graduated college. Lucy, on the other hand, was the child of immigrants who were unfamiliar with the US higher education system and assumed that everyone in the US had to take on debt to go to college. These resources—or cultural capital—can help parents and their children avoid taking on excessive debt in college. When talking to her parents about loans, Lucy said, "They told me not to worry about it, that it was going to be fine, that I would pay it off. And so I kind of just—I didn't pay attention to my student loan debt after that conversation with my parents."

Institutions can serve as a safety net for students, but success in an institution is often predicated on the students' knowledge of and position within that institution. Even at elite institutions, the aid that students need is more easily accessed by those with social and cultural capital. Research by Janice McCabe and Brandon Jackson shows that Black, second-generation college students are often able to work with parents and counselors, and use their academic and social capital to unlock institutional resources to finance their college education.[51] However, they find that first-generation Black college students—like Lucy—often piece things together on their own and have more difficulty tapping into the available resources at an institution. As Anthony Jack notes in his work *The Privileged Poor*, you need more than financial aid to succeed in college; you need knowledge about how that institution works to unlock its resources.[52] Lucy echoed this in her experience:

> *I remember feeling very bitter. And that was throughout my entire educational journey, because I felt like there was some sort of—I don't know how to describe it, but it just felt like there was access to knowledge the certain people had that I didn't that allowed them to know about opportunities, or to maybe try to negotiate a better financial aid package, or something. Because I didn't have access to that knowledge, I couldn't. And I've always been pretty distrustful—even when I was at [college], I was always distrustful of just how financial aid packages were generated. Because I didn't understand why they thought that my estimated family contribution should be as high as it was, given that my parents literally didn't have the money. And so I felt like I was being asked to take out loans that I shouldn't have had to take out. But I didn't know how to navigate that, or negotiate. So yeah, honestly, I mean, I know that taking out loans is a choice, and it's a responsibility, but when I was an undergrad, I really did feel like I didn't have any other options, and so yeah, I just compiled the debt so that I could get through.*

Even though she was at an elite institution, Lucy had the same difficulty navigating and comprehending financial aid as many of our other respondents at less-resourced institutions. And for her, that made it worse. "Some of my friends that were in the same bracket that I was I felt like were smarter in navigating the system. So many of these people were [undergraduate advisors], and so they got their room and board for free. And when I came to understand how that operated, I felt so stupid. Because I was like, 'Wow. How many thousands of dollars would I have saved if I [was a resident advisor]?' Right? [I was] feeling not as resourceful, and not as smart as it related to cutting the cost of my education."

Lucy blamed herself for her situation, echoing broader societal narratives of debt and personal responsibility, and yet she also felt it was deeply unfair. "I was very angry because I felt like I was leveraging my future, in a way. And I was being asked about all this money, and I felt like—I don't know, I just felt like, why did I have to borrow all this money? I remember feeling very annoyed, and I felt kind of like I fell through the cracks, in a sense. It just didn't make any sense to me. A lot of stress. A lot of anger, bitterness, and resentment. Just wondering why me, which sounds very—almost like a victim mentality, and I understand that. But at the same time, it's hard when you see other people who are in similar situations as you, but they end up with different outcomes. So it's like, okay, well, what went wrong in my situation?"

Lucy's question is a good one. Why were others able to navigate the institution and graduate without debt while she was not? For many of our interview respondents, this was the core issue that animated how they thought about their student debt. Yes, student debt helped them get to college, but it felt unfair. Why should they have to take on more debt because their parents were not able to help them pay for the college? Debt may indeed be a resource, as Rachel Dwyer and colleagues say, but it's a resource that needs to be repaid. And in the end, that repayment looms large in the minds of students as they leave college.

Now that she's left college, Georgia thinks about that repayment a lot, her mind constantly returning to her debt. "I definitely think that I've grappled with financial anxiety because of my loans, and also just because of my family's financial situation, which I guess is interconnected with the loans because I had to get loans because of my family's financial situation. But I have developed a stress culture around saving money because I want to be prepared to pay back my loans when it's time." That time to repay comes soon, only months after students leave college. For many borrowers, including most of our respondents, that's when they first realize just how much trouble they are in.

4

Life After College: "It Just Seems Like You're Going to Pay Forever"

When Jourdin graduated college, she had a hard time finding a job. Everywhere she applied, the story was the same: prospective employers said they wanted somebody with experience, and she did not have it. She took a job as a nanny to get by, but when her private and federal student loans came due, she did not have enough to make ends meet. "I was making like $800 a month, so I was like I'm definitely not paying any student loans. The only thing I was paying for was myself. That's the only thing I can afford." Later, when she lost her job, she was able to defer her government loans interest-free but had to put her private loans in forbearance, and the interest continued to accrue on her loans. Over the next few years, Jourdin felt trapped in a cycle: she would find a job. She would get laid off. Her loans would go unpaid. "There's only so many times you can do [forbearance]," she said. "There's no saying how many times you can lose your job, how long you'll be out of a job. It's great to have zero payment, but they're putting interest on it every single day. It's just like . . . it just seems like you're going to pay forever." So far, Jourdin has avoided defaulting on her loans, but only just.

Previously, we documented the crisis of debt accumulation among Black college-goers. Many of these same students will struggle for years to repay their debts. Numerous studies analyzing financial aid, credit report, and survey data reveal that many borrowers are not making progress paying down their debts after leaving college, and rates of delinquency and default have skyrocketed, especially among Black borrowers. Although student loan experts often point out that those who accumulate high debt loads are not necessarily the same people who struggle with repayment, Black borrowers are disproportionately represented in both groups.

The figures are quite striking. Black borrowers have the highest rates of default and delinquency, and they are high across the distribution of student debt. Black borrowers with small amounts of debt, large amounts of debt, those with degrees, and those without, all struggle to repay their loans. Default rates among Black borrowers exceed that of white borrowers independent of whether they completed their degrees.[1] Within six years of leaving college, almost two-thirds of Black college graduates and virtually all (96.3 percent) of Black college noncompleters have put their loans in forbearance, when lenders grant a temporary pause on federal loan payments usually stemming from financial hardship.[2] Forbearance offers temporary relief to borrowers in distress, but interest on loans continues to accrue, causing loan balances to increase. After twenty years in repayment, the median Black borrower still owes 95 percent of their original loan balance, compared to 6 percent for the median white borrower.[3] No matter the statistic, the story is the same: Black young adults are leaving college with substantially more debt than their white counterparts, and this disparity only grows over time after college. Our quantitative research shows that racial inequities in young adult social and economic roles—such as unemployment and underemployment—are a key reason why racial disparities in debt grow over time. But this is only part of the story.

For the borrowers we talked to, experiences with loan repayment are an amalgamation of factors, including the size of the payment, limited knowledge regarding how the process works, interactions with servicers, and the administrative burdens associated with the process. Failure to pay student debt can have severe consequences. Loan defaults and delinquencies get reported to credit agencies, lowering one's credit score, which makes future borrowing more expensive and sometimes impossible. Defaulted accounts can go into collections, which incur fees, ballooning outstanding balances. Debt collectors can contact employers and garnish wages, and income tax refunds and Social Security benefits can be withheld. Then, there is the psychological toll. In addition to the stress associated with financial strain and harassment, borrowers report that harassment from debt collectors also contributes to poor mental health. Rep. Ayanna Pressley (D-MA) described in a webinar sponsored by the Center for Responsible Lending on Student Debt in December 2020 that she does not own a landline phone because of the trauma she received from student loan debt collectors' repeated calls and harassment. While some of the borrowers we interviewed viewed their student debt as just another bill, others expressed how completely all-consuming their debts and efforts to pay it had become.

The student loan repayment system exploits structural inequalities that disproportionately impact Black borrowers. In this chapter we highlight the experiences of Black student borrowers as they navigate through this system. We focus on three main aspects of loan repayment: the early repayment phase and managing payments; the ramifications of falling behind; and efforts to seek assistance through income-driven repayment (IDR) programs.

SHOCK, CONFUSION, SUCCESS, AND STRUGGLES IN THE EARLY REPAYMENT PERIOD

> *Six months after I graduated, I got a call from them like, "So now you got to start paying it back." And I remember having a whole conversation with them, they wanted the amount that was equal to the rent that I was paying at the time. And I just remember thinking, "There is no way that I can do this." And I kind of was freaking out about that and then we ended up—I think at the time ended up doing an income-based plan. But I definitely remember the first phone call with them and they wanted me to pay $600 a month and I was like, "I can not do that."*
>
> —Shola

The start of loan repayment is best encapsulated by knowns and unknowns. Most borrowers are acutely aware of the six-month grace period before their first payment comes due—before one of at least eight or nine of the loan servicers that the US government contracts with reaches out asking for the first payment.

Because over 80 percent of borrowers hold loans through the federal Direct Loan program, most borrowers begin repayment, by default, in the Standard Repayment Plan. This plan is designed to equally divide the outstanding loan balance (including interest) into monthly payments for ten years, with a minimum payment of $50. This plan is designed to work best, and the payments are most manageable, for those with $30,000 or less in debt—which is less debt than is held by the average Black borrower. Among those who borrow, the average loan debt of Black college graduates in 2015–16 was $34,010, and the median amount was $32,523.[4] When disaggregated by institutional sector, the numbers only increase. Public four-year graduates hold an average of $30,613 ($29,750 median), private four-year graduates average $36,093 ($35,693 median), and for-profit graduates' averages are the highest at $42,046 ($45,000).[5] The average Black graduate with debt is not the ideal candidate for the standard plan.

Jourdin struggled with repayment from the jump because she had trouble securing a job. But if we table her employment status, Jourdin was entering a loan repayment system where the standard default plan was not designed to work for people like her. Even without considering their ability to get a job or manage any financial crisis that might loom on the horizon, the average amount of debt owed by Black borrowers places them at odds with the standard, default, and most attractive repayment plan offered by the government. What makes the standard case the most attractive? All the alternative plans (e.g., extended, graduated, or IDR) lower monthly payments while extending the repayment period and increasing the amount of interest borrowers will have to pay. Consequently, the alternative plans—and the better plans for many Black borrowers—are often the more expensive plans. After they leave college, Black borrowers unknowingly enter a loan repayment system that is not designed to meet their circumstances or needs. Then comes the shock, frustration, and struggle.

The borrowers we spoke with were quite knowledgeable about how much they borrowed, but they were still shocked when they received their first student loan bill. Like Jourdin, all of the borrowers knew how much they borrowed and did not dispute the total principal balance on the first bill; and yet, attempting to reconcile how much they borrowed with what they owed in monthly payments was difficult. Lucy recounted her experience when her first student loan payment came due: "The details are a bit hazy, but I think the first time when I had to start repaying, I think I saw something ridiculous like $900 a month, and I was like, 'Oh my goodness, I can't afford this. This is crazy. How is it that I borrowed so much money that now the money that I have to pay back is, like, one month's rent? I don't understand.' That was definitely surprising."

Mateo echoed these sentiments and said, "It was a bit of a sticker shock." Expressions like *sticker shock* were a constant refrain, with many borrowers comparing the magnitude of their loan payments to other bills, just as Lucy did. Nelson's monthly payment was over $1,000. He exclaimed, "When I see a bill for over $1,000, one of the first things I'm thinking, 'Hey, that's double rent, right?'" So, if borrowers knew how much they owed, why the shock and awe? Because the assumptions baked into the Standard Repayment Plan seemed to be completely divorced from their present economic situation.

In her interview, Kirsten raised the issue about lack of transparency in the system that made it difficult to understand. "I don't know anything; I just knew that I got to borrow. There was going to be interest," she said. "But I'm still [not] very knowledgeable about the payment process and how that works and what company gets to have your loans and request it back. So, it's still a very confusing process to me." Kirsten articulated her frustration with repayment at multiple points, including the interest, the payment process, and the distinction between loan servicers and providers. She is not alone. Most (though not all) of our interviewees expressed similar sentiments about the lack of transparency in the system. But time and again, borrowers like Kirsten blamed their lack of financial education rather than the system itself.

To be clear, the repayment system is complex by design. The system operates on information asymmetries and opacity. Payment plans that work best for many borrowers—such as IDR—are "opt-in" and require that borrowers file and refile paperwork every year and provide proof of income, employment, or residency. To top it off, loan servicers often outsource customer service to third parties, which is meant to complicate and deter borrowers from making changes. We should not be surprised that borrowers were oft confused. Many of the borrowers we spoke to could not afford the Standard Repayment Plan, which was the first problem. But if borrowers deviate from the standard plan, they are plunged into a complex system that is difficult to navigate. There are multiple actors, plans, and consequences all meant to ensure that the debt is repaid, and borrowers who fail to do so are punished.

Many of the borrowers we interviewed saw their loan balances increase—known as *negative amortization*—over the course of repayment. This issue continually came up as a source of confusion, frustration, and anger. Confusion with why what appears to be a relatively low interest rate leads the loan balance to increase. Frustration with loan balances that increase when borrowers put their loans in forbearance and deferment. Anger over repayment schedules that make borrowers feel as though they cannot make progress. Alyssa was frustrated when comparing how much she owed to how much she borrowed. "Looking at how much interest has accumulated. You can see how much you took out, and then it's like 'Oh, so I actually owe this much more. Even though I only took out this amount.' That . . . definitely shocked me." Yasmine concurred. "You hear about it, but seeing it in real time is something different."

Even though Yasmine, Alyssa, and Kirsten felt flummoxed by their rising balances, the reason is not that they lack understanding of compound interest or lack financial literacy. Instead, it is the loan system itself that creates confusion for borrowers. Many borrowers, especially Black borrowers, hold a combination of loans, unsubsidized and subsidized federal loans and private loans, because they have greater financial need. Subsidized loans are lower cost because interest does not accrue until borrowers leave college, whereas interest accrues on unsubsidized loans as soon as they are dispersed—often years before a borrower enters repayment. But subsidized loans have more stringent annual borrowing limits than unsubsidized loans. These limits lead to a situation where interest rates accumulate for a longer period of time on the largest loan balances. For this reason, Kirsten found it frustrating to balance her loan payments across her unsubsidized and subsidized loans, and felt it was much harder to make progress on her larger unsubsidized loans.

Those initial reactions of shock and awe quickly evolved into panic when these borrowers realized they did not have the money to pay. This experience is common among Black borrowers. Black borrowers are more likely to default on a greater share of their debt, suggesting that they experience issues with nonpayment earlier in the repayment period than white borrowers.[6] Debra was overwhelmed when her first bill came in. "They sent me an email saying that my first loan payment was $460. Who has an extra $460 to just give back immediately? I'm just starting to work. And the student loan officers don't understand everyone's work situation. I had to call them and tell them that I'm a contractual worker, and my contracts are not always long and not always permanent," she described. "On top of that I also support a household that I live in. So until I can move out on my own and I'm just taking care of me, I can't actually give you $460 a month."

Borrowers like Debra were frustrated with the lack of awareness of servicers who seemed to have no understanding of or sympathy for this disconnect, and a system that did not recognize that—unlike many white borrowers—Black borrowers are often financially supporting family members and in precarious labor market positions. Economist Susan Dynarski has argued that there is mismatch between student debt repayment timing and realized labor market returns in young adulthood.[7] The design of the Standard Repayment Plan does not take into account the reality of entry-level positions and the labor market frictions that occur early in an individual's working life, such as delayed paychecks. When we asked Abella whether she was able to keep up with loan payments when she entered repayment, she replied, "No, not at the beginning. Because starting off on a teacher's salary, the reality of it is you still have to do a month in the hole and you're still catching up on everything. You're trying to settle into a new place, and you have this expense, that expense. So it was kind of hard to keep up with."

Black young adults with college credentials enter into a labor market that is structurally not designed for them and yet must contend with a student loan repayment system that assumes their job prospects and earnings are the same as their white young adult counterparts. As young adults, Black college graduates are more likely to be unemployed or underemployed—defined as holding a job that does not require a college degree—in large part due to discrimination in the labor market. Audit studies that experimentally manipulate the race of a job applicant and hold all other candidate qualifications and experience equal reveal that Black college graduates are less likely to receive job offers and receive offers for lower-paying positions with fewer options for career advancements than white college graduates.[8] In other words, it is discrimination—not ability—that underlies racial disparities in employment and wages.[9] Lucy expressed her frustration with her difficulty finding a job, in spite of her credentials. "[In high school and in college,] they give you all the fluff about having a college degree. [They say] 'It's going to let you find a job; don't worry about your debt; you can major in whatever you want; you'll find a job; you'll be okay,'" she sighed. "So I didn't think about it. I thought I'll find a nice-paying job after college; it's not a big deal. And then I found out, like, Oh."

Most of the borrowers we talked to, like Lucy, struggled with loan repayment right after leaving college. But a minority experienced some initial success and were able to make progress on their loans. Those who were most successful shared a few traits in common: they were more financially secure or could elicit help from relatives. Calee was older, in a two-income household, and described her household as financially secure—though that would later change. Anthony was married and was working with his spouse to pay down the debt together. Although Black young adults are less likely to be married than white young adults, married households, Black or white, are wealthier than nonmarried households.[10] While wealth (and debt) may influence racial inequalities in the timing of first marriage, it may also be that the economic security of marriage makes it easier for youth to repay debt.[11] Charity mentioned that her grandmother paid off a $500 loan and intended to send her money. Monique shared that her parents had amassed some savings to pay down the loans they acquired for her schooling. But while studies show that support from parents reduces the risk of loan default, financial assistance from family or friends was not an option for most.[12] Not only are Black young adults less likely to receive assistance, but they were more likely to assist parents, siblings, and other family members financially, like Danielle who was financially supporting her mother and brother. Rather than one's own financial literacy, positive repayment experiences were mainly tied to financial stability, having a partner present who could help manage bills, and a relative that could assist. But these were the exceptions rather than the rule. And these early successes did not always ensure long-term victory. Most struggled to keep up with their payments and fell behind over time.

"EVERYBODY HAD THEIR HAND OUT EXCEPT FOR ME": LOAN DEFAULT AND NONPAYMENT

When Alexis defaulted on her student loans, she felt that she had no choice. "I wish I didn't do it," she said. "I wish I didn't stop paying, but it was something I needed to do because it was just like I can't live like this. I felt like everybody had their hand out except for me." While only 20 percent of the respondents we interviewed defaulted on their loans (similar to national estimates of Black four-year college graduates), most of the borrowers we talked to had some experience with nonpayment. Many who fell behind did so because they were constantly triaging debts and had to prioritize other bills, or they had unexpected expenses and household shocks that left them with nothing left over to pay their loans. In response, they scrambled—spent countless hours on the phone with servicers seeking out extensions or different repayment options and took on side jobs to make ends meet. These borrowers experienced extreme financial strain because of their student loans, and they were forced to make hard choices that many white borrowers never have to make. We also see these patterns in national data. According to a recent study by Elizabeth Martin and Rachel Dwyer that uses data from the Survey of Consumer Finances, student loans are associated with substantial financial strain among Black households. No such link exists among white households.[13] The financial strain of student loans is racialized. This means that many Black borrowers must routinely accept the possibility of delinquency and default due to no fault of their own.

For many, like Alexis, the decision to pay every month came down to a financial trade-off in which failing to pay their loan was the least disastrous option. As Charity so aptly describes here, her student debt payments had to be deprioritized if she wanted to reduce the risks of financial exigency. "It feels like a luxury bill because it's not immediate," she said. "My lights could be cut off any time, I could be evicted at any time, but if I have options with not paying them off, I'm going to take [that] type of situation."

Every time her student loan comes due, Anya feels as if she's forced to make an impossible choice: pay her rent or pay her student loans. Virgil, a 2015 graduate, agreed. "When they ask you for $500 a month, and you only bring home $2,300, then you have to be like, 'I can't give you $500 and change on a loan when my rent is $700." Both feel as though their loan servicers do not understand, or care, about their situation.

When unexpected expenses arose, these financial challenges soon became a crisis. Two years into repayment, Virgil's mother became ill and needed caregiver support. As a schoolteacher in a low-income neighborhood, he has had to purchase supplies totaling a couple hundred dollars for his students. Virgil knows that his income on paper implies that he can afford the designated monthly payment in his IDR plan, but the economic realities of his life do not play out on paper, and time and time again, he did not have enough to pay.

Virgil has lost track of the time he has spent on the phone with his loan servicer—either because he was calling them to explain why he could not pay and to ask for assistance, or they were calling him to hound him over missed payments. "It's been kind of stressful because the reality is they don't care if I got ill. They don't care about an emergency. All they care about is their money," he said. "And that's one thing that I've learned as an adult and finally just be having to just provide for myself, is that the bill people, they don't care about what's happening in your life. They want their money. And if you don't have the money, they will come get the car. You'll come home and find the things on the street and, so yeah, their responsibility is they don't take into account what is happening in my real, everyday life. That is the hardest part."

Shola shared similar experiences when she called her loan servicer and took extreme measures to ensure that she would be able to pay her rent on time. "There are things you can't plan for that happen or if an emergency happens. . . . And I called and told them, 'I don't have the money right now,' and they essentially said, 'Too bad.' I felt like they didn't really care about any of that. They asked their six to seven questions and they pick out this number," she said, referring to the questions that servicers ask to determine whether borrowers might be eligible for alternative payment plans. "[I told them] I was literally at the point where I had to choose between rent and paying my loan payment, and I said, 'If I have to choose, I'm going to pay my rent.' And honestly, I ended up closing the account that they were drawing from because I just didn't have it at the time." To prevent the servicer from directly withdrawing funds, Shola closed her bank account. While that decision may have avoided a short-term financial burden, it kicked the can down the road and created additional burdens as she fell behind on her student loan payment and could no longer access her closed account.

The perception that servicers are unwilling to assist or do not want to understand their situation is a major source of stress. Charity, a twenty-six-year-old graduate, described the anxiety associated with her loan servicer interactions. "What I didn't know is that you basically have to beg them . . . 'I'm barely making it now, so I can't really pay it.' And so it gives me a lot of anxiety. I didn't realize how much anxiety it would be to constantly call these people and tell them like, 'Can you please just hold off? You'll get your money.'"

These experiences not only are stressful but also take an enormous amount of time and are a constant, chronic feature of life. Lisa, after spending hours on the phone with her servicer, decided she had had enough. After repeated poor interactions with her loan representatives, Lisa stopped reaching out to them. "I have to talk to them sometimes," she said. "But they're not the easiest to deal with. Long wait times and then some people are not knowledgeable about the question that you may ask. And you get transferred from department to department to department and it's like, 'I really don't want to call y'all anyway,' and I really don't want to be on hold for hours, so I end up hanging up." Agnes felt lost and angry when her loan changed hands, which made it harder to figure out who she should be talking to. "Sallie Mae, prior to her transforming into her evil twin, Navient, I remember having aggressive conversations with the person that would call about my loan payment," said Agnes, referring to the corporate split between Sallie Mae and Navient in 2014, when Sallie Mae could no longer offer both private and federal loans. Navient was created to service federal loans, and Sallie Mae continued to provide private loans.

Some of this frustration stems from the fact that the loan servicers are private companies, even if they are working on behalf of the federal government. Information asymmetries abound throughout the student debt system due to these configurations. Lisa described trying to complete a form on the servicer website. "Sometimes when you fill out forms online with them, you'll click on something and the link leads to the IRS, and it's like, I don't feel comfortable with doing that online. So, I'd rather talk to them and deal with them over the phone," she said. Because the servicers are not the owners of the loans, they have more incentive to maximize their profits and less incentive to work on behalf of the borrower. This arrangement, not surprisingly, leads to distrust. Claudia summed it up best here when she said, "I think it's hard to know what's going on sometimes. It's hard to communicate with the servicer. They're really good at communicating with me if they want money, but if I need to contact them, it's like I have no idea who to reach out to."

Federal loan borrowers who experience financial hardships do have options to avoid default, and many of our interviewees took advantage of these options. Borrowers can seek deferment or forbearance, which allows them to pause their payments temporarily. Jaydnn was able to put his loans in forbearance to avoid defaulting, and he was grateful for it. But these solutions are just that: a temporary solution to a chronic (repayment) problem. For example, those who apply for forbearance or deferral can do so only for twelve months, and in most cases, interest continues to accrue on loans. This means that borrowers who go into forbearance often see their loan balances and monthly payments increase when they start paying again. Lisa experienced this firsthand when she lost her job and applied to defer her student loan payments, only to discover that her expected monthly payments increased fivefold, from $200 to $1,000. Unable to pay, Lisa put her loans back in forbearance. In this sense, forbearance offers temporary relief in exchange for longer-term financial pain for borrowers who are chronically struggling to repay their loans. Jourdin, who had both private and federal loans, said she felt as though she was trapped in a cycle of deferments that ultimately made it harder and harder for her to pay her debts. "Just coming up as a young professional, I was making nothing when I graduated. So, I had to put my [federal] loans on forbearance right away. And then, my monthly payments went up. Then I lost my job a few years later. Put it in forbearance again. Monthly payments went up [again]. And I was like, 'Hey. Why did it go up?' And they're like, 'Well, when you put in forbearance, you had to catch up.' I'm just like, 'Why can't you just add it on the tail end, instead of making my payment higher?' They're just like, 'That's just what it is.'"

In spite of these frustrations, Jourdin was thankful that she was able to put her federal loans in forbearance when she hit tough times. She had a harder time with her private loans, however. "Sallie Mae is just like, this is it, you can't change anything. There's nothing you can do," she said. The private student loan market is less regulated and offers fewer protections or alternative repayment plans for borrowers. Unlike federal loans, private lenders are not required to offer deferment or forbearance during periods of economic hardship, and many do not. Interest rates on private loans are also considerably larger than federal loans, and borrowers are more likely to fall behind on these larger payments when they experience hardship.[14] Jacqueline, a thirty-year-old with private and federal loans, said she had trouble with her private loan servicer. "They don't care how much money you're making. This is your interest rate. This is your payment." Maria, who has private loans through Chase Bank, called and told her servicer she was not making enough money to make payments. They replied, "Well, are you going to get another job?" She eventually applied for food stamps.

While not all interactions with loan servicers were as awful as Maria's, many borrowers felt as though the canned solutions offered by servicers—either over the phone or on their websites—did not work for their unique situations. They blamed themselves and expressed frustration that they did not understand or have the system already figured out. Jaydnn, and many other borrowers we interviewed, said he spent all of his time researching different options and finally found a repayment option—IDR—that worked best for him. Unfortunately, many found these options only after they had already fallen behind.

SEEKING RELIEF: THE PROMISE AND PERIL OF INCOME-DRIVEN REPAYMENT

Despite issues with servicers, missed payments, repeated deferments, delinquency, and default, virtually all the borrowers we interviewed wanted to pay their debts and believed it was their obligation. To do so, they needed a long-term solution that would make their payments more manageable. For the vast majority of (federal loan) borrowers, the most attractive long-term solution is IDR. Designed to reduce the burden of repayment, IDR programs cap eligible borrowers' payments as a percentage of their income. In principle, IDR seems like a relatively simple and effective way to alleviate the burden of student debt. In practice, it is inefficient, inequitable, and burdensome for Black borrowers.

About one quarter of federal Direct Loan borrowers are in IDR, which consists of Income-Based Repayment (IBR), Income Contingent Repayment

(ICR), Pay as You Earn (PAYE), and Revised Pay As You Earn (REPAYE) plans.[15] In existence since 1994, IDR was expanded to include all types of borrowers during the Obama administration in response to rising default and delinquency rates. These plans differ in the amount required to repay (e.g., 5 percent, 10 percent, 15 percent of discretionary income), length of repayment period, and who qualifies based on loan type eligibility or debt to income. The typical IDR plan has borrowers pay 10 to 15 percent of their discretionary income, and any remaining balance is discharged after twenty to twenty-five years of repayment, depending on the plan.

Recent data indicate that Black borrowers are overwhelmingly represented in IDR plans relative to borrowers from other race and ethnic backgrounds, and that a majority of Black borrowers have enrolled in IDR.[16] That such a large percentage of Black borrowers are in IDR plans underscores the central theme of this chapter: Black borrowers are struggling to repay their loans, and they need help. Many Black borrowers—and most of those we interviewed—were emphatic when they said that IDR was not enough to reduce the burden of their debts. Instead, our interviewees described IDR plans that were administratively burdensome and difficult to access, did not provide sufficient financial relief, and left them saddled with growing debt burdens.

The first challenge with IDR is that it is complex and administratively burdensome to access. Many of the borrowers we talked to expressed frustration with getting and staying enrolled in IDR. Danielle lost track of the time she spent on the phone with her servicer trying to figure out whether she was eligible for IDR. Later, after being enrolled for a year, she had to recertify her income. Enrollees in IDR have ten days to return their paperwork to certify their income to their servicer, and if they do not, they are returned to a standard repayment plan.[17] Due to a delay in processing her paperwork, Danielle was automatically switched back to a standard repayment plan and defaulted on her loans. Now she has to get out of default before she is allowed to return to IDR. "It's a hassle just even dealing with them and making sure they get through the paperwork," Danielle said. "And even if you sent it, sometimes they don't get it. Or they might decline it. Right now, I'm in a phase where they declined some of my paperwork, and they said they sent out a letter. It's just really hectic dealing with them in general." Danielle was not alone; Jaydnn and Abella also expressed encountering issues with the paperwork and providing proof of income. Claudia expressed fears that technology failures would interrupt her ability to submit payment, and

Khadija had difficulties navigating the website. These challenges—confusion around eligibility, delays in paperwork—are all too common among borrowers. According to data from the Department of Education, fewer than half of borrowers in IDR are able to recertify their income on time. Others simply do not have information about these plans: IDR remains surprisingly underutilized despite being the best available option for many borrowers in distress.[18] These administrative burdens are all tied to the design of the programs being opt-in, meaning borrowers have to apply for enrollment and to stay in the program.

The IDR process is administratively burdensome, but that is not the only reason for the confusion; loan servicers also bear some responsibility. According to a report from the Consumer Financial Protection Bureau (CFPB), student loan servicers often do not share information about IDR plans with borrowers, and some have denied access to IDR even when borrowers are eligible. These problems are more common among Black borrowers, who are more likely to have issues with loan servicers than their white counterparts.[19] It bears noting that servicers have a financial incentive to steer borrowers away from IDR and toward more profitable options, such as forbearance, where they can still make money from interest payments.[20]

These barriers to IDR exacerbate racial disparities in debt repayment.[21] A recent analysis by Ben Kaufman at the Student Borrower Protection Center shows that, among borrowers who are having difficulty repaying their loans, white borrowers are twice as likely to stay enrolled in IDR as Black borrowers.[22] This puts Black borrowers, like Danielle, under financial strain and at a greater risk of default, whereas their white counterparts are better able to benefit from IDR.

A second challenge with IDR is that it does not provide the repayment relief that it was designed to provide, especially for Black borrowers. Among the borrowers we talked to who were in IDR, nearly all of them were emphatic that it was not enough to prevent them from struggling to repay their loans. "Once I got on the income-driven repayment plan, they were still saying that I owed, not six hundred and something dollars, but I say it might have been like two-something maybe," Anya said. "[But] it was still a lot because what they don't do is calculate your expenses, your rent, and things like that; they just calculate how much you get, and that's that. That's just not realistic because, [in the city where I live], my rent alone is almost $1,300. You see what I'm saying? So I'm like, 'I can't give you guys that, it is what it is.'" Under an IDR plan, most borrowers are expected to pay 10 percent of their monthly discretionary income, which is calculated as the difference between the household's adjusted gross income and 150 percent of the federal poverty line for their state and family size.[23] This formula has been criticized for failing to account for local cost of living, tax burdens, and other expenses—much like the federal poverty line itself.[24]

Anya is a good example of how IDR is failing Black borrowers on this front. Anya has a combined $70,000 in debt from her undergraduate and master's degree training, is twenty-nine years old, single, and does not have any children. She lives in a major metropolitan area on the East Coast and makes approximately $60,000 per year before taxes working in a white-collar job. After taxes and other deductions, she takes home just under $3,100 per month.[25] She is enrolled in the REPAYE program, and based on the IDR formula, she is expected to pay $289 per month on her student loans.[26] While that payment may seem manageable, Anya pays $1,300 per month for her apartment, plus $270 per month for utilities. Her other living expenses—such as groceries, transportation, cell phone, and other debts—total to around $1,000, not counting the money she sends home to help her family with their bills. That leaves Anya with very little left over to pay her student loans, and almost no wiggle room if she has an unexpected expense. "It's like, 'I can't pay you what you guys are asking me for; I just can't,'" she said. "And I have a lot of other stuff that I got to do, that I need to do, and that I need to pay on. And rent is a priority, and so it's just like, 'How am I going to really pay this?' Because if it's up to them, I'm going to be broke, seriously. So it's just kind of like I don't know how I'm going to pay for it. I really don't. I don't." Frustrated and overwhelmed, she is barely keeping up, and she is one unexpected expense from defaulting on her loans. And if she does, she will be reverted to the standard repayment plan, because loans in default do not qualify for IDR—making it out of reach for those who are in the most need.

A third challenge with IDR is that it has not delivered on its promise as a loan forgiveness program. In addition to reduced payments, the prospect of loan forgiveness at the end of the extended repayment period is an attractive feature of IDR for many borrowers. Claudia was counting on this loan forgiveness. "That is my plan right now," she said, sounding resigned. "Making the income-driven payments and seeing what happens in twenty-five years." But what does it mean to have your debts forgiven at the end of the repayment period? It means that the borrower's federal debt was so large that it necessarily took over twenty-five years to pay given the repayment schedule. Or, that the borrower's income remained low enough for several decades that their payments were too small to make a significant dent in the loan principal. Neither is an ideal situation.

There is mounting evidence that IDR plans, instead of providing relief, are leading Black borrowers to have negative amortization on their loans—meaning they owe more on their student loans than they originally borrowed.[27] Using credit panel data, Marshall Steinbaum shows borrowers with outstanding balances that exceeded their original loan balance are concentrated in areas with zip codes where the majority of residents are Black, which he attributes in part to high enrollment in IDR plans. Olympia, who is enrolled in an IDR plan, expressed her frustration. "I think the most difficult part is watching my balances grow even though I make a payment every month," she said. "And it seems like it's doing nothing." Steinbaum argues that IDR programs will never solve the student loan crisis because they were designed to address a liquidity problem—young borrowers often lack the money to pay down their loans—when the student loan crisis is a wealth, or solvency, crisis. It is akin to putting a band-aid on a broken leg.[28]

For Black borrowers in financial distress, IDR is often their only lifeline, and yet many found it frustrating, difficult to navigate, and insufficient—not unlike the standard repayment plans. Some tried other loan modification options, such as loan consolidation, and found it similarly wanting. Still others put their hopes on the Public Service Loan Forgiveness (PSLF) program, and are holding their breath that they will qualify after making their qualifying payments, even though this program has similar administrative burdens and hurdles to navigate. During our interviews in the summer of 2019, there were widespread media reports that 99 percent of PSLF applications were being denied.[29] Mounting disillusion with the PSLF was palpable among our interviewees. Kellyanne hoped she would qualify for PLSF, but she was resigned that it probably wouldn't work out. "[I'm probably just going to] keep paying it for the rest of my life, I guess," she said. "Right now, in this current moment, that's my backup plan."

The student loan repayment system is not working for Black borrowers. When faced with repayment troubles, many of our borrowers spent hours talking to loan servicers, trying to figure out a needlessly complex system that was not designed for them and left them overwhelmed, frustrated, and without hope. When Sarah told us about how she was struggling with debt repayment, we asked her if she reached out to anyone else—family members, friends, mentors—to help. "No, not anyone," she said. "I don't think that I would have—I wouldn't feel comfortable asking the people that I know who have money, and then my family just wouldn't be able to really—I mean they would if they needed to, but it would be so much more of a burden on them . . . I don't want that to be a burden on anybody because . . . those are my decisions. So I just try to deal with it." For some of our respondents "going it alone" felt like the only honorable path forward, in part because they felt responsible for their situation and didn't want to be judged for their debts. But for others, it was more complicated.

As a first-generation college student, Kirsten said her role is to provide for her extended family, not to be a burden. "Now that I have accrued all this debt, I still need help when the purpose of me getting all these loans was to be financially stable to not need help," she said. So, it's kind of like, how did we do all this work but still end up in a situation where I still need help?" Debra, a twenty-four-year-old college graduate, was more blunt: who do you turn to if you're struggling when you know everyone is struggling? "Honestly, as a Black person, you don't have anyone else to call besides yourself because you know everyone else's financial situation. And if you have an inkling of your financial situation, as a regular Black single-parent household, then you have an idea for every other single-parent household." Resigned, alone, and with nowhere to get help, Debra and Kirsten worried about the future.

5

The Hidden Costs of Debt Repayment

In October 2020, the *New York Times* profiled young white newlyweds Hayley Messner and Tanner Cemper, who put off getting married until they could pay down their student loans.[1] The story paints a picture of two responsible young adults who worked together to navigate their debts so they could marry, free of financial worry. As the *Times* tells it, they enrolled in financial planning classes, cut up their credit cards, and eschewed nights out to save money. The story—like many media profiles on student debt—underscored the importance of personal responsibility and financial literacy for successful debt repayment. What it failed to highlight are the structural realities that facilitated their financial position: Mr. Cemper had a high-paying position at his family's construction firm. Ms. Messner also came from a wealthy family, and both were able to live with friends and family until they got on their feet. It's easy to prescribe financial literacy when you have the resources to act on that advice. This is not to say that this couple did not work hard, nor are they undeserving of their happiness. But the situation for the Cempers is overwhelmingly different than it is Black borrowers, who rarely have these opportunities and have more burdensome debts. Unlike many white borrowers, Black borrowers have yet to experience a happy ending. As Tressie McMillan Cottom said, "We cannot 'financial literacy' our way out of this."[2]

Previously, we outlined the difficulties experienced by Black borrowers when entering repayment. In this chapter, we ask: What are the other, hidden, costs of debt repayment? How does it impact lives, relationships, decisions, work, and well-being? Just as debt accumulation and repayment are racialized, we argue that the negative consequences of student debt for young adults' well-being are racialized and are more severe for Black college-goers, compounding their disadvantage in spite of their degrees. Repayment comes not with a sense of triumph, but with a profound sense of self-blame, regret, severe psychological distress, and dashed dreams. For most of the people we talked to, the stress of debt repayment is financial: they worry about how they're going to make ends meet, start a family, and meet their career goals when they can barely repay their debt. For some, their debts affected their work, family plans, and ability to live independently as they transitioned to adulthood. Still others experienced a deep-seated shame; they felt they had made all the wrong decisions and had nobody but themselves to blame. Seeking relief, many continued to follow the *education gospel* to graduate school, in the hopes that an advanced degree could improve their financial situation and fulfill their dreams. Instead, it too often led them deeper into debt as they tried to find a way out.

SELF-BLAME AND REGRET: INTERNALIZING THE PERSONAL RESPONSIBILITY NARRATIVE

When we asked our respondents how they felt about their student loans, most said they wished they had done *something* differently. But many had trouble pointing out exactly what that *something* was. Olympia said: "Every time I think about it, I see the number and I'm just like, 'Why did I do this to myself? What could I have done? Should I have went to [a different school]?' And so I always question, did I make the right decision? I don't know." Danielle added: "It's overwhelming to think about the debt, and I wish I would've known more about college prior to getting these loans." Alexandra didn't point to a single factor and instead pointed to a littany of decisions that she wished she could do over. "I just wish I was more aggressive. I won scholarships, but I wish I was even more aggressive in winning more scholarships. I just wish I knew, like, 'Hey, you should really set up a business in high school.' So then, I'd be able to pay for college outright."

Our respondents had difficulty pinpointing what, exactly, they had done wrong, or what they wish they knew. Some, like Alexandra, had unreasonable expectations for their younger selves. But one thing was clear: they placed the blame squarely on themselves. They blamed themselves for falling into debt, for picking the wrong school, for not looking hard enough for scholarships, or for selecting the wrong major. "Nobody else pushed me into these decisions," Kirsten said. "Those are my decisions."

Debt and personal responsibility have long been linked. Historically, debtors have been stigmatized as irresponsible and irrational, whereas those who were debt-free were seen as paragons of responsibility and self-worth.[3] The word *debt* is a morally charged term that in many cultures is synonymous with sin.[4] In some religious communities, debts are still seen as sinful, something Malik said he experienced in his Christian church groups: "I interact with white Christians, and some of them think it's sinful to have debt, even student loan debt. And so there is something spiritually, like God doesn't like me because of what I did to further my education. And that's not just a stigma, that's an obstacle to overcome. It's rough out there." Even as student debt hits record highs, it remains stigmatized: just as the *New York Times* lauds white couples for making good decisions as they pay down their debts, other media outlets use questionable data to make specious claims that debtors are squandering their loan money on spring break, drugs, and alcohol.[5]

The stigma of debt is a social mirror: when Kirsten and millions of others look into it, they find themselves wanting. If debt is a personal failure, they must have failed. But at the same time, many recognize that the deck is stacked against them and have a hard time squaring their personal experience with the cultural narratives that underlie the stigma of debt: *sure, I made some mistakes, but what else was I supposed to do?* Naomi felt conflicted. "It's like, on one hand, I should've done more education for myself. But then I feel like 'No, they kind of make you feel like it's okay.' So that financial literacy part is missing . . . [but] I kind of feel like I've been manipulated a bit." Virgil framed his choices against the consequences he feared it would have for his family:

> *It is definitely scary because, in a way, it makes me feel like I made a mistake. But I also look at it and been like, "What other option did I have?" This is what was presented to me. Culturally, we push college. And you've got to have degrees before people even look at you now, especially if you want to get a good job. But also, the job market isn't what it used to be in that just because you have a degree, it does not mean you're going to find a job. So I consider myself very lucky to have a job and to have the degrees that I have, but also, I'm almost resentful because I feel like I made a mistake. And I feel like I've put myself in a position that I can't control and I feel like I will go to my grave owing somebody. I don't want my people worried about—the people who I leave behind worried about the choices that I've made.*

Debtors distanced themselves from other borrowers who, from internalizing the dominant cultural narrative, they know to be irresponsible. Jared, who accumulated approximately $30,000 in debt in college, said he had no choice but to borrow, but thought that others were less responsible. "Some people cash those checks and go splurge or ball out," Jared said, referring to the refund checks that some student borrowers receive when taking out loans for college. "But to me, that wasn't what I was trying to do, because I knew that if I took out more, that'd be more I'd have to pay for. And so I was cognizant of that." Naomi emphasized that she was not irresponsible like other borrowers, saying, "I don't go shopping, really. Unless I really need it as part of my daily survival, I tend to stay away from it. It makes me feel guilty when I do spend money, so I don't eat out because I always feel guilty." Like dancing a two-step, these respondents had both internalized the personal responsibility narrative while cognitively distancing themselves from those whom they saw as irresponsible. This presents a collective action problem for debtors: How could you organize politically when you believe you've been cheated but also believe that those who share your position got there through their own bad choices? But more immediately, it makes people feel isolated and miserable.

"LIKE A DARK CLOUD OVER MY HEAD": STRESS, PSYCHOLOGICAL ANGUISH, AND A CERTAINTY OF HOPELESSNESS

When Lisa started repaying her debt, it was all she could think about. She thought about it while she was at work, it kept her up at night, and she was reminded of it every time she got a letter from her loan servicer. Lisa said her student debt is "like a dark cloud over my head," following her around as she goes about her day. "It just feels like I'm never going to be able to pay if off. And that's kind of depressing sometimes."

Anxiety, depression, dread, fear, worry: these were common themes among our respondents, whose debts loomed large in their minds. Virgil said he couldn't stop thinking about his debt. "Every time they send me an email, I get a little nervous seeing the email pop across my phone because I feel like I never know what they want or I know that they could be asking for more money. Definitely stresses me out all the time." Malik did not think about his debt when he was in college, but "now that I'm facing the monster, I'm not going to lie to you . . . sometimes I find it soul crushing." One reason debt is stressful, or, as Malik more eloquently put it, "soul crushing," is that it is chronic. A constant, recurring "dark cloud" that doesn't go away. Unlike event stressors, which have a discrete start and end point—think losing a loved one or getting a divorce—chronic stressors are ongoing, are unpredictable, and chip away at one's mental health over time.[6]

It seems obvious that student debt creates psychological turmoil; it was certainly obvious to Lisa, Malik, and Virgil. But research on the mental health consequences of student debt has been decidedly mixed. Although some scholars find evidence that student debt is related to psychological anguish, others find that those saddled with debt have no different, or even better, mental health than those without debt.[7] Some have argued the reason is that student debt is not nearly as stressful or distressing as some believe—something that everyone we talked to would disagree with.

We offer another explanation: the racialization of student debt leads to more pernicious consequences—psychological and otherwise—for Black borrowers. Throughout this book, we have shown how student debt is racialized in ways that lead Black college-goers to both accumulate more debt and have more difficulty repaying that debt. And, if debt is noxious because it is difficult to repay, then it makes sense that these consequences would be more pronounced for the borrowers for whom debt is most burdensome. Recent research that teases apart the consequences of student debt for different racial and ethnic groups shows support for this explanation.[8] For example, in a study on student debt and sleep problems, Katrina Walsemann, Jennifer Ailshire, and Gilbert Gee find that student loan debt is associated with sleep problems for Black but not white young adults. Student debt, in other words, is racialized in both its causes and consequences.[9] Daniel is familiar with this feeling. "Sometimes when I just wanted to sleep, this was on my mind," he said. "[You] can't run away from your own thoughts."

Sociologist Patricia Drentea argues that debt creates anxiety, fear, and distress in part because repaying debt is chronically stressful. The financial strain of not knowing how you're going to make the next payment, the email reminders that show your outstanding balance has barely moved (or perhaps gone up) in the past year, the calls from loan servicers if you fall behind on your payments—all make debt a unique chronic stressor in modern life.[10]

Jacqueline feels anxious about her debt because she doesn't know how she's going to keep up with her student loan payments while also paying her other bills. "I'm always stressed. I feel like money and finances is something that's always on my mind," she said. "And that's probably because I'm always working [to pay my debts]. So I feel like I'm always working, always thinking about money. I have a very strict budget that I must follow. It's impacted my mental health because I'm always thinking about it." For Jacqueline and others, debt is stressful because it adds another financial ball to an already precarious juggling act. With nowhere else to turn, Jacqueline took on second and third jobs to help make ends meet—leaving precious little time for her to unwind or spend time with her family, leaving her exhausted all the time. This is another reason debt can be so stressful: it creates difficulties in other areas of life and makes it impossible to achieve any semblance of work-life balance. The stress of debt begets more stress.

Charity also felt anxious and stressed as she tried to keep up with her student loan payments, and it only got worse when she fell behind and went delinquent on her loans. "It's a cause for anxiety," Charity said. "It's a very big cause for anxiety because my grandma calls me almost every single day saying, 'I got this paper for you. I got that paper for you. You need to start paying your loans back. Call these people.' Sometimes, I know what she's calling for, so I don't answer." Charity started to feel better after her doctor prescribed her medication to treat her depression, but her precarious economic position meant it was only a temporary fix. "And then I left Alabama, so I didn't have access to it anymore. That's when the depression came back."

Even those who can keep up with payments felt exasperated and frustrated with their progress on their loans. Yasmine was stretched thin trying to keep up with payments, but the stress was manageable at first. Until she logged on to her servicer's website and saw that all of her efforts didn't seem to be putting a dent in her balance. "I mean, as I've gotten older and I'm out of college, [it's] more frustration of having the debt," she said. "Because I think last year, I may have paid over $1,200. But the principal went down about $700. It does not seem to be declining as much as it should be."

"A Certainty of Hopelessness" is a legal standard used by courts when considering whether to allow student loans to be discharged in bankruptcy. They very rarely are.[11] This expression is also an accurate description of extreme psychological distress and despair that were common among our respondents. Many felt as though their debts would follow them to their graves and that there was nothing they could do to change their fate. "It's almost like there's a chain," said Alyssa. "I'm chained to this loan. I feel like I'm going to be repaying this for the rest of my life." "I literally want to cry," Jacqueline added. "I used to jokingly say that I would probably die with a balance, and I don't want to die with a balance. But I feel like that's my reality. That it feels like it's impossible to pay off what I owe." Virgil struck a similar tone. "I resign that I'll be paying student loans for the rest of my life

. . . unless I win the lotto or become some big superstar," he said, laughing, trying to lighten the mood. Linda said her student debt "almost feels like a forever debt, like a debt that would—when you talk to people, a debt that was never meant to be repaid. This is just going to be you're owing to the government for the rest of your life."

When you ask people why they go to college, many will tell you they go so they can have a shot at a brighter future. But for the people we talked to, debt clouded that future. Linda had a hard time envisioning what that looked like with her "just choking, terrible, monkey-on-my-back debt. I think of the amount of money that I have to make in order to live a decent type of life and build some sort of something for myself, even while trying to pay off this debt." Lucy shared these worries. "It just feels like my debt is just this heavy, oppressive force that's always with me, or that affects how I think about my life . . . how I think about, I don't know, everyday life decisions. It's just always in the foreground or background. It's just always there." Like a dark cloud, student debt follows them around, leaving them asking, *How can I build a life with this hanging over my head?* The answer is not so clear.

DASHED DREAMS IN THE TRANSITION TO ADULTHOOD: RELATIONSHIPS, CAREERS, AND INDEPENDENCE

Things have not worked out the way Jacqueline had planned. At thirty, she's single, and although she has a full-time job, she says it's a job to "get by" and not a "career job." She has a hard time making rent but doesn't want to burden her family by returning home. She doesn't feel as though she'll ever have a career that will help her attain a comfortable life. When Jacqueline borrowed private and federal loans to make it through college, she thought she would be able to repay them easily and move on with her life. But that's not the case. "I feel like it still limits what I thought my life at thirty would look like."

Leaving school, exiting the parental home, entering the labor market, starting a family—these are the key markers of what sociologists call the *transition to adulthood*.[12] In market-based economies like the United States, attaining these markers to adulthood in a timely and orderly fashion is often a prerequisite for long-term financial security and socioeconomic attainment. Yet for the most recent generation of young adults, all available evidence suggests that the transition to adulthood is becoming more delayed and complex: people are leaving school later, living with their parents longer, are at a higher risk of returning or "boomeranging" back to the parental home, and are starting families later.[13] Recent cohorts of young adults are also less wealthy, make less money early in their careers, and have more debt than their parents' generation had at their age.[14] Few social scientists would argue that rising student loan debt is the sole force driving these broad demographic changes, and yet Jacqueline's experiences beg the question of whether and how student loan debt is impacting the life chances and choices of a generation of young people, particularly young Black people. "It's my generation—the Millennials," Jacqueline said. "We are having kids later, we're getting married later, we're buying homes later, because of this debt. And I am a true example of that."

Into the Red, Back to the Nest: Student Debt and Returning to the Parental Home

Alyssa did not plan on moving back in with her parents when she left college. After getting her degree from a public HBCU in the South, Alyssa did what most young people do when they graduate from college: she started applying for jobs. "But," she said, "either I wouldn't get a call back, or I wouldn't make it to the interview [stage]." After searching for a job and being out of work for three months after graduation, Alyssa started at a temp agency and was assigned a part-time job in HR at a local manufacturing company. She was already in a financially precarious position when the student loans came due. "It's like I'm coming out of college—what job do you think I have that I can afford this?" Alyssa called her mom, who suggested she come back home to save some money and get back on her feet.

When Alyssa moved back home, she joined the millions of young Americans who have "boomeranged" back to the parental home, or never left. Data from the NLSY97 show that most young people (88 percent) exit the parental home at some point during young adulthood, but of those that do, more than half (58 percent) "boomerang," or return home.[15] The risks of returning home are greater for Black young adults, which scholars argue are a result of two key factors: that Black youth have more difficulty making ends meet when they leave the home and that Black youth have stronger connections to family than do white youth.[16] Student loans are part of this story.

To understand why people return home, it is useful to think of *push* and *pull*: factors that might *push* young adults back toward their parents' doorstep or *pull* them back. Push factors tend to be external to the family and reflect ongoing difficulties in young adults' lives, such as money problems, losing a job, getting a divorce, or experiencing mental health issues.[17] Pull factors tend to be closely related to family dynamics, including circumstances like family health problems that pull young people back to the home to care for their parents or other family members, and strong relationships with family members. It is easy to think of student debt as one of these *push* factors: if young people are having difficulty repaying their student loans, their loans might *push* them back home. Corinne put it more succinctly than most: "I don't think I would have moved back in with my parents if I didn't have [student debt]."

Many of our respondents described their experiences moving back home in this way. Alyssa's account was one of being pushed home due to her debt. Naomi, too, wasn't making enough money to afford rent and student loans, so she moved back home six months after graduating from a large public university in the Midwest. Naomi managed to save enough money to get back on her feet and move out of her parents' home after a couple of months, but a few years later, she found herself back on their doorstep after aggravating an old college injury. When she found out she would need surgery and would no longer be able to work, she said, "My parents stepped in. They were like, 'You can come back home.'"

Nobody we talked to planned on living with their parents indefinitely. Living with parents was a way to help them reset and get their finances in order. Melody, a twenty-five-year-old college graduate who recently moved back home, said, "I plan on staying home . . . maybe two years. Like when I'm twenty-six, twenty-seven, then I'll move out. But I just need to make sure my loans are paid off." Although many young people think of living at home as a temporary "reset," still others have difficulty seeing an exit strategy: if they couldn't afford to pay their loans before moving back home, how could they afford it if they moved back out? "It is something I think about late at night: How am I going to pay this off?" Alyssa asked herself. "I'll think myself into a funk. I'm ready to move out into my own place, but I can't because I don't have a job that pays well enough where I could move out."

While student loan debt can *push* people back home, for some, their decision to move home could best be described as being *pulled* back due to familial obligations. Danielle felt as though she had to move back home because it was the only way she could keep up with her bills and help at out at home. When Danielle was in college, she sent money home to help her mom, who was caring for her severely ill little brother. After Danielle dropped out of college, she struggled to keep up with her student loan payments while still sending money back home to her mom. Then her mom got sick and ended up in the hospital. "I had to come back to her house to help out with her and my brother," said Danielle. "And I'm the only one who has an income outside of what they get for Social Security." Unlike others who were pushed home by their student loans, Danielle was pulled home. She said that her loans have become harder (rather than easier) to repay now that she's moved home and become the primary caregiver and provider for her family. "It's just really overwhelming for me. It's just [another] bill that I have now."

Melody described her reasons for moving home as a combination of *push* and *pull* factors. When in college, Melody would send money home to her mom to help pay for groceries and utility bills. She continued this practice after she graduated college, but her job in retail made it difficult to pay her loans and help at home. She ultimately decided to move home, both as a strategy to pay down her debt, and so she could continue to help her mom like she did when she was in college. But she worries about how she can continue to assist at home and pay her student loans while also finding time to study for her exams for nursing school. "I feel like I can't fully focus and study for my boards because I'm always thinking, 'What if something happens? How can I pay [afford] that?' Because I'm already helping out at home. Another expense to think about. And what if I don't pass? What am I going to do? Because when the government wants their money, they want their money."

Whether they were pushed home, pulled, or some combination of the two, Black young adults are returning home at least in part because of their student loans. In figure 5.1, we show that this is yet another way that the consequences of student loan debt are racialized. In research with our colleague Cody Warner at Montana State University, we found that student debt is associated with a higher risk of returning home for Black but not white four-year college-goers.[18] For Black youth, student debt is a liability that makes the transition to adulthood more fragile and increases the risk of "boomeranging." For white youth, it is a resource. The upshot is that student loans are making it more difficult for Black youth to attain residential and economic independence from their parents and are fueling racial disparities in the transition to adulthood. In this sense, student loans are a stumbling block that impedes Black college-going young adults as they set out from

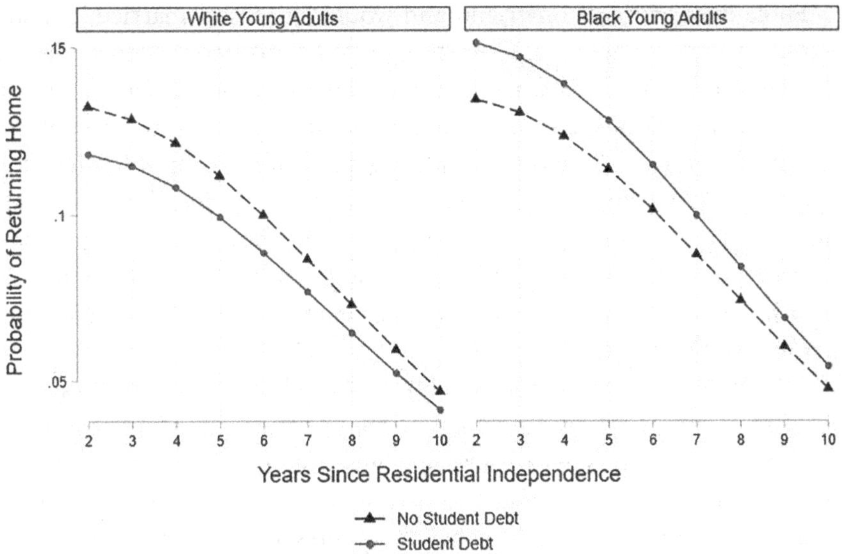

FIGURE 5.1 Student debt, race, and the probability of returning to the parental home

Source: National Longitudinal Study of Youth, 1997 Cohort

the starting gates to adulthood. As they find themselves stumbling out of the gates, it is difficult for them to imagine starting a family of their own.

"When You Get Married, It's Not Your Debt and Their Debt. It's Our Debt": Student Debt and Family Formation

When Malik was in college, he imagined a future with white picket fences, a spouse, and some children. Today, his reality is quite different. "I am single. I don't make very much money, but I have this high debt level. And so there are things in my life that, I wish . . . ," he paused, and trailed off. Even though young people today are more likely to delay marriage, cohabit before or instead of marrying, and put off having kids than previous cohorts, these changes have been starker for student loan debtors.[19] Our discussions with Black borrowers point to two key reasons: financial strain and the real and perceived stigma of debt among those looking for partners. For those who do get married and start a family, their student debt continues to play a role in shaping the dynamics of their romantic relationships.

Shola lives with her boyfriend and would like to get married, but she worries about her finances. "Something that I think about is how much it costs to get married," Shola said. Three months ago, Shola defaulted on her student loans. Now, she cannot envision getting married—the cost of the wedding, or their ability to start a life together—if she cannot pay her student loans. "I'm bringing all of this debt into this . . . So just thinking about how that's going to affect those things, or could affect those things in the future, is very discouraging." It's been enough for her to pump the brakes on any plans to get married. For the time being, she says, she will continue living with her partner.

Like many other young adults today, Shola is choosing cohabitation over marriage, for now at least. Cohabitation has become the modal relationship form for young adults, with more cohabiting than married before the age of thirty. Social scientists argue that part of this decision reflects the state of young people's finances today: cohabitation presents a welcome alternative when marriage feels financially out of reach.[20] When faced with the choice between cohabitation and marriage, many young people who are struggling with student loan debt are choosing the former. In one of the first studies of student loan debt and family formation, we found that young women with student loan debt were choosing cohabitation over marriage, more so than those without debt.[21] For many of the Black young adults we spoke with, debt was but one of many financial barriers to marriage.

Student debt may be a financial barrier to marriage, but it can also cause tension between couples. Student debt is a frequent topic of conversation between Jada and her boyfriend, who are planning to have a child together. The way she describes it, their combined student debt is almost like the third member of their relationship—the center of attention and sometimes a point of contention. Other respondents in serious relationships described their debt in the same way. Anthony, who is married, feels stressed out when trying to navigate his wife's loans. "I've never had an issue [with my federal student loans]. My wife's loan? It's a different story. She has Sallie Mae and some of those other private companies." Anthony says that his wife's private loans have caused arguments, in part because her loan servicer has been so aggressive about—and less flexible with—loan repayments. For those in serious relationships, student loan debt creates what Abby Stivers and Elizabeth Popp Berman refer to as *relational work*: the labor that goes into maintaining, navigating, and negotiating intimate relationships.[22] All relationships require work, but Stivers and Popp Berman argue that student debt compounds that work and can strain relationships. These disagreements can be magnified when individuals bring different amounts of debt to the relationship, such as Anthony and his wife, because it sets the groundwork for financial conflict, resentment, and blame.[23]

Student debt may feel like a daunting stressor for those in serious relationships, but it also poses problems for singles on the dating market. When we asked Malik, a recent college graduate, what has been the hardest thing about managing his loans now that he's in repayment, his answer surprised us: "This might be a little off-topic, but interacting with women!" he laughed. "When you get married, it's not your debt and her debt. It's our debt. My debt level is slightly more than twice the national average. If I go on a date, that's fine, great. But when we get serious several months later, you have to talk about your finances. And when it comes out, they're like 'Oh my gosh.' And so that's the thing that holds me back, if you will, in terms of taking these major milestone-like steps in terms of finding a wife and marriage."

Malik may have been half-joking, but he is not alone. Kirsten, who graduated from a public college in California, is single and worries about her debt. "I just started recently dating, and I've had to work through that," she said. "I had never thought it was a big deal, but then you're going into a partnership with a lot of debt. So how do you work through that debt, and what does that mean for your future with them if you have children? I definitely thought about what people would marry into, which would be my loans, and if that's an option. [But] I understand that those are luxuries that I'm not afforded at the moment, and I probably won't be for a very long time."

For most of the single young people we talked to, the stigma of debt loomed large. "I'm sure a potential partner doesn't want to be with me with this debt because they don't want to have to take it on themselves," Naomi said. "I just think of it as something as potential partners maybe will look down on me; I'm taking away rather than bringing something to the table. I feel like within my generation and culture, we're very like *get money*. So nobody wants to be with somebody with debt. They want to be with somebody who's getting money and making moves." Naomi's concerns are a clear demonstration of the sense of worthlessness that comes with internalizing the stigma of debt. But they also highlight how, when a culture values money above all else and when life becomes commodified, those with debt are found to be wanting.

Lucy had more practical concerns: time pressures. "I feel like I'm always living with this sense of pressure. It even affects my ability to do something as simple as building a relationship with someone," she said. "I don't feel I have the luxury of just being able to spend hours at a time talking to someone because it's like, okay, well it's been an hour and a half. I need to go apply for a job or something. I need to figure out a way to make money . . . I do worry about marriage prospects, though, because, my gosh, who would want to marry me with all the debt that at I have? That's really scary. Or what if I meet someone who has just as much debt as I have. Will we ever get out of debt? This is just scary." Lucy isn't just in debt; her life has come to revolve around debt. *Like a dark cloud over her head*, debt is shaping all of the decisions she makes, and makes her feel she should always be working to pay down her debt. She is not alone.

"I Don't Feel Like I Have a Life Because I'm Working to Pay Bills": How Student Debt Reorients Career Plans

Lucy was unequivocal when we asked how she felt about how her student debt affects her life. "Oppressive. Literally oppressive," she said. "I have a friend who's debt-free. She's never taken out a loan in her life, and I see the contrast between her life and mine. Now she's working on a startup, and she is so free with how she uses her time because she doesn't have to worry about paying anyone back. Whereas for me, I feel like all my time is figuring out how to make money so I can pay back my loans." Lucy feels as though her student debt has reoriented her life around paying bills. Instead of thinking about what she wants to do with her life and her career, she's thinking about what she has to do to pay bills now, which shapes her short- and long-term career plans.

For our respondents, the pressure to pay student loans made their working lives feel transactional and commodified: they were working to pay bills, and nothing else. Jacqueline described her life as a constant hustle in service of paying her debts. "I have a full-time job, and I've always had at least one or two additional part-time jobs," she said. "I don't feel like I have a life because I'm working to pay bills. I remember there was a meme circulating around on the Internet: *I went to college to get a job to pay for college.* I literally feel like that's my life."

Instead of pursuing her dreams, Lucy and Jacqueline worked to pay the bills, which they feel blocked them from career opportunities. "I can't afford to do anything for free," Lucy said."No unpaid internships, which can often lead to amazing opportunities. I can't do that. I feel like I have to trade my time for dollars because I have all this debt I have to repay." Black young adults like Lucy and Jacqueline often have difficulty advancing in their early careers and are underrepresented in paid and unpaid internships during and after college.[24]

Other borrowers made career decisions that might qualify them for loan forgiveness—even if they're not sure that they'll ultimately qualify. Malik would prefer not to work as a food service worker at his alma mater, but he has stuck with it because he has been told his job will qualify him for public service loan forgiveness, because the university is a nonprofit. "I just feel constrained in this job because it's a stable state public-service-loan-forgiveness-qualifying job, and that's a long time to be on the hook at the same place," he said. "But at the same time, that's a lot of money that I'm on the hook for. It's a lot to walk away from."

Young people are often told to "follow their dreams" and "pursue their passions" when they leave college, and think about how long-term career plans align with those goals. But those who are struggling to repay their student debt need to make decisions that will help them now—not later. Research on student debt and career decisions resonates with the stories we heard from our respondents: debtors are working longer hours, and they're taking the highest-paying jobs they can find that help them pay the bills now, even if those jobs don't have as much potential for wage growth in the long run.[25] They don't have the luxury to follow their passions; they have to follow the money.

Sociologists argue that college graduates today operate on the "passion principle"—striving for careers that allow them to pursue their passions and follow their dreams.[26] The ability to pursue these passions, however, often depends on social position. After all, how can you have the freedom to pursue your passions if you are discriminated against because of the color of your skin, you can't afford to make rent, and you are falling behind on your student debt payments? When Linda was in college at a private college in the South, she got her degree in education and wanted to make a difference teaching in low-income Black communities. After college, she followed her passion. But when her student loans came due—she had borrowed around $20,000 in undergrad—she couldn't afford to make the payments. She was able to defer payments for a while, but as she watched her balance grow, she worried about how she would pay her loans. "I'm like, what kind of soul-selling job do I have to work in order to be able to pay off all this debt?" Recently, she went back to graduate school to try to open up her career options, but she feels that student debt has reoriented her career plans. Before, she never thought about salary; she thought only about her passion. Now, she says, "Student debt is affecting the types of jobs I want and accept versus the types of jobs that I really think are going to be helpful [to society]." Virgil, too, is a teacher, but it is not his passion. "I feel like I work [as a teacher] because I have to," he said. "I'm staying in teaching because I have to pay bills. I'm less likely to take the safe move that I know that I need to take to try and pursue my artistic dream. I know that I need to make a move, but I won't because I know that staying in teaching is going to keep a check in my bank account every month." Sarah went to school for social work and hoped to help communities of color, but found she wasn't making enough money in her first job and found a higher-paying—but less-satisfying—job. "Switching to the job I have now pays substantially more, so as I think about next moves, it feels like I need to stay in this sort of position," she said. "I mean it's not necessarily what I thought of in going into social work. I thought I'd be doing more community-based work with people. But that stuff doesn't pay well."

At every turn these borrowers are trying to make the practical choice, even if it comes at the expense of pursuing the career they would prefer. Critics of student loan debtors have often argued that debtors made bad choices—not only that they borrowed too much or too little, but that they also make bad career and major choices that funnel them into low-paying jobs that make it difficult for them to repay debt.[27] Such critiques are part of *deficit narratives* that seek to frame Black people's outcomes as individual flaws rather than structural problems. But this, like all *deficit narratives*, is false. For example, a study by Natasha Quadlin finds that Black students who take on loans in college are more likely to major in "applied" fields, such as business and nursing, rather than the humanities or the social sciences.[28] Quadlin argues that these findings suggest that students may be more likely to gravitate toward "practical" majors when they know they'll have loans to pay after they leave college. Student loan debtors aren't making bad decisions; they're being practical. But these practical choices were not enough to save them from their student debt. Instead, they felt stuck—stuck with jobs they didn't want and stuck with debt, even if they feel they're making the best decisions they can.

So what comes next? Agnes, Linda, and Lisa are teachers; they knew they weren't going to get rich, but they hoped this work would be rewarding and provide them with enough to make a decent living. "I went into education knowing that I wouldn't be a millionaire," Lisa said, "[but now] I know that just being a teacher, I'll never be able to pay off [my student debt]." Lisa feels dejected and out of options—so much so that she now says she regrets going to college. Recently, she had a frank discussion with her parents: what can she do? Their answer: Go back to school. "My dad would like me to pursue a PhD," she said, "but I'm like, I'm never going back to school [laughter]. I'm not doing that." But for Agnes, Linda, and many other Black young adults stuck in what they feel are dead-end jobs and too much debt, going back to college comes with the promise of opportunities they could not attain with their bachelor's degree.

FOLLOWING THE EDUCATION GOSPEL TO GRADUATE SCHOOL

Sandra felt stuck in a dead-end job. So, after working as an administrative assistant at a construction company for four years, she decided to enroll in an online master's program in business from a private nonprofit university. "Going back to school is a way to help pay down my debt," she said. "I'm trying to find a job where I can get paid a good amount of money." For her, graduate school checks all the boxes: it comes with the promise of financial security; it allows her to pursue her passions, keep her options open, and because of that, will help her pay down her debt. It seems like the most sensible, practical solution. Or that is what she hopes, anyway. The reality is that while going to graduate school may seem like a good solution, it comes with a great deal of risk and more debt. A lot more debt.

When she decided to go to graduate school, Sandra was participating in a cherished American tradition: don't like your station? Get an education! She followed the *education gospel* to graduate school. Sandra is part of a growing number of young Black college graduates who choose to go on to graduate school after leaving college. Although Black students are underrepresented in graduate school—in large part because they are also underrepresented in undergraduate education—among those who graduate from college, Black college graduates are more likely to enroll in graduate school than their white counterparts.[29] Much of the growth in graduate enrollments has been driven by students of color.[30] Such statistics could be seen by some as evidence of racial progress, but the story is more complicated.

In the past decade, the total number of people enrolled in graduate school has increased by nearly 40 percent, and this growth has been driven by enrollments in terminal master's degree programs.[31] On the demand side, this increase in enrollment represents a creeping credentialism in the United States: as more people attain a college degree, employers ratchet up requirements for positions, and applicants look for ways to stand out.[32] On the supply side, graduate programs—especially master's degree and other certificate programs—have increased as colleges and universities have become more tuition dependent and desperate for revenue.[33] Because many graduate programs exist in part to generate revenue, they are both costly and often lack the more robust financial aid support of undergraduate programs, even at elite schools that have a reputation for financially supporting undergraduate students.

Alexandra went to get her master's degree in education at an Ivy League university because she wanted to set herself up for the best career opportunities. She knew that the university was well-resourced and had several financial aid and scholarship programs for students, and she planned to leverage those resources to help defray costs. But she was in for a rude awakening. "Everyone knows [the university] has a huge endowment, but the scholarships are restricted . . . so you search through the database and contact your school to let them know which scholarships you qualify for." After finding several scholarships she qualified for, she alerted the graduate school so that they would distribute the funds. "When I contacted the graduate school, they were pretty much like 'Oh, well, we don't participate in any of these.' It became such a big issue that the director for financial aid made a general announcement that there will be no negotiation of financial aid [for master's degree students]." Olympia had a similar story. "I remember looking at the financial aid award letter, and I was like, 'These heifers only going to pay for one class? That's it?'" This is a common problem among graduate students: even as the cost of attending graduate school has increased, opportunities to receive aid—scholarships, fellowships, student assistantships—have declined.[34]

After getting frustrated with the lack of financial aid at her university, Alexandra went to the financial aid office to try to figure out what to do. "When I had a meeting with the financial aid [officer], her response to me was literally, 'We see that you recently paid off loans, so you're familiar with the process.' So basically saying because I recently paid off loans, it should be no problem for me to take out more," she said. "What I've realized is that us master's students are pretty much paying for a lot of other people to come to school for free, and we're paying with interest on that. What's constantly being reiterated by administration is, 'Oh, we don't have funding for that,' and it's just like, 'Is this [an Ivy League university], or is this a community college?' I don't understand."

Both Alexandra and Olympia felt as if they were reliving the choice they made when they were undergraduates: if they wanted to complete their education, they would have no choice but to borrow. But because the costs are so high and the aid is so low, the numbers add up quickly. Olympia, who borrowed around $10,000 to fund her undergraduate degree over four years, accumulated closer to six-figure debt during her two-year master's degree. "[In undergraduate] I had a lot of scholarships that covered the majority of the cost," she said. "In my master's, the loans covered the majority of the cost. So my graduate degree debt is absolutely ridiculous." Alexandra borrowed around $45,000 to pay for her master's degree, in addition to the $28,000 she took out as an undergraduate.

Kirsten managed to avoid taking on debt as an undergraduate in part because she attended a college that had robust financial aid programs for students of color, but graduate school was another story. "All loans," she said. "That's where the juicy stuff happens. I knew that graduate school, especially master's programs, they are really rare in supporting grad students. So they give a little assistantship stipend, which was like $6,000 a semester. And then for the rest, for the first year of my master's program, I took out a Direct PLUS Loan [for] about $12,000. And then I took up the full $20,500 loan for both years in my master's program. And then pretty much from my second semester of my master's program up until I left my master's program, I had a side job. I worked at Lowe's; I worked as a research assistant in a couple of labs to try and supplement the income. It was never really enough."

Some scholars who study student loan debt ignore graduate school debt or argue—either implicitly or explicitly—that we should not care about debt accrued in graduate school. Their reasoning goes something like this: the numbers may be eye-popping, but nobody is forcing students to continue their education into graduate school. Besides, those who get graduate or professional degrees often end up in high-wage careers that make their large debt loads manageable. But what this narrative misses is that many Black students are not going to graduate school as some sort of vanity project, but because they're seeking the financial security that their bachelor's degree never provided them. And while the rewards to graduate degrees may be larger, so too are the risks.

The financial risks of graduate school are high and are racialized. Five- and six-figure debts—like those held by Kirsten, Olympia, and Alexandra—are not uncommon among Black graduate students and are becoming more common. Black students owe substantially more graduate debt than the average—around $71,000 in 2016, compared to approximately $54,000 owed among white and Hispanic graduate students.[35] All available evidence suggests that the situation is becoming more dire. Between 2000 and 2016, Black-white disparities in outstanding graduate student debt nearly *quadrupled* in size, and racial disparities in graduate school debt are several orders of magnitude larger than racial disparities in undergraduate debt.[36]

Six-figure debts—the kind that are extremely difficult to repay, even among high earners—are also troublingly common among Black graduate students, and becoming more so. In a recent analysis, Robert Kelchen found that in 2000, it was rare for students of any racial background to accrue more than $100,000 in student debt (around 1 to 2 percent of all borrowers), and racial disparities were relatively small. But by 2016, he found an "astonishing" disparity—with nearly one in three Black graduate students owing more than $100,000, compared to only one in ten white students.[37] Alexis, one of those Black graduate students, has six-figure debt between her undergraduate and graduate education. "To be over $100,000 in debt, it just seems like it's going to be a burden that's going to be with me for a very, very, very long time," she said. "And again it's helped me get my degrees. But this is not the position I wanted to be in five years ago." So what explains racial disparities in very high debt loads? Kelchen had the same question after investigating this topic. He found that these racial disparities were not attributable to fields of study—again, it's not that Black students are making bad choices—but instead he argues that structural racialized inequalities, such as the racial wealth gap, play a more important role.[38] Just as undergraduate student debt is racialized, so too is graduate student debt.

Academics, policy makers, and others have long argued that the eye-popping graduate student debts are nothing to worry about because those with graduate degrees make more than enough to cover their debts. But Virgil would like a word. Virgil first went to graduate school to get his master's degree because he felt as though he had to. "[After college] I was making upper thirty thousands per year, and I still can't really make ends meet. I felt like I need to get my master's degree so I can make more money as a teacher, so I can at least make mid-forties a year," he explained. "And so, I'm not going to be able to make ends meet while I'm going through this process. So I took out some more federal loans. And here I am getting in more debt to try to make more money." But as he took on more debt—$30,000 in total during graduate school—Virgil became disillusioned: why was he taking on so much debt just so he could make a few thousand more a year in his job? "And then the really crappy part is that I just lost motivation. I was like, 'I don't want to do this. I don't understand why I'm having to do this just so that I can make more money.'" Going back to graduate school was a failed Faustian bargain for Virgil: he was hoping to trade his passion for financial security, but instead he was left disillusioned and in debt.

Virgil, like so many other Black graduate students we talked to, felt cheated and regretful, and eventually decided graduate school wasn't worth it. He left school without his master's and is now saddled with graduate school debt levels without the advanced degree. "Even with a master's degree in education, hypothetically, I could have a master's degree, work for thirty-five years in education, and not even make $60,000. And I just really think that it's woefully unfair and that with the amount of work that teachers are expected to do and the nature of the work that we do, that something has to change. And I'm just not sure I want to continue to be a part of that." Virgil makes an important point here: even had he completed his degree, it's not clear the risk would have been worth the reward. Virgil and other Black graduate students take on substantially more debt than their white counterparts and yet have lower wages after they leave school. One of the few studies on graduate student debt by James Pyne and Eric Grodsky shows that in addition to higher debt burdens, Black graduate degree holders make less than their white counterparts—a difference that holds for all types of advanced degree holders, including master's, doctoral, and professional degree holders.[39] These wage gaps—just like the racial debt disparity—have increased in the past two decades.[40] Even PhDs can't bridge the racial economic divide because "umbrellas don't make it rain."[41]

Virgil tries to retain his sense of humor through it all. "The major thing, right now, is they're asking for their money back. And they're asking for an amount that I can't pay. And the sad thing is that I've also considered just going back to school," he laughed. It was a running joke among many of our respondents that they might go back to school to defer or delay debt repayment, but the undercurrent of that dark humor was an even darker reality: many of them had no idea how they were going to get out from under their debt.

Kirsten thinks about these things a lot. When we asked her how she thinks her debt will affect her in the long run, she paused. "I think in the short term, positive, because it helps me kind of [be] able to live, be able to afford rent and a car, and not even luxuries, just basic necessities [while in graduate school]." Her debt got her a degree, and nobody can take that away from her. "I think in the long term, it will be negative. What I've accrued in the long run, it's going to bite me in the butt because I'm going to have to take care of that on top of trying to navigate a new job, a new place, purchasing a home. I don't know when it'll be an option but not for a very, very long time."

6

Student Debt and the Reproduction of the (Fragile) Black Middle Class

Now in her late twenties, Olympia has plans. She would like to settle down, save some money, and buy a house. But she worries about how she is going to make that happen. Olympia has $61,000 in debt between her undergraduate and master's degree programs, and her balance continues to increase. "One of my main goals is to buy a house at some point before I'm forty. But I'm really worried that my student loan debt could prevent me from getting a good deal on a house. I know student debt is the biggest thing on my credit report right now, so I know that's impacting my credit score." There have been times when Olympia has struggled to make her payments on time, but every now and again she finds herself with extra money left over at the end of the month. When that happens, she has a decision to make: "Do I need to save this money or put this money towards student loans and make an extra payment for that month? And being aware that if I focus on paying on this debt as much as possible, it's taking away from other resources of buying a car, buying a house, and all that other stuff." If Olympia is going to be paying down her debt—and putting all of her extra income and savings toward that debt—how will she build a nest egg and save for her dream home? Or even have enough to tuck away for an emergency sitaution? It is a question she asks herself all the time. "I just always think of how this can impact my socioeconomic mobility, economic prosperity in America, especially for students and people of color and how it's preventing a lot of us from reaching other goals that we were told we could reach if we go to college. So it's definitely on my mind a lot. It's something that I just think about."

Olympia's struggles highlight a grim reality for Black people in the United States. We often think of college as a solution for inequality, or an "engine of upward mobility," but that engine doesn't appear to be working for Black college-goers like Olympia. Instead, it appears to run faster and smoother for white college-goers than for everyone else. If college could reduce racial inequality, one might think that the racial wealth gap would shrink as education increased. But in fact, the opposite is true. The racial wealth gap is widest among college-educated households.[1] College, it would seem, is exacerbating racial inequality rather than alleviating it. We argue that the racialization of student debt is part of this story.

We previously outlined how struggles with student debt repayment materialized, created feelings of despair, and complicated the transition to adulthood for Black borrowers. Whether it was the magnitude of the debt, their inability to make progress, difficulties with making the minimum payment, or the need to juggle student debt with other financial obligations, many of our respondents believed that they may never repay their debts or would spend the rest of their lives doing so. Aware of the fragility of their economic position, they faced a future built not on the strength of their educational credentials, but on the weakness of the financial foundation tied to that decision. If this is what it meant to be a part of the college-educated Black middle class, then debt, not wealth, was a defining characteristic.

As our society begins to grapple with the near inevitability of taking on student debt to attain a college degree, it has also unveiled the inner machinations of wealth production and the intractability of racial wealth inequality within our society. In this chapter, we explore the economic consequences of racial disparities in debt: if racial disparities in debt are wide and increasing over time, what are the consequences for racial economic inequality?

PLANNING FOR THE FUTURE AND FALLING SHORT

Many borrowers know that the opportunity costs associated with debt repayment are high. As Yasmine, a thirty-two-year-old community college and four-year college graduate, articulates here, "I mean, I would have more disposable income if I didn't have the debt. My net worth would be plus $17,000 right now if I didn't have the debt. So I mean, in the abstract sense, it has impacted it. And every month, every dollar that I put toward the debt is less money that I can save or invest in something else." Yasmine is right. All else equal, by age thirty, having student debt is associated with lower net wealth, financial, and nonfinancial assets compared to those without debt.[2] If Black borrowers like Yasmine are paying down their debts when their white counterparts are purchasing homes and saving for retirement, then it is unlikely they will be able to catch up or surpass them. And for those who are falling behind on their loan payments—like Yasmine—their ability to save for the future and accumulate wealth is further hampered. In this way, the racialized student loan debt disparities that emerge in young adulthood can exacerbate racial wealth inequalities.

It seems obvious that having student debt means you might be less likely to buy a home, or having debt prevents you from saving money. But this does not seem to be true for everyone. Using the same NLSY97 data that we analyze, Min Zhan, Xiaoling Xiang, and William Elliott find that those who leave college with student loans have lower net worth than those who do not, but this association is stronger among Black than white young adults.[3] The financial consequences of student debt are racialized. If debt is a millstone that weighs down one's ability to generate wealth, it is a heavier millstone for Black young adults.

"I Want to Buy a House, but I Don't Think It's in the Cards Right Now Because I'm in Too Much Debt"

Jaydnn, a thirty-year-old college graduate who came from a middle-class background, doesn't know where to begin. He feels as though he cannot plan for his future, let alone make big decisions like buying a home, until he pays off his debt. His situation has made him start to question his ability to attain his goals. "I think it's made me feel hesitant to want to make big financial steps in terms of like purchasing a house or starting a family," he said. "Knowing that I have these monthly payments looming and how much they are, it's been challenging to figure out how exactly could I begin to think about affording a house with these loans. That's one thing that's been really challenging." Jadynn's hesitancy was a common refrain among our interview respondents. Here, he explains how his student debt not only makes it hard for him to save for buying a house but also makes it nearly impossible to plan for a future where that wealth is a possibility. If you are not able to conceive of how to achieve a particular goalpost financially, then the realization of that goal becomes less feasible.

Linda, a first-generation college graduate, envisions becoming a homeowner one day. But it is hard for her to see how that will happen. "I want to be able to buy a house. My mom wants to retire. So I'm trying to figure out how to help her when she's not working and taking care of things that need to be taken care of," she paused, and sighed. "I can't do anything. I can't buy a house, definitely not in [in this city]. So I have to think about what my life is going to look like after this, and it looks like I won't be able to do any of that. I'll be living with my mom in her house and trying to pay her bills, and I won't be able to maybe get my own place for a while." For Linda, the homeownership dream remains out of reach given her debt and geographic location. The housing market in the city where she lives is one of the most expensive in the US. And, like many other borrowers, she won't be able to realize her dreams with financial help from her familial networks, but instead must ask how she can attain her goals while she is trying to navigate both her debts and her role as a financial caregiver. Of course, there may be unmeasurable nonpecuniary returns to Linda's situation, such as the support and assistance that proximity to family provides, but her arrangement comes coupled with a lower likelihood of wealth generation or financial security.

Like Linda, many of our respondents expressed feelings of regret and sadness that they would not be able to attain homeownership in the foreseeable future. Their student debt, coupled with their precarious economic situations, impeded their ability to become homeowners. Charity put it this way: "As far as trying to buy a house—I want to buy a house, but I don't think it's in the cards right now because I'm in too much debt. My debt-to-income ratio is too high. It's too, too high, and I know that. And I'm not trying to get, I guess, in more debt trying to buy a house. I'll rent until I can't." And if it was not the magnitude of the debt, others knew their history with defaulting on their loans might even make it impossible to qualify for a mortgage with a manageable interest rate.

Debra sees it all as deeply unfair. "All of it, to me, sounds like financial discrimination," she said. "So when you look at all that debt, you realize that you're spending more than what you're trying to spend trying to acquire a house. But they don't really want you to buy a house. You've got to pay high-interest rates if you tried to include a house in your spending, even if you, actually, have the money for it. They still say, 'You almost have too much debt.' That's where it gets complicated, at least for me, right now."

In the United States, homeownership has long been seen as the pinnacle of the American Dream. But this long-term stable financial foundation—one that forms the basis of middle-class life at least since the middle of the twentieth century—has always required either familial wealth or government financial assistance (in the form of access to low-interest mortgages) to acquire. White young adults, for example, are far more likely to get money from their parents for a down payment, because white families have the savings, home equity, or other forms of wealth to put down large sums of money on their children's future homes.[4] Jaydnn and many Black borrowers cannot rely upon familial wealth to help them achieve homeownership. Homeownership, as a vehicle to middle-class status, creates wealth for those who have access, and wealth is what buys access. In a racially stratified society, this also means that systems that support white American wealth accumulation through homeownership do not support Black Americans. Far fewer Black Americans have ever become homeowners. At its peak prior to the 2007–09 Great Recession, Black homeownership rates reached just under 50 percent compared with 77 percent for white Americans, and homeownership as a wealth-building enterprise has been all but nonexistent within the Black community.[5] Black households who are able to own homes encounter housing market discrimination and residential segregation that diminish the value of their home and its appreciation over time. Black homeowners are unable to extract wealth or build their wealth via home equity similar to their white counterparts. Andre Perry, Jonathan Rothwell, and David Harshbarger find that the property values of houses located in majority Black neighborhoods are devalued by half compared to equivalent homes in neighborhoods without Black residents.[6]

The deck is already stacked against Jaydnn, Olympia, Charity, and other Black college graduates who aspire to buy a home and achieve "middle-class" status. Student debt compounds that disadvantage and is but one more barrier in a long, historic line of barriers to home ownership. Over 70 percent of our interview respondents said that they feel as though their student debt prevents them from purchasing a home. That student debt is negatively associated with homeownership and home equity means that for many Black borrowers wealth generation may continue to be an elusive goal.[7]

While several respondents talked about how student debt hampered their dreams of homeownership, others spoke about adjusting their dreams and goals for the future. Jared, a thirty-one-year old graduate, lightheartedly joked that he would be downgrading his future desires and would settle for a lesser alternative. "I'd like to have a lot more savings. I'd say I'm doing pretty well. But had I not had student loans or had they been forgiven or something, I'd have a better car. I'd have probably a bigger house or more children. Things of that nature. But I'd say I pretty much probably live the same. I don't need to have a Maserati or anything like that. *But just to have the option to have that stuff is what I would be looking for.*" It was not because Jared felt undeserving or his preferences had changed, but that his student debt had rendered "the option" of setting such lofty goals out of reach. He settled for less. Jared's hopes for a nicer car or a bigger home might seem trivial in comparison to Jaydnn's struggles to purchase a home. But the point is that the cuts from these debts are sometimes deep and sometimes superficial. Either way, they still cut. Our society tells children to dream big, but for Black children the messages are: *you're dreaming too big* or *you have to be more realistic.*

"You're Almost Stuck:" Student Debt, Asset Accumulation, and Access to Credit

Debra, like Olympia, feels stuck. She can pay down her debt, but that means she cannot save money for the future. When she first took out student debt, she thought it was great because it helped her to get to and complete college. But now her opinion has changed. "It's negative now. Before, it was positive. I do want to pay it. But I don't want it to hinder me from my own timeline of acquiring capital for my family. Capital assets is what gets you where you need to be. So if I don't have the ability to leverage what I have economically, you're almost stuck—I'll be stuck in the same place for a good little minute."

"Being stuck" was a common theme among our interview respondents. For some, this meant that they were not able to contribute to their savings and their retirement, which made them anxious about the future. They felt as though they were standing still while everyone else passed them by. For others, it meant that they couldn't access credit—to get a new car, to open a business—that could help them move forward. And for those in the most dire straits, it meant that they had to turn to high-cost loans and credit cards just to stay "stuck" and not fall behind.

Much like the prospective homeowners we profiled here, some felt as though they would never be able to save for the future with all of the bills they have right now. Jaydnn and Khadija are setting aside money to pay for their loans, but they wish they could have saved or invested their money to secure their future or start emergency savings funds. "Not only am I paying a lot of money," Jaydnn said, "I'm also missing out on the savings and the interest I can get from that savings or other ways to invest money. So I'm kind of missing out in two ways. You know?" Khadija added: "The money that I'm making right now isn't going towards what I want in the future but what I've spent on in the past."

Jacqueline, too, worried about how her student debt would affect her long-term plans for retirement. A recent meeting with a financial advisor confirmed her fears. "My financial advisor [told me] I wouldn't be able to retire at what would be a 'traditional retirement age' based off just how much I was making and how much debt that I have. And just to reiterate, my only debt is my student loans."

Jaydnn, Khadija, and Jacqueline are stuck, paying down debt instead of saving for their future. Robert Hiltonsmith, a senior policy analyst at Demos, argues that this is one key reason that student debt impedes wealth acquisition. According to his analysis, four-year college graduates with debts of $50,000 can expect a lifetime wealth loss of nearly $208,000—most of which comes from lower retirement savings.[8]

Student debt can also shut off opportunities to build assets because debtors lack access to credit. Earlier, we discussed how Charity said her debt was too high to qualify for a low-interest mortgage. Many other borrowers who had fallen behind on their payments or defaulted also found it difficult to get access to credit to help them get ahead. Danielle, who is the primary caregiver for her sick mother and little brother, felt as though doors kept closing after she defaulted on her loans. "With the late payments and all that, with me being late on the payments or not being able to make payments, it's affecting my credit. So it limits me on things that I can do. So if I do want to get a loan for something, my interest rate is out of this world. So it's making all aspects of my life difficult, honestly." Lisa, too, ran into problems when she bought a car so she could have reliable transportation to work and was only able to get a high-interest rate loan. She has been trying to refinance to get a better rate, but she's striking out. "I tried to refinance my auto loan. And then, I was denied based on my credit history. And I don't have anything major on my credit outside of student loans. I don't have credit cards. I don't have anything else. This impacts my finances and just my ability to own a car. I can't get a car at a decent rate. I'm paying high rates. I feel like I'm being punished for the debt that I've incurred from school. [It's] like a punishment."

Troubles with debt repayment can lead to other difficulties outside of the credit market, as Shola discovered. Shola feared that her brief history of loan default would leave a mark on her credit history and prevent her from other opportunities. "I think the past three months, three or four months, I was defaulting on my loans. But when you go to apply for something that's not necessarily financially based, they still want your credit score. So just thinking about how that's going to affect those things, or could affect those things in the future is very discouraging." Shola is right to be concerned.

Employers, landlords, and even insurance companies routinely check credit histories when reviewing applicants, and increasingly base their decisions on credit reports.[9] Defaulting on student loans makes it harder to get a job or secure an apartment, and studies show that Black borrowers are punished more heavily for poor credit scores than whites.[10] Households with student debt are also more likely to be credit constrained, denied credit, and less likely to be able to pay their bills on time.[11] Calee experienced all of this at once, when going through a particularly challenging time. "My credit was bad because my loans had gone into default, so I couldn't access consumer credit. When I separated from my husband, then I had the financial blow of separating, being a single parent, trying to rent an apartment, not having good credit, and just struggling financially."

Years before Calee separated from her husband and defaulted on her loans, she was having trouble making ends meet. She had dropped out of college and had a hard time finding a job that paid enough to keep up with expenses. At first, she was able to keep up with her student loan payments, but then it got harder to pay all of her bills on time. She applied for a credit card, and at first, the credit card made it easier to keep up with her bills. It was a safety net when times were tough. After she separated from her husband, Calee relied more on credit cards to weather the storm, but she could only get the highest-interest credit cards (around 35 percent APR) because of her credit. Soon, not only did she find herself struggling to pay her student loans, rent, and care for her child, but she couldn't pay her credit card bills either.

Without access to emergency savings, some of our interview respondents turned to high-interest unsecured debt—like credit cards—to make ends meet. Credit card debt and other forms of unsecured debt are often used to supplement inadequate wages and paper over financial insecurity, especially in the wake of stressful and expensive life events like divorce, job loss, and illness.[12] Maria, who is proud of the progress she has made paying down her private student loans, reluctantly turned to credit cards after her husband lost his job. "I am a pretty financially sound person," she said. "I'm not over here buying trips I can't afford or clothes I can't afford and stuff like that with my credit cards . . . [It's just that] my husband had been out of work. It's been more out of necessity."

Although credit cards and other high-interest loans may help borrowers weather adversity, they come at a high cost. These debts are substantially harder to repay than other forms of debt, in large part because they do not help borrowers build wealth, they have high interest rates, and balances can be carried forward from month to month—which happened to Calee regularly. Exhausted and out of options, Calee filed for bankruptcy. "I actually did file bankruptcy to get rid of the consumer debt," she said. "[I did it] with the awareness that the only debt I would have then at that point would be my student loan debt to focus on." Anthony, too, got into trouble when his roommate lost his job, moved out, and he was stuck paying rent on a two-bedroom apartment. "So there is a point where I had to make a decision between paying credit cards or my rent," he said. "And I paid the rent because I need a roof over my head. So a lot of my credit cards went into collections at that time. And it was a huge stressor." While these respondents faced challenges above and beyond their student loans, this is a subtle way that student debt undermines wealth: without a safety net, and no wealth to draw from, some borrowers took on more debt just so they could stay "stuck" without falling behind. In extreme cases, they ended with debts in collection and bankruptcy.

Student Debt and the Racial Wealth Gap

Our respondents' stories highlight the economic burdens of student debt for short- and long-term financial security. The stories vary in severity: for some, student debt means they will not get their dream car. For others, it makes them feel as though they'll never be able to buy a home and start their families. For those struggling the most, it cuts off opportunities, denies them access to credit, and plunges them deeper into debt. Unlike many of their white peers, they could not rely on inheritances to improve their financial status, so they prayed for debt cancellation.

Their stories reflect vast racial disparities in wealth that have persisted *across* generations, but racial wealth disparities also increase *within* generations because wealth begets wealth. Using data from the NLSY97, we estimate that the racial wealth gap among college-going youth more than doubles over the course of young adulthood—from a disparity of around $22,000 at age twenty-five to more than $56,000 by age thirty. As you can see in figure 6.1, Black college-goers are "stuck"; their wealth barely increases from the ages of twenty-five and thirty, while white wealth more than doubles.

Social scientists have long studied the origins and reproduction of the racial wealth gap and have argued that the wealth gap represents the sedimentation of centuries of systemic inequalities and vicious racist policies—from the institution of slavery, through "redlining" practices that denied

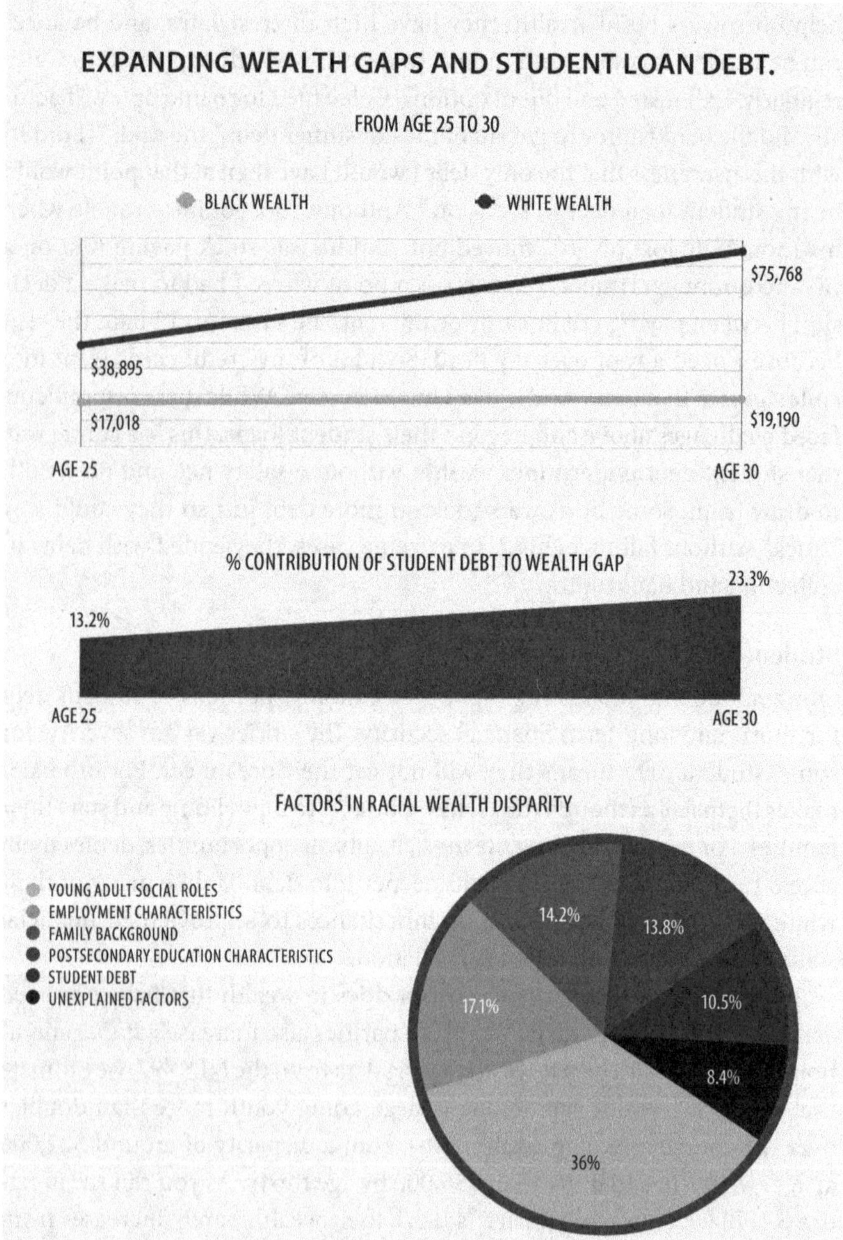

FIGURE 6.1 Student debt and the growing racial wealth gap

Source: National Longitudinal Study of Youth, 1997 Cohort; Image courtesy Jeffrey Himpele, VizE Lab for Ethnographic Data Visualization

Black people access to homeownership, Jim Crow, and racial segregation.[13] But when we saw the data on rising student loan debt among Black youth, we wondered whether rising student debt may explain part of the story among recent cohorts of young adults. That is: does student debt help us understand the wide racial wealth gaps that exist among college-going households? In a paper published in the *Sociology of Race and Ethnicity*, we tried to answer this question. Using the NLSY97 data, we found that racial disparities in student debt accounted for around 13 percent of the racial wealth gap at age twenty-five. In other words, if we could somehow snap our fingers and make Black debt equivalent to white debt, the racial wealth gap among college-going young adults would fall by around 13 percent. Troublingly, we found that the contribution of student debt to the racial wealth gap increased over time: by the time borrowers reached age thirty, student debt accounted for almost one quarter of the racial wealth gap.[14] When Yasmine said that her net worth would be higher if she didn't have student debt, when Olympia reflected on how she felt student loans affected her ability to attain economic prosperity, and when Debra said she felt "stuck" because of her student loans, they were right. But they did not need our statistical models to tell them that. To be sure, plenty of white people have stories about how their student debt has held them back; the issue is that this debt affects Black young adults to a much greater degree. Student debt is racialized, and it contributes to the racial wealth gap.

AN ENGINE OF UPWARD MOBILITY? INTERGENERATIONAL WEALTH, HIGHER EDUCATION, AND "MIDDLE-CLASS" ATTAINMENT

For many of our respondents, college felt like the only option. They had been told their whole lives that a college degree would buy them access to financial stability, prosperity, and a ticket to a "middle-class" life. This is indeed the overarching cultural message that we have internalized in the US. But if we define the middle class in terms of financial stability and security, it is far from clear that college provides access to the middle class for Black Americans. In fact, given the lack of intergenerational wealth among Black families, it's not even clear that there is a definable Black middle class.

Naomi grew up in what she called the "middle-middle" class. Her family was comfortable; her father was a dentist, and her mom worked in hospital administration. She said there was never any question that she would go to college. She remembers her parents telling her from a young age: "You're going to go to school. You're going to get good grades. And you're going to go to college because we went to college." Naomi says the message was clear: "If you want to have a life, you're going to go to a college." Her two older siblings went to college, and in her household, going to college was seen as the only way to "make it." But now, Naomi highlights the fragility of that middle-class position. Over time, she noticed cracks in the façade of her middle-class upbringing. "My parents both came from working-class low-income families, which means you're the one sibling who 'made it.' You're supporting your siblings and their children as well. And that went on, even in [my dad's] practice. His practice was basically in the hood, and his patients would not pay him. And so that meant less in our home." Later, Naomi would realize that her parents were barely getting by and were deeply in debt. Today, she sends money home to her parents to help out.

Naomi recalls how her father spoke about college when she was growing up: "On top of my dad presenting it as the best years of life, which is interesting because that's more of an idea for typical privileged kids from what I understand, because it is a space more for—I guess you could call it social maintenance, right, rather than a space where you're trying to gain some level of social mobility." But Naomi's precarious, or fragile, middle-class upbringing made her question whether college can truly buy financial stability. "I went into it, I think, in between the maintenance and the mobility part, growing up with the idea because I felt I'm kind of stuck between two worlds in a way because of my identity, even where I grew up." On the one hand, Naomi hopes that college can help her "preserve" or "maintain" the middle-class position she was raised in. On the other, she sees the fragility associated with her upbringing and hopes that it will also bring upward mobility to a more stable, secure position. This tension between the role that college should be serving for middle-class Black families and their children raised a question for Naomi: can a college degree buy the financial security and stability that is supposed to be afforded by a middle-class status?

For many of our respondents, there was the shared belief that middle-class status was attainable via a college degree. But like their parents and many generations prior, their debt accumulation and lower wealth levels reflected their fragile economic position. Throughout the entirety of our respondents' lives, the Black-white wealth gap, the difference in mean or median net worth between Black and white households, has either remained stagnant or increased. The racial wealth gap is even higher among college-educated households, where white households have fifteen times the median wealth of Black households.[15] This gap increased significantly post–Great Recession as college-educated white households got wealthier and the wealth of Black households was decimated by the Recession and has remained stagnant since.[16] Even among families with college-attending children at the top of the wealth distribution—the most privileged families—Black families had about 60 percent of the home equity ($92,555) of white families ($154,627) and almost half the financial assets ($46,579 versus $81,827).[17] It is not just that Black households tend to have less wealth; the typical Black household has essentially no assets and rarely holds or has access to any appreciating assets to generate or increase their net worth.[18] Because middle-class Black families often lack the equivalent wealth, access to well-resourced neighborhoods, and social connections of middle-class white families, their security and status are more precarious and fragile.[19]

Despite vast racial wealth disparities, wealth is often missing from discussions of college as an "engine of upward mobility." Many go to college to acquire skills that will make them competitive in the labor market, and the economic value of a college degree has historically been a story about labor market wages and earned income, with a college education being one of the key engines of social mobility in the United States.[20] Lifetime earnings for those with a bachelor's degree are, on average, about $1 million more than for those with a high school diploma. And, while lifetime earnings for Black college degree earners are substantially lower than white degree earners (around 20 percent lower), there is no question that college is associated with income and wage gains among Black households.[21] The economic value of a college degree—especially in a labor market that offers virtually no opportunities for those without a college degree—has never been more clear. This income-based narrative, however, masks the broader economic factors—like wealth—that shape educational attainment and mobility, and has, until recently, ignored the role of student debt and its disproportionate burden on Black students and families. It also perpetuates myths related to how and whether a college degree can buy entry into the middle class for Black college-goers.

Using wealth, and not just income, to understand middle-class status, disrupts notions of college as an engine of upward social mobility. In a recent paper, William Darity and colleagues call income and occupational-based conceptualizations of the middle class "a White-centered narrative." They argue that wealth-based measures of class reveal the Black middle class to be much smaller than previously estimated and that the Black middle class is "subaltern"—the most privileged tier of an otherwise marginalized community.[22] For most, wealth in the US provides insurance against financial risks; serves as a mechanism of social mobility; and serves as a means of solidifying access to social, political, economic, and educational opportunities. In addition to providing a more complete picture of the household financial portfolio, wealth also captures the fragility of the Black college-educated financial position. When we consider that racial wealth gaps are largest among the college educated, it is clear that higher education is not as effective a mechanism for upward mobility—and entry into the middle class—for Black people as it is for whites. Moreover, because of their weaker wealth position, having a college education and beyond is less protective of middle-class status: highly educated Black people are far more likely to experience more downward mobility and indebtedness than more highly educated whites.[23] A college degree may buy higher incomes, but it's not buying wealth for college-going Black Americans, particularly in an era of debt-financed higher education.

To further illustrate this point, we asked whether a college education is associated with attaining a wealth-based measure of "middle class"—having at least median wealth (or higher)—among Black and white young adults.[24] We find that, by age thirty, Black young adults have about half the chance of being middle class (according to their wealth) relative to whites. And, a college degree seems to buy entry into the middle class for white young adults but not Black young adults: Black young adults with a college education are no more likely to be "middle class" than Black young adults with less than a college degree. White college graduates, on the other hand, are around 65 percent more likely to be "middle class" compared to whites with less education. College-educated Black young adults who fall short of being "middle class" are also more likely to have high student debts. These results provide additional evidence that a college degree is not an engine of upward [wealth] mobility for Black young adults, and student debt is a key reason why.

When we use a wealth-based measure of class, it also becomes clear that young Black women are less likely to be middle class than Black men. Although we have not engaged with intersectional theories or discussed gender dynamics in this book, it is Black women, not Black men, who make up the majority of our interviewees (around 80 percent). While one could argue this is a quirk of our interview sample, it also reflects the growing presence of Black women in higher education. Young women are more likely to attend college than young men, but this gender disparity is wider among Black young people. White women have the highest graduation rates at 39.62 percent, followed by white men, 31.24 percent. The gender disparity in college completion is even greater among Black Millennials, where Black women complete college (22.76 percent) at almost twice the rate of Black men (13.36 percent). Yet, the median wealth of Black male Millennials ($8,105) is 2.5 times greater than Black female graduates ($3,316). According to the American Association of University Women, female borrowers hold over two-thirds of the outstanding debt. As rates of enrollment and degree completion among women continue to exceed male students at the certificate, associate's, and bachelor's degree levels, there is mounting evidence that women are far more likely to have education debt, with Black female borrowers holding some of the highest loan balances.[25] The student debt crisis is both racialized and gendered.

None of these findings would surprise Naomi, as a Black college-educated woman. She came from the fragile Black middle class, and she feels as though she's going to end up like her parents—educated but financially insecure. Her parents wanted her to go to college to do better than they did, but she feels stuck and that she is going to end up right where she started. Not only is educational attainment not a guarantee of a wealth-based middle class (and never really was), but student debt is also impeding wealth accumulation and undermining her chances for social mobility. It's not just that student debt is making achievement of those goals out of reach, but that attaining these education goals never really meant securing middle-class status for Black Americans. And for the few who did, it was a temporary, oftentimes one-generational achievement. Disparities in student debt have become an additional policy-created mechanism contributing to divergences in outcomes related to the higher educational experience, but are also reproducing long-standing racial inequalities in wealth, particularly among college-educated populations.[26]

Black students take on a great deal of financial risk in pursuit of higher education. They incur this risk in a society that requires expensive credentials of populations that are underresourced, are the least wealthy, and face systematic barriers to wealth-building opportunities.[27] Under these conditions, they accumulate more debt, have more difficulty repaying that debt, and suffer greater economic consequences for incurring that debt. In an era of debt-financed higher education, college does little to reduce racial inequality, and these racialized processes are contributing to a fragile Black middle class, whereby the Black college-educated are more socially and economically fragile and at risk for downward mobility than middle class white families.[28] Student debt is the latest mechanism by which racial inequalities are reproduced across generations.

7

Upstream and Downstream Solutions

In May 2019, billionaire investor Robert F. Smith made waves with what many thought was a revolutionary intervention in the student debt crisis. At the end of his commencement speech to the 2019 graduating class of Morehouse College, he forgave the student debt of all the graduating students in the audience. In his thirty-five-minute address, Smith told the graduates before him about how their education gives them the opportunity to better themselves and their communities. But he juxtaposed these themes of hope against the barriers and systematic exclusion that have plagued the Black community for generations: the broken promises of the Freedmen's Bureau after the fall of slavery, the New Deal social safety nets that denied benefits to most Black workers, and the vicious redlining practices that categorically denied homeownership to Black families. He told the story of his daily rides to school on bus #13 and how forced busing policies in his hometown gave him an opportunity to get an education but left most of those in his community behind. Smith called on the graduates to "help make things better" and to use their newfound privilege as college graduates to lift up and liberate those around them. And then, as if to provide an example of what he meant, Smith said, "On behalf of the eight generations of my family that have been in this country, we're going to put a little fuel in your bus. My family is making a grant to eliminate [your] student loans."[1] Robert Smith's $35 million commitment to forgive the debts of Morehouse's class of 2019 (and their families) changed the lives of the young Black men in attendance that day. For them, debt would not—in the words of Stacey Abrams—"be a millstone that weighs them down." This gift, Smith hoped, would allow them to lift up others and pay it forward.

Smith's gift was a generous act of philanthropy. At the same time, it revealed the limits of private wealthy donors, and perhaps even the notion of debt forgiveness, for solving the student debt crisis. Smith's gift erased the debts of the young men lucky enough to graduate from Morehouse in 2019, but what of those who graduated in 2018 and left college with an average of $40,000 in student debt?[2] Or the young Black women who are barred from attending Morehouse but have greater debts than Black men? Or those—like Anthony—who did not graduate? How can they lift up and liberate their communities when their debts continue to be "a millstone that weighs them down"? Smith's gift, while laudable, is an individual solution to a structural problem.

In this book we have argued that the student debt crisis is racialized—that the historic rise in student debt and the risks it creates for economic, social, and psychological well-being disproportionately fall on Black college-goers. Scholars have spent the past decade arguing whether student loan debt represents an accumulation crisis, a repayment crisis, or a completion crisis. We have shown that, for Black college-goers, the answer is not "either/or" but "all of the above." Black college-goers—like Virgil, Lucy, and Naomi—are drowning in their debts in a way that white college-goers simply are not. We documented how the legacies of racism and racial inequality in the US have left Black Americans with no choice but to borrow and leave them struggling to repay that debt long after they leave school. While these loans may help Black youth gain access to and persist in college, student loans are an imperfect tool for college accessibility that creates new financial risks for young people in the pursuit of a college degree. To be sure, there are some Black Americans for whom the risk pays off—who either avoid taking on excessive debts or can repay their debt easily after landing a great job—but the numbers don't lie. For every person like Elise who avoided taking on debt or can easily manage their debts, there are thousands of Black Americans like Virgil, Lucy, Naomi, and Anthony who are the real face of the student debt crisis. These are the people who followed the *education gospel* to college, who believed, like many of us, that a college degree comes with the promise of upward mobility and stable middle-class lives. But for these and many other Black Americans, higher education has failed to deliver on that promise, like so many other American institutions that came before it. Instead of providing a pathway to the middle class, higher education has been an anchor keeping them in place. Instead of building up and strengthening the Black middle class, debt-financed higher education has made the Black middle class more fragile, more out of reach, and perhaps more illusory than it was before. The question then remains: What should, or could, be done about it?

When we hear politicians—such as Virginia Foxx or Brian Kemp—talk about student debt, they talk about individual deficits. They argue college students should make better decisions, take fewer risks, be more prudent with their money, or improve their financial literacy. But throughout this book we have made the case that Black Americans' struggles with student debt are rooted in centuries of systemic racism and racial inequality in this country and ultimately reproduce those racial inequalities. Systemic problems cannot be solved with individual-level solutions. It is akin to saying that if Black people worked a bit harder or had a stronger grasp of compound interest rates, then all would be well. It is, in effect if not its intention, a racist argument that does more to legitimate and justify racial inequality than it does to remedy that inequality.

Reducing or eliminating racial disparities in debt—and alleviating the suffering of Black borrowers—will require structural, not individual-level reforms. These solutions must simultaneously help those who are currently struggling with debt and prevent the next generation from repeating it. Medical sociologist Irving Zola used the metaphor of a raging river to describe solutions to social problems.[3] In Zola's story, a witness sees a person drowning in a swift river current and struggles to pull them to safety. A few minutes later, another person floats by, in need of assistance. And then another. Eventually, the bystander—exhausted from pulling people out downstream—decides to go upstream to investigate why people keep falling into the river. The metaphor implies that we can design *downstream* policies that help those who are drowning now, but we can also go *upstream* to prevent people from falling into the river in the first place. Solving the student debt crisis requires both upstream, downstream, and even midstream policies. Downstream policies may provide more immediate relief and be more politically feasible, but without upstream and midstream solutions that tackle root causes and focus on prevention, we will be forever pulling drowning people out of the river. As Tressie McMillan Cottom said, "Student debt cancellation without higher ed reform won't work. And higher ed reform without debt cancellation won't work either."[4] In what follows, we outline some of the policies that could assist Black borrowers who are drowning in debt, rein in debt-financed higher education, and make inroads toward addressing centuries of systemic racial inequality.

DOWNSTREAM SOLUTIONS: PULLING DROWNING DEBTORS OUT OF THE WATER

Debt Forgiveness

In our interviews for this book, nearly everyone we talked to had something to say about debt forgiveness. Some, like Kellyanne, planned to take advantage of the Public Service Loan Forgiveness program. She hoped she would be eligible for forgiveness under the PSLF's rather arduous eligibility criteria and repayment schedule, even though she knew that most applications were being rejected at the time. "My plan is to get it forgiven, and if it's not, then it's just going to blow my plan out of the water," Kellyanne said. "So, then what do I do?" Others hoped that the political winds were shifting and that their debts would be forgiven. "I really need to have a 2020 president who will forgive them," laughed Jaydnn. A decade ago, debt forgiveness was a fringe idea and held political support only for those students who were defrauded by for-profit colleges. But today, debt forgiveness is a mainstream political policy position; Elizabeth Warren and Bernie Sanders both proposed debt forgiveness plans during the 2020 presidential campaign. As of this writing, under pressure from progressive Democrats, President Biden has begun exploring his legal authority to forgive up to $50,000 in federal student debt via executive order.[5]

Debt forgiveness would lift a heavy financial burden off a generation of Black young adults and their families.[6] For Alyssa, it would mean she could save up enough money to move out of her mom's house. For many others, like Virgil, Malik, Jaydnn, and Lucy, it would give them the financial peace of mind to take the next step—to get married, start a family, or pursue their dream career. For almost everyone, including Lisa, it would ease the chronic anxiety she feels from worrying about how she will make her next payment. While it is hard to know what would happen if we could snap our fingers and eliminate student debt, a recent study by Marco Di Maggio, Ankit Kalda, and Vincent Yao tries to do just that.[7] In their study, Di Maggio and colleagues exploit a natural experiment, or a random shock, that led to debt forgiveness. National Collegiate, the country's largest private student loan company, lost a series of lawsuits because it failed to prove that it owned the loans it was collecting on. The judge then ordered these debts to be discharged. Overnight, the debts of thousands of borrowers were forgiven. Di Maggio and colleagues followed the borrowers who won these lawsuits and those who did not. What they found was that the lives of borrowers whose debts were forgiven improved dramatically. They had one less bill to triage, their finances improved, and they started paying down their credit cards and other debts. No longer weighed down by their debt, they began to move more freely about the country, getting better jobs, and improving their incomes and credit scores. Within three years, their incomes had increased by about $4,000, equivalent to about two months pay for these borrowers. Now imagine this scenario on a national scale. Debt forgiveness not only would benefit those borrowers affected but could also stimulate economic growth, increasing income, productivity, and consumption.[8]

Debt forgiveness can be an effective policy to combat the student debt crisis, but it will only be as effective as its design and implementation. The most effective policy is one that is *bold, accessible, and inclusive*, providing the most relief possible to the most borrowers. A *bold* policy is one that forgives all or most student debt. More timid policies—such as President Biden's proposal to forgive up to $10,000 in debt—will not offer relief to millions of Black borrowers, who accumulate substantially higher debts than their white peers and are more likely to hold six-figure debts. Even the most popular proposals that cap forgiveness at $50,000—such as Elizabeth Warren's plan—will only partially help Black borrowers who are deep in debt.

An *accessible* policy is one that borrowers can easily benefit from. One of the main criticisms of the Public Service Loan Forgiveness program is that it is administratively burdensome. To qualify, borrowers must first work for an employer that qualifies for the program, apply, and make standard payments for ten years, during which time they cannot miss a payment or depart from the payment schedule; they also are not allowed to modify or consolidate their loans, or else the clock is reset. At the end of the ten-year period, borrowers must then reapply for the program and confirm their eligibility. As we write this book, more than 90 percent of borrowers have been denied for one reason or another—having the wrong loan type, failing to meet the repayment criteria, not holding an eligible job.[9] A debt forgiveness program that is administratively burdensome to access and that few people can benefit from is not a forgiveness program; it is a broken promise. Any debt forgiveness program must learn from the mistakes of the PSLF and provide borrowers with clearer guidelines, annual reminders and information on forgiveness, and auto enrollment processes that minimize paperwork and confusion.[10]

Finally, an *inclusive* policy is one that is open to all borrowers, or the most borrowers possible. Most of the discussion surrounding student debt forgiveness focuses on federal loans and the students who borrow. Less discussed is the fate of private loans, which have less favorable terms and are more difficult to repay than federal loans. While the president may not have the legal authority to forgive private loans via executive order, Congress could pass legislation to forgive private student debt, and has considered bills that forgive private loans for for-profit-goers and students with disabilities.[11] Graduate students are often ignored in discussions of debt forgiveness, but as we show in chapter 5, Black graduate students carry substantial debt burdens and have just as much trouble paying their debt as undergraduate borrowers.[12] Also absent from discussions of student loan forgiveness are the parents of students, who have increasingly taken on and struggled to repay PLUS loans.[13] As debt balances grow among older adults, and older Black adults in particular, PLUS loans should be included in discussions on debt forgiveness.[14] In a recent interview with CNBC, Persis Yu, the Director of the National Consumer Law Center's Student Loan Borrower Assistance Project, summed it up nicely: "One of the takeaways from these student loan forgiveness programs is that trying to parse out who deserves cancellation and who doesn't is actually really hard. The most efficient, the fastest way and the way to ensure that you actually are getting relief to people who need it is to give it to everyone. That is the most equitable way to make sure that you're not wasting government resources slicing and dicing the student loan portfolio and spending money to keep money from other people, instead of just getting it to the folks who need it."[15]

Although universal programs are less administratively burdensome than targeted programs, critics of debt forgiveness argue that it is a regressive social policy, that its benefits would accrue to wealthy populations—such as doctors, lawyers, and other high-income groups—who both have higher debt loads and are more likely to attend college and accumulate debt than those who are less socially advantaged.[16] Some, like economist Darrick Hamilton, reject this reasoning and argue that all policies benefit those with less need (Type 1 errors, or "false positives") and miss those with the most need (Type 2 errors, or "false negatives"). "All policies have type 1 and type 2 errors," Hamilton argued at the *Dignity and Debt* workshop at Princeton University. "Simply because some privileged white folks may get their debt forgiven does not mean we should ignore the real suffering that student debt has caused among college-goers of color."[17]

Far from being regressive, debt forgiveness may actually reduce Black-white social and economic inequality.[18] Charlie Eaton, Adam Goldstein, and Laura Hamilton say that the idea that student debt cancellation is regressive is a "myth," in part because it ignores the racial distribution of student loan debt and the racial wealth gap. In a 2021 Roosevelt Institute report, they show that student debt cancellation would disproportionately benefit Black, low-income, and less wealthy borrowers because "people from wealthy backgrounds (and their parents) rarely use student loans to pay for college."[19] They argue that, for that reason, more substantial plans like Elizabeth Warren's proposal to forgive $50,000 would be more progressive than smaller plans that cancel only a small portion of debt (e.g., $10,000) because Black families hold larger loan balances than white families. In another analysis of Elizabeth Warren's proposal to forgive $50,000 in debt, Raphaël Charron-Chénier, Thomas Shapiro, Louise Seamster, and Laura Sullivan showed that 80 percent of Black households would receive full student loan cancellation, compared to 73 percent of white households.[20] The evidence that student loan debt forgiveness is a progressive social policy is mounting.[21]

Not only would debt forgiveness reduce racial disparities in student debt, but several different independent research teams using different data sources have found that it could also reduce racial wealth disparities. Charron-Chénier and colleagues, using the Survey of Consumer Finances, found that debt forgiveness would lead to greater relative wealth increases among Black households—in part because wealth levels are so low in Black households.[22] Our own analysis of the NLSY97 data, which we described in chapter 6, shows that if we could snap our fingers and make student debt levels between Black young adults and white young adults equal, the racial wealth gap among college-going young adults would decrease by nearly 30 percent.[23] Other teams of researchers have found the same pattern: debt cancellation is not only progressive, it could also reduce (but not eliminate) the racial wealth gap.[24]

In sum, debt forgiveness policies can undoubtedly lift the burden of debt off Black borrowers, who have been the hardest hit in the student debt crisis. Debt forgiveness is also likely to reduce racial disparities in student debt and has the potential to reduce racial wealth inequalities. It is not a silver bullet—and a one-time debt forgiveness policy will not prevent future generations from falling into debt—but it is a start.[25] President Biden appears to be warming up to legislation on debt forgiveness.[26] However, a policy must be bold rather than timid, accessible rather than burdensome, and inclusive rather than exclusive, in order to be effective.

Income-Based Repayment: Fixing a Broken System

Critics of debt forgiveness proposals argue that we already have a progressive debt forgiveness program in the United States: income-driven repayment (IDR).[27] But IDR has not delivered on its promise as a loan forgiveness program, and when loans are forgiven, Black borrowers will pay the price.

Borrowers enrolled in IDR are eligible to have their loans forgiven after making payments for twenty to twenty-five years, but forgiven debts are treated as taxable income. This means that borrowers who are promised the relief of debt forgiveness will be greeted instead by a tax bomb. How big would this tax bomb be? The Institute for College Access and Success has calculated tax burdens on loan discharge for several different scenarios, and all result in tax burdens of several thousand dollars. For example, upon their loans being discharged, a divorced social worker with two children who left school with $55,000 in loans from undergraduate and graduate school could expect to receive a tax bill of approximately $12,000 if they are enrolled in the REPAYE program and over $19,000 if enrolled in PAYE.[28] This would more than double the household tax burden for the year.

These tax burdens would disproportionately burden Black borrowers because they have higher debt burdens than their white counterparts, and their balances grow faster after leaving college. In her recent book *The Whiteness of Wealth*, Dorothy Brown, a professor of law at Emory University and expert on the tax code, writes "Today, [B]lack Americans of all income levels are . . . invisible when it comes to shaping policy, but are paying more in taxes than their white peers because our tax laws were designed with white Americans in mind."[29] IDR's debt discharge tax bomb is yet another example of how the tax system is stacked against Black Americans and contributes to racial and economic disparities. Of course, this needn't be the case: Public Loan Service Forgiveness does not treat debt discharge as taxable income, and neither should IDR plans.

In chapter 4, we identified three key challenges with IDR programs, as currently designed: they are difficult to access and administratively burdensome to stay enrolled in; they do not offer adequate financial relief for Black borrowers; and they leave too many saddled with too much debt for too long. That is, IDR is not sufficiently *bold, accessible, or inclusive*. But it needn't be that way. A streamlined IDR that is simpler, more accessible, and more equitable could be an effective downstream tool for alleviating financial distress among borrowers.

As it is currently implemented, IDR is inefficient, burdensome, and inequitable, the result of a complicated application and certification process, and perverse financial incentives among lenders. But increasingly, researchers point to a simple fix that could alleviate some of these problems: make IDR the default repayment option for borrowers. When borrowers leave college, they are placed in a standard ten-year repayment plan by default and have to "opt in" and apply for an IDR plan.[30] Susan Dynarski and others have advocated for making IDR the default option, giving borrowers the option of "opting out" of IDR if they prefer to be in a standard repayment plan. Such a move would be simple but effective. In a recent study, James Cox, Daniel Kreisman, and Dynarski showed that only one-third of borrowers chose to enroll in an income-based repayment plan when the standard plan was presented as the default option and they had to "opt in" to an IDR plan. But when borrowers were presented with IDR as the default option and given the option to "opt out" to a standard plan, the researchers found that the vast majority—63 percent—of borrowers chose the IDR payment option.[31] Making IDR the default option would not only increase take-up, but if correctly implemented, it could also cut lenders out of the application (opt-in) process and reduce default rates. Additional changes—such as streamlining the recertification process by having the IRS verify income (rather than relying on borrowers to submit paperwork)—would keep more people enrolled in IDR once they are there and reduce administrative burden.

To make IDR truly affordable and offer debt relief, changes also need to be made to reduce monthly payments and account for local differences in the cost of living. And those in default must be allowed to enroll in IDR, so people like Anya do not have to choose between paying their rent and paying their student loans.

The challenges to IDR are robust, but there are clear solutions. One promising fix comes from the Center for Responsible Lending and the National Consumer Law Center, which have proposed a new IDR plan, the Affordable Budget-Conscious (ABC) plan.[32] According to calculations by these groups, this new plan would reduce monthly student loan payments under current IDR plans by more than $100 per month for many borrowers and would save borrowers thousands of dollars over the life of the loan. Under the ABC plan, Anya would be able to more easily afford her monthly student loan payments. This plan solves these problems by doing the following:

1. Setting monthly payments to no more than 8 percent of discretionary income. The ABC plan reduces monthly payments relative to traditional IDR plans in two ways: it reduces monthly payments to 8 percent from 10 percent; and it calculates discretionary income as the difference between adjusted gross income and 250 percent of the poverty line in a given state (as compared to 150 percent for traditional IDR plans), which allows for more nondiscretionary income to be put toward rent and other essential expenses.
2. Reducing complexity in the system by streamlining the application process and recertification process.
3. Automatically enrolling all borrowers who are delinquent or default on their loans into the program, thus opening IDR to the most distressed borrowers.
4. Making discharged debt nontaxable, similar to the Public Service Loan Forgiveness program.

Fixing the broken IDR system is an important downstream solution to the student debt crisis. But relying too heavily on IDR as a downstream solution also creates risks for Black borrowers. For many, enrolling in IDR means their loan balance might increase, as their payment is lower than the accumulation of interest, and it ensures Black borrowers are saddled with more debt for a long period of time. IDR may have been created to address the repayment crisis, but it is a band-aid that does not address how and why borrowers are struggling to repay their loans or got into debt in the first place.[33] To address those issues, we need midstream and upstream solutions that focus on prevention.

MIDSTREAM SOLUTIONS: MAKING COLLEGE AFFORDABLE

The student debt crisis is at least in part, if not in its entirety, a crisis of college affordability. In chapters 2 and 3, we highlighted borrowers who felt they had no choice to borrow if they wanted to go to college. They talked about being surprised by how much they were expected to pay in the first year of college, and how they had difficulty paying not only for tuition but also for books, rent, and other living expenses. They talked about the difficulties of navigating a Byzantine financial aid system that put them at risk of losing their financial support. They also spoke of financial aid packages that swung wildly from year to year, of changing family circumstances—a parental job loss, an illness—that made college more difficult to afford over the course of their career. We also showed how the vast disparities in resources and support across institutions led to disparate outcomes and debts. Some students felt supported financially and socially and in turn borrowed less, whereas many others attended historically underfunded institutions that left them without a safety net. Making college more affordable for Black students would prevent many from accumulating excessive debt loads. We argue that this could, at least in part, be achieved by making financial aid more generous and less complex; reversing decades-long trends in defunding college and reinvesting in and refunding institutions of higher education that serve Black students; and, more boldly, making the first two years of public higher education free for all to attend.

Fixing Financial Aid

Virgil, Lucy, Naomi, and others we interviewed all expressed frustration in their experience accessing and receiving financial aid. Virgil missed a deadline, and his grandfather put his first semester tuition on his credit card. Lucy's parents had difficulty filling out the FAFSA form, and she remains convinced that it cost her valuable aid that would have prevented her from taking on debt. And Naomi's aid was never enough to cover the cost of tuition, room, and board, and she felt as though she often had to pass up opportunities—special classes, study abroad, internships—because she had to work to keep up with expenses. In chapter 2 we discussed how scholars have proposed that simplifying or eliminating the FAFSA—for example, by reducing it to a one-page application, or using tax information collected by the IRS to determine aid eligibility—would make it easier for students like Virgil and Lucy to access funds.[34] Doing so would also make it cheaper and more efficient for college financial aid offices and the federal government to administer.[35]

Beyond simplifying aid to make it more *accessible*, financial aid must be more *bold* to help make college more affordable. For example, the Pell Grant—a key source of financial aid among low-income Black students—has not kept pace with rising college costs. When it was first introduced in the 1970s, the Pell Grant, on average, covered nearly 80 percent of the total cost of college—including tuition, room and board, and fees. Today, the Pell covers less than 30 percent of the total costs of college.[36] What this means is that students like Virgil have to pay more out of pocket, take on more debt, work long hours, and lose out on opportunities in college. President Biden has proposed doubling the Pell Grant to reverse the historical decline in its value.[37] Others have proposed more modest steps of indexing the Pell to inflation to slow its decline.[38] In the end, increasing student aid—including but not limited to the Pell Grant—would increase access to and persistence in college, and reduce debt.

The Consolidated Appropriations Act of 2021, which was recently signed into law, takes some small but important steps toward meeting these goals and improving the accessibility and generosity of financial aid. Among other things, this legislation simplifies the FAFSA by reducing the number of questions on the form and making it easier for vulnerable students to recertify their status as independents. It also makes financial aid more generous, by changing how the expected family contribution (EFC) is calculated; it will now be referred to as the Student Aid Index. For the first time, the EFC/SAI can be negative, which will allow the neediest students to receive more aid than the cost of attendance.[39] Financial aid reforms like these are critical for helping students and families keep up with rising college costs, but they do not address a key root cause of this problem: the defunding of higher education.

Reinvesting in Public Higher Education

When state funding for public higher education is cut, colleges become more reliant on tuition for their revenues, and often pass these costs on to students and families by way of higher tuition and fees and cuts to institutional financial aid. Making college affordable will not be possible without reversing this trend and (re)funding public higher education. Doing so will require a massive reinvestment of public funds in higher education, which begs the question: how could we pay for all of this? Many scholars and policy experts—including Laura Hamilton, Sara Goldrick-Rab, among others—have argued that this money could be raised by ending tax breaks for wealthy, elite, private institutions and redistributing this revenue to public colleges and universities.[40] Others, like higher ed policy experts Dominque Baker and David Deming, suggest that this could be achieved via state and federal partnerships.[41]

In earlier chapters, we argued that the defunding of higher education has been racialized—that funding has been limited and cuts deeper at HBCUs, MSIs, and regional colleges and branch campuses that primarily serve students of color. For too long, colleges that primarily serve students of color have been underresourced and done less with more. So if the defunding of higher education has been racialized, the refunding of higher education must correct these disparities and be targeted toward the very institutions that have been long-starved. There are some signs that progress is being made toward this end. The passage of President Biden's American Rescue Plan included an unprecedented reinvestment in HBCUs, including $2.6 billion in funding in 2021, tripling the typical funding that these schools typically receive. But while this level of funding may be unprecedented, Dominique Baker argues that this one-time injection of funds pales in comparison to the high cost of decades of racist policies that have starved these institutions.[42]

Scholars and activists have also made inroads to raise awareness and funding for the regional public colleges and branch campuses that disproportionately serve Black students. For example, the Michigan *One University* campaign has strived to equalize state funding appropriations across all Michigan campuses. Historically, flagship campuses (like University of Michigan–Ann Arbor) have received the lion's share of state funding and can rely on a steady stream of donations from alumni donors. But branch campuses—like Dearborn and Flint in Michigan—lack a wealthy alumni donor pool, and cuts in state appropriations tend to hit these campuses the hardest. Campaigns like the *One U* campaign seek to redress these disparities, and lobby for more equitable distribution of state funding. Although the *One U* campaign is specific to Michigan, it provides a model for other state colleges and universities to follow. Armed with these resources, these institutions would be able to provide more support for Black students.

To reduce debt burdens among Black students, we must reinvest in higher education, stop the decline in state appropriations, and redirect resources to institutions that serve students of color. Private colleges and universities with large endowments can be partners in this effort. Those colleges that say they are supportive of equity, diversity, and inclusion should put their money where their mouth is and use their vast financial resources to admit and support a larger and more diverse student body.[43] Too long we have been relying on underfunded colleges to do less with more to serve Black students. Public schools like Georgia State—where Black students have been supported socially and financially—should become the norm rather than the exception. As we said in chapter 3, the message here is simple: Black students do better, and accumulate less debt, at institutions that support them financially and socially. We need to invest in these institutions so that they can achieve this goal.

Free College

At the end of every interview for this book, we asked our respondents a question: *Do you think college is worth it?* In spite of the challenges they faced, the high costs, and debt, nearly all of them said, resoundingly, "Yes." Virgil agreed that college was worth it, but he added, "I do not think that the ends justify the means." He questioned the *education gospel* that preaches the necessity of college for success in a country where the costs of college are so high. "It's unfortunate that we went through this phase or we're going through the phase where we keep telling people that college is the way. [But] if college is the way, then we've got to figure out a way to make college free. That's how I think about it," he said. "If you're saying to be a productive adult citizen in the United States of America, you need a degree, then if we're saying that culturally, then we've got to say college is free." Virgil has a point: if a college degree is the new high school degree, then like public high school, college should be free. Sara Goldrick-Rab, founder of the Hope Center and an early proponent of free college programs, concurred with Virgil's opinion in a *Wall Street Journal* op-ed. "It's time for a new approach," she writes. "America became great in part because it decided to offer elementary and secondary school to the masses, propelling innovation and economic growth. It simply needs to remember and reinvest in that smart decision, this time including public higher education."[44]

If we believe that the student debt crisis is primarily driven by high college costs, then making college free seems like a sensible solution to student debt burdens. Once considered a radical idea, polling now shows that the majority of the public—including the majority of Republicans—support a two-year free college or debt-free college option.[45] Goldrick-Rab, whose plans provided the blueprint for national free college proposals—such as those included in Bernie Sanders's College for All plan and President Biden's American Families plan—first proposed the Free Two Year College Option (F2CO) with Nancy Kendall in 2014.[46] In this proposal, Goldrick-Rab and Kendall lay out a plan to make two years of college free for all who want to attend. Under their plan, students could enroll in a community college or a four-year college and receive free tuition, as well as an income support that would cover the costs of room and board (or rent) and other expenses. This point is crucial: we know that students not only struggle to pay tuition but also have difficulty keeping up with living expenses while in college. Goldrick-Rab and Kendall propose this program could be entirely funded not by new taxes, but by redistributing existing higher education funding. For example, they propose that the federal government would cover tuition for all students, with additional funds going to schools that serve low-income students (who are disproportionately students of color). State funding for higher education could then be directed to pay for books, fees, and other expenses for students.[47]

In the past several years, state and local programs that offer free college have been on the rise. They include community- and state-based *College Promise* programs (such as the Kalamazoo Promise program that began in 2005) as well as states that have passed free college legislation (including California, Illinois, New Jersey, New York, and Massachusetts).[48] Researchers have also created scholarship programs that mimic free college in order to study its effectiveness.[49] The question that remains is: Does free college actually work to promote college access, retention, and reduce debt?

The answer, so far, appears to be a qualified yes. When implemented and funded properly, the evidence suggests that free college programs increase college attendance, promote persistence, and reduce debt among vulnerable students.[50] But not all free college programs are created equal. Free college programs are less effective in achieving these ends if they are contingent on merit or school performance (e.g., grade restrictions). Such programs punish low-income students who are at risk of dropping out and reward wealthier students who are more academically prepared for college.[51] In addition, first-dollar programs that disperse funds to students before taking into account other sources of aid tend to work better than last-dollar programs that disperse funds to students only after discounting other forms of aid. First-dollar programs work better because they allow students the opportunity to access other forms of aid that can help them cover the cost of room and board, supplies, rent, or childcare, whereas last-dollar programs do not. The devil is in the details, but free college has the potential to increase college access and reduce debt burdens for the next generation of college students. A national program—such as the proposal in President Biden's American Families plan—would ensure that all students have access to a free college option, regardless of where they live.

Opponents of free college argue that we cannot afford it. But we argue that we can no longer afford the high-cost, high-aid model of higher education. Even if free college required additional tax revenue to work properly, the societal benefits of increasing access and persistence in college would arguably outweigh the costs.[52] Astra Taylor, a writer, activist, and advocate for free college and debt forgiveness, put it this way: "Pushing for free college has a double meaning for me. It should be free in the sense that it doesn't cost anything, but it should also be free in the sense that it frees people to pursue the things they're interested in and to become whole citizens. In other words, contra Reagan, the state *should* be in the business of subsidizing curiosity because that is good for society. That's good for democracy."[53] There may be other benefits: to the extent that for-profit schools thrived when public colleges and universities were defunded, these reinvestments in higher education could slow or reverse the growth in exploitative for-profit schools that disproportionately bury Black students in debt.[54]

Midstream policies that reinvest in higher education—increasing financial aid, funding institutions of higher education, and free college options—are necessary tools for solving the student debt crisis among Black students and families. These aren't the only policies or tools that might be effective; reinvesting in community colleges and regulating for-profit colleges would also be transformative.[55] Yet, even these bold policies will not undo centuries of systematic racism that underlie the student debt crisis.

UPSTREAM SOLUTIONS: DISMANTLING THE LEGACIES OF RACISM AND CLOSING THE RACIAL WEALTH GAP

Throughout this book, we have argued that racial disparities in student debt accumulation and repayment reflect historical inequalities and injustices that date back centuries in the US and reproduce and exacerbate these inequalities in the present day. The sedimentation of these historical inequalities has created and maintained the racial wealth gap, which far exceeds racial disparities in income. Midstream reforms to higher education, no matter how bold, cannot remedy the stark economic divides by race that have created and perpetuated the student debt crisis for Black college-goers. To truly solve the student loan crisis among Black borrowers, we must go upstream to close the racial wealth gap and begin to reverse the historical injustices that drive it.[56] Stratification economists William Darity and Darrick Hamilton suggest two solutions that would help close the racial wealth gap: a race-neutral "baby bonds" program and race-targeted reparations for slavery.

Baby bonds are a race-neutral program, first proposed by Manning Marable, that promises to close the racial wealth gap. Baby bonds are a progressive program that would complement existing old-age programs like

Social Security and provide all newborns with a publicly held trust of up to $60,000, with larger trusts going to children born into poorer families.[57] Why baby bonds? In a 2019 TED Talk, Darrick Hamilton put it this way: "The reason why we should create these trusts is simple. Wealth is the paramount indicator of economic security and well-being. It provides financial agency, economic security to take risk and shield against loss. Without capital, inequality is locked in. We use words like choice, freedom to describe the benefits of the market, but it is literally wealth that gives us choice, freedom and optionality . . . it is wealth that begets more wealth."[58] For Hamilton and Darity, baby bonds fulfill the promise of FDR's Economic Bill of Rights, giving everyone the capital they need to pay for college, secure a down payment on a home, start a business, and have the power to take control of their lives, all while reducing economic and racial inequality.

A 2020 paper by Naomi Zewde shows the potential of baby bonds to reduce the wealth gap.[59] Using data from the Panel Study of Income Dynamics, Zewde poses a counterfactual question: what would the racial wealth gap among young adults look like today if they were born into a country with baby bonds? She finds dramatic differences. In the real world we live in right now, white young adults have sixteen times the wealth of Black young adults ($46,000 versus $2,900). In a world with baby bonds, she finds that this racial gap is much smaller; on average white young adults would have approximately $79,000 in wealth, and Black young adults would have around $58,000. Zewde argues that these wealth disparities are likely to decrease further across subsequent generations, as Black families build wealth over time. In other words, baby bonds would lift all boats and drastically reduce the racial wealth gap. To date, Cory Booker's America Opportunity Accounts Act has been the only legislation proposed to make baby bonds a reality, rather than a counterfactual experiment.[60] At an estimated cost of only 2 percent of federal expenditures—less than the cost of current federal programs for tax credits and subsidies—baby bonds have the potential to unravel centuries of economic and racial inequality.[61]

For William Darity, baby bonds are an important start, but not a silver bullet for erasing the racial wealth gap. He argues that only a race-targeted reparations package can close the racial wealth gap and compensate the descendants of slavery for centuries of exploitation, violence, and racism. Reparations for slavery is not a new idea. The US government once promised newly freed slaves "40 acres and a mule," but they defaulted on this promise and many others like it. Darity proposes that the United States finally repay this debt and make direct payments to the descendants of slavery on the order of $267,000 per person, which would erase the racial wealth gap. "If the goal is to end the subaltern status of Blacks in American society, a comprehensive national program will need to be designed and implemented that is aimed directly at removing racial wealth differences," write Darity and colleagues in a recent paper. "That strikes us as reparations—the authentic path toward racial justice and authentic closure of the economic distance between Black and white America."[62]

The goal of reparations is lofty, but it is inching ever closer to a political reality. The late Congressman John Conyers introduced H.R. 40—a bill to fund a committee to study and develop a reparations proposal—in every legislative session between 1989 and 2017. After Conyers died, Congresswoman Sheila Jackson Lee and the late Congressman John Lewis introduced H.R. 40 in subsequent sessions. For almost four decades, Congress ignored H.R. 40. But in April 2021, after the murder of George Floyd, Breonna Taylor, Ahmaud Arbery, and too many other Black men and women made the issue of racial justice impossible to ignore, the 117th Congress finally voted to approve H.R. 40.[63] While the bill only establishes a committee to study the topic, it remains an important first step. The public, too, appears more receptive to reparations than at any other point in history. A 2020 poll shows that the majority (50 percent) of the US public supports H.R. 40, and 56 percent said that they thought Congress is "doing too little" to address racial inequality, including nearly half of white Americans.[64] Slowly, the winds may be moving in the direction toward change. Upstream, midstream, and downstream solutions—including but not limited to the policies and programs proposed here—are necessary to solve the student debt crisis among Black Americans. Critics might argue that we cannot afford these investments. To that, we would respond that we cannot afford to continue to allow Black Americans to be financially punished for pursuing the American Dream of higher education.

For these changes to become a reality, however, we need public pressure and collective action that represent a broad array of coalitions. Activist groups like the Debt Collective have worked tirelessly to make the public aware of student loans through the lens of economic and racial justice and have organized the first student debtor's union. On the legal and policy side, advocacy groups like the Student Borrower Protection Center, The Hope Center, and the National Consumer Law Center have fought to protect students of color from predatory practices and have been on the vanguard of upstream and downstream policy reform. Only a decade ago, debt forgiveness and free college were fringe ideas. Today, these proposals are a core part of the Democratic Party platform, in large part due to the efforts of these organizations and others like them. These are hard-won victories, and it is necessary for these groups to work together and form broad coalitions to enact change. Much like how labor unions have partnered with civil rights groups, community organizations, and other groups to achieve victories, these debtors unions and advocacy groups can do the same.[65] Partnerships with the Black Lives Matter movement, for example, would help further frame the student loan crisis as a racial justice issue. We need these groups to continue to remind the public, policy makers, and politicians that debt-financed higher education is a failed experiment that has disproportionately burdened Black families. Higher education may come with the promise of upward mobility and secure, stable middle-class lives for white Americans, but in an era of high college costs and rising debt, that promise is one of many that has been broken for Black Americans. It is time that we fulfill that promise.

AFTERWORD

The COVID-19 Pandemic

About five months after we completed the interviews for this book, the COVID-19 pandemic swept the United States. Businesses and schools were shuttered to control the virus, leading to a historic spike in the unemployment rate. As of this writing, the virus has taken the lives of over 950,000 people. The pandemic has been especially painful for Black Americans, who disproportionately suffered loss of life and livelihood, all while bearing witness to the brutal murders of George Floyd, Ahmaud Arbery, Breonna Taylor, and countless others at the hands of the police or vigilante racists.[1] And still, the racial wealth gap continues to grow in the pandemic.[2] Amid such great pain, writing about student loans felt almost trivial, but in July of 2020 we checked in with our interviewees to get a sense of how their lives, and their debts, changed in the wake of the pandemic. Many were still worried about their student loans, but Kellyanne had more pressing concerns. "I'm worried about my Black family in a time where systematic racism is hurting my people severely," she said. Dylan agreed. "The world is imploding and I'm Black."

In March of 2020, the federal government suspended all federal student loan payments. Overnight, most loans owned by the Department of Education were placed in interest-free forbearance through at least September 1, 2022, meaning that borrowers would not need to pay their loans and interest would not accrue. For many borrowers, this automatic pause was a lifesaver. Shola took advantage of the pause to try to save money. Sandra was able to send money back to her mom, who fell behind on bills in the pandemic. Olympia says she finally feels a bit of relief. "I am thankful that I do not have to pay student loans during COVID," she said. "It provides me the opportunity to use that money towards other expenses such as keeping up with rent."

In many ways, the federal coronavirus pause is an example of an accessible *downstream* policy discussed in chapter 7. It also set the precedent for the federal government's ability to stop collecting federal student loan payments. Borrowers were automatically enrolled in the program (opt-out, rather than opt-in), which eliminated administrative burden and the need for onerous paperwork that is so often a stumbling block for borrowers. But the temporary pause is a short-term solution to a long-term problem. Shola hopes that this pause will help her save money so that she can pay her student loans more easily when the program ends, but she worries that if she loses her job, she'll be right back where she started. And, the most vulnerable borrowers are left out of the federal loan pause. Jourdin continues to struggle because her private loans are not eligible for forbearance. She asked her private student lender if she could defer her loans, but they declined her request. So far, she has been able to keep up with the minimum monthly payments, but the interest on her loans continues to compound.

In addition to the pause, the federal government passed the Coronavirus Aid, Relief, and Economic Security (CARES) Act, which provided further relief to borrowers and colleges. As part of the CARES Act, postsecondary institutions received over $12 billion in federal aid, a lifeline in the wake of massive pandemic-induced budget shortfalls. The CARES Act also allocated an additional $1.05 billion to minority serving institutions. As we discuss in chapter 3, these institutions are historically underfunded, had less cash reserves in the pandemic, and catered to a student body that was more vulnerable in the pandemic than majority white institutions. These funds were immediately put to use, allowing these schools to shore up their budget shortfalls. It also enabled them to provide financial aid to students in need.[3] Florida A&M University, a Historically Black University in Tallahassee, used $16 million in aid to pay off the outstanding unpaid tuition balances for all of its students. Echoing Robert F. Smith's comments to Morehouse graduates, FAMU President Larry Robinson said in a graduation speech, "This is an indication of our commitment to student success and our hope that your time [here] has been transformative as you take on the challenges of the day, go out and make a difference."[4] To revisit a point from chapter 3, the lesson here is simple: when institutions are properly funded, they can better invest in and support their students, reducing the need for and burden of student debt.

The American Rescue Plan—the follow up to the CARES Act—quietly provided additional relief to borrowers in income-driven repayment (IDR). Borrowers in IDR are eligible to have their debts forgiven after twenty to twenty-five years of payments, but all forgiven debts are treated as taxable income as we discussed in chapter 7. Under this new provision authored by Senators Bob Menendez and Elizabeth Warren, any debts that are discharged via IDR through 2025 will no longer be taxable.[5] This provision eliminates surprising "tax bombs" for borrowers in IDR, but some progressives hope that it's one small step toward a stand-alone debt forgiveness plan. Today, other changes are on the horizon: the Public Service Loan Forgiveness (PSLF) program is on the verge of being overhauled in an effort to reduce the complexity and administrative burden and increase the accessibility of the program. With any luck, similar changes will come to increase accessibility and generosity of income-driven repayment.

The COVID-19 pandemic laid bare the social, economic, and racial divides in the United States, but it also revealed that while money cannot fix all problems, it can fix some. Just as unemployment insurance and COVID-relief stimulus checks provided economic relief for millions of Americans, the pause on student loan payments and funding to institutions of higher education provided economic relief to borrowers and the institutions that serve them. Such changes are welcome and needed, but they only nibble around the edges of the student debt crisis. Without systemic solutions to the student debt crisis, we are likely to find ourselves back where we started, with a generation of Black college-goers buried in debt. Claudia says that one of the reasons she voted for Biden and Harris in the 2020 election was that she wanted to see action on student debt forgiveness. So far, she has been frustrated by the lack of progress. We share her frustration but see opportunities for change. History shows us that pandemics—like this one—are often catalysts for massive social and economic change because they show that the status quo is untenable. As we come out of two years of loss, pain, and sorrow, we have an opportunity to change course and correct historical injustices. Let's not waste it.

METHODOLOGICAL APPENDIX

When we first started this project, our plan was to write a quantitative book: to draw on our training as quantitative social scientists and our decade-plus of quantitative research on student loan debt to document vast racial disparities in debt accumulation, repayment, and its consequences. We knew from the quantitative data that racial disparities in student debt are pervasive, grow across the life course, and have pernicious consequences for inequality among the current cohort of young adults. However, survey data are blunt instruments that can tell us a great deal about *what* is happening but can be limited for understanding *why*. As we worked on this project, it became apparent that the numbers were incomplete: we were missing the stories, experiences, and narratives of the Black borrowers that underlie the numeric disparities. Ultimately, we relied on both quantitative and qualitative data for this book. Here, we elaborate on our data collection and analysis, and identify some limitations of our approach.

QUANTITATIVE DATA: THE NATIONAL LONGITUDINAL STUDY OF YOUTH, 1997 COHORT

Most of the quantitative data in this book—and the data from our published research—are from the National Longitudinal Study of Youth, 1997 Cohort (NLSY97). The NLSY97 is a nationally representative, longitudinal dataset of a cohort of young people (N=8,984) that is collected and maintained by the Bureau of Labor Statistics.[1] Respondents in the NLSY97 were between the ages of twelve and seventeen at the first wave of survey collection in 1997, were followed annually through 2011, and have been followed biennially through the present day.

The NLSY97 is an ideal data source for understanding racial disparities in student debt. The NLSY97 follows a large sample of college-going youth

(N=5,688) from a cohort that holds historically high levels of student debt during their transition into adulthood. While this cohort holds lower debt levels than the cohorts that followed them, they are now old enough—in their mid-thirties—so that we can gain some understanding of the consequences of student debt for well-being in young adulthood. Additionally, because the NLSY97 is a longitudinal study that has followed respondents for much of their lives, it includes a plethora of information about young people's family background—including their living arrangements in childhood and adolescence, parents' wealth—as well as annual data on their college experiences, and labor market and socioeconomic well-being after college. The NLSY asks respondents to report their student debt at several different points in their lives: (a) annually while respondents are enrolled in college; and (b) over the course of young adulthood at roughly ages twenty, twenty-five, and thirty (as part of the debts and assets modules). These longitudinal data on debts and assets allow us to track trajectories of debt accumulation and repayment across the early adult life course, the mechanisms that explain these trajectories, and how debts are associated with well-being in young adulthood. Although the self-reporting of student debt raises concern about measurement error, borrower self-reports and official lender (credit) reports are extremely similar for nearly all forms of debt, including student loan debt.[2] Moreover, self-reported student debt levels in this sample are comparable to national estimates for this cohort (mean student debt is $22,540 in the NLSY97 at age twenty-five), suggesting that respondents in the study are representative of this cohort of student loan debtors in the United States.[3]

Over the past decade, we have leveraged the NLSY97 data to better understand the scope and correlates of racial and socioeconomic disparities in student debt accumulation after college; racial disparities in the repayment of student debt across the early life course, and the factors that explain these growing disparities; and the consequences of student debt for racial socioeconomic inequality and well-being during young adulthood.[4] We rely on these findings, and new analyses of these data, in this book. All analyses were completed using Stata.

QUALITATIVE DATA

In our analysis of quantitative data, we compare the experiences of Black and white young adults, focusing on *between-race* differences that reveal vast racial disparities in student debt between Black and white borrowers. Our goal with the qualitative interviews, then, is to understand the diverse experiences, perceptions, successes, and failures *among* Black borrowers, in ways that could both enrich what we know from the quantitative data and reveal new insights. Our research design is therefore aligned with the sequential confirmatory mixed methods approach.[5] We hoped that these interviews would allow us as researchers to better understand the larger social forces that shape the debt burdens experienced by Black borrowers, while also providing our respondents with the opportunity to describe their experiences and struggles with student debt in their own words.

In 2019, we conducted forty-nine interviews with Black young adults who attended colleges in the United States between 2005 and 2015. These respondents are former college students from the same age cohort as NLSY97 respondents (between the ages of twenty-five and thirty-five at the time of interview), who had a diverse range of (four-year) college experiences. To recruit interview respondents, we advertised the study on social media (Facebook, Twitter, LinkedIn) and alumni email listservs for Black Greek life organizations, and recruited from our local networks at a large midwestern public university and an East Coast Ivy League university. We also used snowball sampling—asking interview respondents to identify potential study participants—to recruit a few additional interviewees. Individuals were eligible to participate in the study if they (1) self-identified as Black or African American; (2) attended a four-year college or university at some point in the last fifteen years; and (3) borrowed student loans for their undergraduate or graduate study. Interviews were conducted over the phone and via Zoom, which allowed us to interview respondents from all over the country, and lasted around one to two hours. Respondents were compensated $30 for their time. Respondents were compensated an additional $50 for completing our COVID-19 study follow-up in July of 2020 (see the afterword).

In our semistructured interviews, we asked respondents a series of open-ended questions that were theoretically informed by our quantitative work on racial disparities in debt. These interviews were designed to elicit respondents' narratives around how they paid for college; their experiences taking on debt and interacting with financial aid offices and lenders; their life while in college; their family's social and economic contribution to their college experience; and their life circumstances, decisions, and experiences with loan repayment after college. The interview was organized into four sections of similar length: (1) college life; (2) family background; (3) life after college and experiences repaying loans; (4) reflections on the role of student debt in their lives today. In section 1, we asked respondents to reflect on their experiences in college, including the number and names of institutions they attended, the challenges they faced, the amount of and type (e.g., federal versus private) of loans they borrowed and how they felt about them, and the conditions that led them to borrow (or not) when they first got to college and as they progressed through it. In section 2, we asked respondents to reflect on the home they grew up in, including their socioeconomic well-being, discussions about and planning for college, and whether the respondents received or gave assistance to their family while in college. In section 3, we asked respondents about their labor market history after leaving college, and their experiences with their student loans and loan servicers when they first entered repayment through present day. In the final section, we asked respondents to express, in their own words (and with probing questions), whether they thought student debt has shaped their lives today, and if so, how and why. We ended every interview by providing respondents with information and resources for student loan repayment. Following each interview, the interviewer (one of the study authors or a research assistant) took notes on key points and themes of the conversation that may have not been clear from the transcript.

We followed up these interviews with postinterview surveys, allowing respondents to share more detailed information about their debt (e.g., how much they borrowed) in the event they did not have access to this information during the interview or were not comfortable sharing information about their debts. Table A.1 shows select descriptive statistics from this survey. A few notable patterns: first, there is wide variation in life experiences, social background, and experiences with debt among Black borrowers in the sample, a key goal of the qualitative interviews. Second, although we selected respondents for the survey nonrandomly, default rates and average debt levels are similar to national estimates of Black borrowers who attended four-year institutions.[6] Finally, the vast majority of our respondents identified as women, which in part reflects that the racialization of student debt is also gendered (see chapter 6).

We used inductive and deductive coding to analyze the qualitative data. Deductive codes were based on our previous research and captured themes that were evident from this work, including but not limited to themes related to economic and social support from family members, financial strain in college, administrative burden in the debt repayment process, and emotional

TABLE A.1 Postinterview survey descriptive statistics

	Mean/Percent	Median
Student Loan Debt Accumulation and Repayment		
Undergraduate loans among borrowers (US dollars)	$36,135	$35,716
Currently making payments on undergraduate loans (%)	66%	
Took out loans for graduate education (%)	59%	
Graduate school loans (US dollars)	$27,287	$18,000
Graduate school loans among borrowers (US dollars)	$46,616	$42,500
Currently making payment on graduate loans, (%)	51%	
Current amount owed on student loans (US dollars)	$63,970	$65,000
Monthly payment average toward student loans (US dollars)	$226	$187
Ever defaulted on student loans (%)	22%	
Ever applied or received forbearance (%)	59%	
Ever took out private student loans (%)	20%	
Feelings About Student Loans		
Difficulty paying student loans on time (%)		
Never or rarely	42%	
Sometimes	18%	
Very often or always	40%	
Assistance from friend / family member paying loans (%)		
Never or rarely	83%	
Sometimes	8%	
Very often or always	9%	
Feelings of lack of progress with student loan payment (%)		
Never or rarely	11%	
Sometimes	9%	
Very often or always	80%	
Feelings that student debt prevented home purchase (%)		
Never or rarely	28%	
Sometimes	18%	
Very often or always	54%	
Feelings that student debt negatively impacted life (%)		
Never or rarely	15%	

TABLE A.1 *(Cont.)*

	Mean/Percent	Median
Sometimes	35%	
Very often or always	50%	
Feelings that student debt prevented reaching of goals (%)		
Never or rarely	37%	
Sometimes	40%	
Very often or always	23%	
Feelings that student debt is/was worth it (%)		
Never or rarely	25%	
Sometimes	43%	
Very often or always	32%	
Feelings of regret due to student debt (%)		
Never or rarely	30%	
Sometimes	32%	
Very often or always	38%	
Sociodemographic and Financial Characteristics		
Highest level of education achieved (%)		
High school	5%	
Bachelor's degree	54%	
Professional degree	41%	
Highest level of education for parent / primary caregiver (%)		
High school	22%	
Associate's degree	10%	
Bachelor's degree	39%	
Professional degree	29%	
Work status (%)		
Student	34%	
Currently out of work but looking	5%	
Self-employed	7%	
Employed for wages	54%	
Annual personal income (US dollars) (%)		
<$25,000	32%	

TABLE A.1 *(Cont.)*

	Mean/Percent	Median
$25,000–$39,999	20%	
$40,000–$59,999	15%	
$60,000–$99,999	34%	
$100K+	0%	
Feelings of having enough money to pay the bills (financial strain)		
Never or rarely	19%	
Some months	10%	
Most months or always	71%	
Always	0%	
Respondent gender		
Man	22%	
Woman	78%	
Respondent marital status		
Not married	85%	
Married	15%	
Respondent age (years)	*28*	*28*

responses to indebtedness. We also used inductive coding to capture themes that arose from the respondents that we did not anticipate. One notable theme that came out of the interviews is what we call "best-laid plans": a recurring theme where respondents recounted their careful financial and college planning and how such planning was not enough to prevent them from falling into debt. Another inductive theme that we called "the hustle" emerged when respondents discussed how they felt their student debt commodified their lives and made their life revolve around making money (chapter 5). These two themes are illustrative of the relationship between our quantitative and qualitative data. The former theme confirms our quantitative findings that financial literacy cannot and does not explain racial disparities in student debt. The latter theme illuminated and enriched our understanding of the nuanced ways that student debt creates financial strain, in ways that have not been measured in quantitative data. To ensure coding consistency, the study authors and research assistants independently read and coded each transcript and noted any discrepancy in codes. The quotes presented in this book are examples of broader patterns that were apparent in the data. To protect the identities of our respondents, we use pseudonyms and omit key details about the colleges they attend, their employers, and place of residence. All qualitative analyses were conducted using AtlasTI, and quotes used in the book were lightly edited for clarity.

LIMITATIONS

Our central goal in this book is to paint a clearer portrait of racial disparities in student debt and to tell the stories of Black borrowers whom we view as the too-often-hidden faces of the student debt crisis. But in writing this book, we also faced several trade-offs that led us to limit the scope of the project. As such, the picture we provide is only partially complete. We highlight three limitations of this book that we hope will spur further investigation.

The most obvious limitation, as scholars who are interested in race, racism, and student debt, is that we omit the stories of borrowers of color who are not Black. In chapter 1, we say we focus on the experience of Black Americans (and Black-white differences) because we know that Black Americans face the highest rate of borrowing and loan default, and because we are interested in the extent to which student debt is linked to historic racial disparities in wealth—an area of study that mainly focuses on the experience of Black Americans because of the relationship of wealth disparities to the institution of slavery and the legacy of Jim Crow. But that does not mean that Latinx, Native American, and Asian American borrowers do not face challenges with student loans that are exacerbated by systematic racism. Indeed they do. As our colleagues in the Lumina Foundation's Borrowers of Color Working group have argued, Latinx, Native American, and Asian American college students face unique challenges in college that are distinct from those faced by Black Americans.[7] In this book, we answer their call by "carefully examining differences among" Black borrowers. But that focus comes at the expense of documenting the experiences of other racial and ethnic groups. We point readers to the excellent work of our colleagues in the Lumina Borrowers of Color Working group—Denisa Gandara, Desiree Zerquera, Christine Nelson, Amanda Tachine, Jameson Lopez, Dominique Baker, Sarah Sattelmeyer, and Joanna Darcus—for a broader discussion of race and ethnic disparities in student loan debt.

A second limitation—of both our quantitative and qualitative work—is that it centers largely on "young adults" who by and large went to college in the years that followed high school. Thus, we may miss nontraditional students who attend college later in life, though we do have information on college-going among our qualitative and quantitative respondents up until at least age thirty. A second issue associated with our focus on "young adults" is that narratives of student debt are centered only on these borrowers. We therefore miss those adults who take on student debt for friends and family members. Though we highlight parents' PLUS loans in chapter 2, our analysis does not center on their experience. Given that we know that Black parents and caregivers are more likely to take on debt—and take on more debt—than their white counterparts, it is likely that the racial disparities in student debt discussed in this book are substantially larger than suggested by our data.

The third limitation is that our focus on four-year college-goers comes at the expense of those who attend two-year colleges. We know that Black college-goers are more likely to attend two-year colleges, and even though these schools are less expensive (on average) than four-year institutions, many of these borrowers struggle to pay for college and with debt after college. In this book, we chose to primarily focus on the experience of four-year college-goers for a few reasons. First, four-year colleges—and four-year degrees—hold a powerful place in the American cultural imagination as key avenues of success and upward mobility. By focusing on the four-year college experience, we hoped to show that Black student debt could not be reduced to a failure to attend or graduate from these vaunted institutions. Second, because we were interested in interrogating the meaning and fragility of the Black middle class, this led us to narrow our focus to a population that (predominantly) attends four-year colleges. We were also unable to contact any interview respondents who attended for-profit institutions during undergraduate coursework (though we did speak to several people who attended for-profit graduate schools). What this means is that we are missing the voices and experiences of those who attend two-year colleges and for-profit institutions. We point the reader to Sara Goldrick-Rab's excellent *Paying the Price* and Tressie McMillan Cottom's *Lower Ed* for a richer discussion of these issues.[8]

We are sure that readers may find other limitations of this book, and we stress that any errors and omissions are our own. But we hope that discussions of these shortcomings will lead to productive conversations that move our understanding of race, racism, and student debt forward.

NOTES

Introduction

1. Kevin Carey, "Student Debt in America: Lend with a Smile, Collect with a Fist," *New York Times*, November 27, 2015, sec. The Upshot, https://www.nytimes.com/2015/11/29/upshot/student-debt-in-america-lend-with-a-smile-collect-with-a-fist.html.
2. Paul Davidson, "Are Student Loans as Big of a Problem as People Think?," *USA Today*, July 7, 2017, https://www.usatoday.com/story/money/2017/07/07/student-loans-big-problem-people-think/101842736/.
3. Janna Herron, "Saddled with Huge Student Loan Debt, Homebuyers Sacrifice More to Purchase a House," November 6, 2018, https://www.usatoday.com/story/money/2018/11/06/student-loans-and-buying-house-tougher-outstanding-debt/1846622002/.
4. Rachel Hinton and Ashlee Rezin Garcia, "A Generation of College Grads Buried in Student Debt," *Chicago Sun-Times*, June 2, 2018, https://chicago.suntimes.com/2018/6/2/18527648/college-grads-buried-student-debt.
5. Federal Student Aid, US Department of Education, "Federal Student Loan Portfolio," 2021, https://studentaid.gov/data-center/student/portfolio.
6. Adam Looney and Constantine Yannelis, "A Crisis in Student Loans? How Changes in the Characteristics of Borrowers and in the Institutions They Attended Contributed to Rising Loan Defaults," *Brookings* (blog), September 10, 2015, https://www.brookings.edu/bpea-articles/a-crisis-in-student-loans-how-changes-in-the-characteristics-of-borrowers-and-in-the-institutions-they-attended-contributed-to-rising-loan-defaults/.
7. Anne Helen Petersen, "Here's Why So Many Americans Feel Cheated by Their Student Loans," *BuzzFeed News*, February 9, 2019, https://www.buzzfeednews.com/article/annehelenpetersen/student-debt-college-public-service-loan-forgiveness.
8. Alisa F. Cunningham and Deborah A. Santiago, *Student Aversion to Borrowing: Who Borrows and Who Doesn't* (Washington, DC: Institute for Higher Education Policy, December 2008), https://eric.ed.gov/?id=ED503684; Jason N. Houle, "Disparities in Debt: Parents' Socioeconomic Resources and Young Adult Student Loan Debt," *Sociology of Education* 87, no. 1 (2014): 53–69, https://doi.org/10.1177/0038040713512213; Brandon A. Jackson and John R. Reynolds, "The Price of Opportunity: Race, Student Loan Debt, and College Achievement," *Sociological Inquiry* 83, no. 3 (August 2013): 335–68, https://doi.org/10.1111/soin.12012.
9. Jacob P. K. Gross et al., "What Matters in Student Loan Default: A Review of the Research Literature," *Journal of Student Financial Aid* 39, no. 1 (2009): 19–29; Mark Huelsman, "The Debt Divide: The Racial and Class Bias Behind the 'New Normal' of Student Borrowing," Demos, May 19, 2015, https://www.demos.org/research/debt-divide-racial-and-class-bias-behind-new-normal-student-borrowing.
10. Judith Scott-Clayton, *The Looming Student Loan Default Crisis Is Worse Than We Thought*

(Washington, DC: Brookings Institution, 2018), https://www.brookings.edu/research/the-looming-student-loan-default-crisis-is-worse-than-we-thought/.

11. Tamara Draut, *Why America's 20- and 30-Somethings Can't Get Ahead* (New York, NY: Doubleday & Company Inc., 2005); Sara Goldrick-Rab, *Paying the Price: College Costs, Financial Aid, and the Betrayal of the American Dream* (Chicago, IL: University of Chicago Press, 2016); Anya Kamenetz, *Generation Debt: How Our Future Was Sold Out for Student Loans, Bad Jobs, No Benefits, and Tax Cuts for Rich Geezers—And How to Fight Back* (New York, NY: Riverhead Books, 2006).
12. Susan M. Dynarski, "An Economist's Perspective on Student Loans in the United States," CESifo Working Paper Series (Munich: Ludwig-Maximilians University, 2015), https://www.cesifo.org/en/publikationen/2015/working-paper/economists-perspective-student-loans-united-states; Looney and Yannelis, "A Crisis in Student Loans?"; Federal Student Aid, US Department of Education, "Federal Student Loan Portfolio."
13. Beth Akers and Matthew Chingos, "Is a Student Loan Crisis on the Horizon?," *Brookings*, June 24, 2014, https://www.brookings.edu/research/is-a-student-loan-crisis-on-the-horizon/; Beth Akers and Matthew Chingos, *Game of Loans: The Rhetoric and Reality of Student Debt* (Princeton, NJ: Princeton University Press, 2016).
14. Judith Scott-Clayton and Jing Li, "Black-White Disparity in Student Loan Debt More Than Triples After Graduation," vol. 2, Evidence Speaks Reports (Washington, DC: Brookings Institution, 2016).
15. At four-year colleges
16. Scott-Clayton, *The Looming Student Loan Default Crisis.*
17. US Department of Education, "College Scorecard Data," 2021, https://collegescorecard.ed.gov/data/.
18. Christian Gollayan, "Lots of Millennials Blew Student Loan Money on Spring Break," *New York Post*, April 1, 2017, https://nypost.com/2017/04/01/think-twice-before-you-spend-your-student-loan-on-spring-break/; Kate Ashford, "College Students Using Loans for Spring Break, Alcohol, Drugs," *Forbes*, March 29, 2017, https://www.forbes.com/sites/kateashford/2017/03/29/loans-spring-break/.
19. Fenaba R. Addo, Jason N. Houle, and Daniel Simon, "Young, Black, and (Still) in the Red: Parental Wealth, Race, and Student Loan Debt," *Race and Social Problems* 8, no. 1 (2016): 64–76, https://doi.org/10.1007/s12552-016-9162-0.
20. US Department of Education, College Scorecard, "University of North Carolina at Chapel Hill," accessed May 9, 2021, https://collegescorecard.ed.gov/school/?199120-University-of-North-Carolina-at-Chapel-Hill.
21. Undergraduate Admissions at the University of North Carolina at Chapel Hill, "Afford," *Undergraduate Admissions* (blog), 2021, https://admissions.unc.edu/afford/.
22. National Center for Education Statistics, *Digest of Education Statistics, 2018* (Washington, DC: National Center for Education Statistics, 2018), https://nces.ed.gov/programs/digest/d18/tables/dt18_330.20.asp.
23. For a detailed account of the factors that explain rising debt, we point our readers to Best and Best's *The Student Loan Mess*, Akers and Chingos's *Game of Loans*, Goldrick-Rab's *Paying the Price*, Christopher Newfield's *The Great Mistake*, and Suzanne Mettler's *Degrees of Inequality* (to name a few), all of which provide very thoughtful, but very different, discussions of student debt.
24. College Board, "Trends in Student Aid 2018," Trends in Higher Education Series (Washington, DC: The College Board, 2018), https://research.collegeboard.org/pdf/trends-student-aid-2018-full-report.pdf.

25. Anthony B Atkinson, Thomas Piketty, and Emmanuel Saez, "Top Incomes in the Long Run of History," *Journal of Economic Literature* 49, no. 1 (2011): 3–71, https://doi.org/10.1257/jel.49.1.3; Lane Kenworthy, "Has Rising Inequality Reduced Middle-Class Income Growth?," in *Income Inequality: Economic Disparities and the Middle Class in Affluent Countries*, ed. Janet C. Gornick and Markus Jantti (Palo Alto, CA: Stanford University Press, 2013), 101–14.
26. Rakesh Kochnar and Richard Fry, "Wealth Inequality Has Widened Along Racial, Ethnic Lines Since End of Great Recession," FacTank: News in the Numbers (Washington, DC: Pew Research Center, 2014).
27. Rachel E. Dwyer, Laura McCloud, and Randy Hodson, "Youth Debt, Mastery, and Self-Esteem: Class-Stratified Effects of Indebtedness on Self-Concept," *Social Science Research* 40, no. 3 (2011): 727–41, https://doi.org/10.1016/j.ssresearch.2011.02.001.
28. Laura Hamilton and Kelly Nielsen, *Broke: The Racial Consequences of Underfunding Public Universities* (Chicago, IL: University of Chicago Press, 2021).
29. Houle, "Disparities in Debt," 53–69.
30. Scott-Clayton, *The Looming Student Loan Default Crisis.*
31. Scott-Clayton, *The Looming Student Loan Default Crisis.*
32. Addo, Houle, and Simon, "Young, Black, and (Still) in the Red," 64–76; Jason N. Houle and Fenaba R. Addo, "Racial Disparities in Student Debt and the Reproduction of the Fragile Black Middle Class," *Sociology of Race and Ethnicity* 5, no. 4 (2019): 562–77.
33. Melvin Oliver and Thomas Shapiro, *Black Wealth/White Wealth: A New Perspective on Racial Inequality*, 2nd ed. (New York, NY: Routledge, 2006); Fabian T. Pfeffer, Sheldon Danziger, and Robert F. Schoeni, "Wealth Disparities Before and After the Great Recession," *ANNALS of the American Academy of Political and Social Science* 650, no. 1 (2013): 98–123, https://doi.org/10.1177/0002716213497452.
34. Darrick Hamilton et al., *Umbrellas Don't Make It Rain: Why Studying and Working Hard Isn't Enough for Black Americans* (Oakland CA: Insight Center for Community Economic Development, 2015), https://socialequity.duke.edu/wp-content/uploads/2019/10/Umbrellas_Dont_Make_It_Rain_Final.pdf.

Chapter 1

1. Stacey Abrams, "Commentary: My $200,000 Debt Should Not Disqualify Me for Governor of Georgia," *Fortune*, April 24, 2018, https://fortune.com/2018/04/24/stacey-abrams-debt-georgia-governor/.
2. Abrams, "Commentary."
3. Ngina S. Chiteji and Darrick Hamilton, "Family Connections and the Black-White Wealth Gap Among Middle-Class Families," *Review of Black Political Economy* 30, no. 1 (2002): 9–28.
4. Michelle Goldberg, "The Debt-Shaming of Stacey Abrams," *New York Times*, August 17, 2018, sec. Opinion, https://www.nytimes.com/2018/08/17/opinion/columnists/stacey-abrams-georgia-governor-debt.html.
5. Steven A. Boutcher, Anna Raup-Kounovsky, and Carroll Seron, "Financing Legal Education Through Student Loans: Results from a Quasi-Experiment in Tuition Remission," *Journal of Legal Education* 67, no. 3 (2018): 755–79.
6. Goldberg, "The Debt-Shaming of Stacey Abrams."
7. Eduardo Bonilla-Silva, "More Than Prejudice: Restatement, Reflections, and New Directions in Critical Race Theory," *Sociology of Race and Ethnicity* 1, no. 1 (2015): 73–87, https://doi.org/10.1177/2332649214557042.
8. Eduardo Bonilla-Silva, *Racism Without Racists: Color-Blind Racism and the Persistence of Racial Inequality in the United States*, 4th ed. (Lanham, MD: Rowman & Littlefield, 2014).

9. Louise Seamster, "Black Debt, White Debt," *Contexts* 18, no. 1 (2019): 30–35, https://doi.org/10.1177/1536504219830674.
10. Tressie McMillan Cottom, *Lower Ed: The Troubling Rise of For-Profit Colleges in the New Economy* (New York, NY: The New Press, 2017).
11. Michael Hout, "Social and Economic Returns to College Education in the United States," *Annual Review of Sociology* 38, no. 1 (2012): 379–400, https://doi.org/10.1146/annurev.soc.012809.102503.
12. Christina Ciocca Eller and Thomas A. DiPrete, "The Paradox of Persistence: Explaining the Black-White Gap in Bachelor's Degree Completion," *American Sociological Review* 83, no. 6 (2018): 1171–1214, https://doi.org/10.1177/0003122418808005.
13. Renee Stepler, "Hispanic, Black Parents See College Degree as Key for Children's Success," Pew Research Center, February 24, 2016, https://www.pewresearch.org/fact-tank/2016/02/24/hispanic-black-parents-see-college-degree-as-key-for-childrens-success/.
14. Rachel Baker, Daniel Klasik, and Sean F. Reardon, "Race and Stratification in College Enrollment over Time," *AERA Open* 4, no. 1 (2018): 2332858417751896, https://doi.org/10.1177/2332858417751896.
15. Ciocca Eller and DiPrete, "The Paradox of Persistence," 1171–1214.
16. Jason N. Houle, "A Generation Indebted: Young Adult Debt Across Three Cohorts," *Social Problems* 61, no. 3 (2014): 448–65, https://doi.org/10.1525/sp.2014.12110.
17. Louise Seamster and Raphaël Charron-Chénier, "Predatory Inclusion and Education Debt: Rethinking the Racial Wealth Gap," *Social Currents* 4, no. 3 (2017), https://doi.org/10.1177/2329496516686620.
18. Houle, "A Generation Indebted."
19. Author analysis of the National Longitudinal Study of Youth, 1979 cohort and National Longitudinal Study of Youth, 1997 cohort. For more information, see: Houle, "A Generation Indebted," 448–65.
20. Baker, Klasik, and Reardon, "Race and Stratification in College Enrollment over Time."
21. Laura Hamilton and Kelly Nielsen, *Broke: The Racial Consequences of Underfunding Public Universities* (Chicago, IL: University of Chicago Press, 2021).
22. Gilder Lehrman Institute of American History, "Ronald Reagan on the Unrest on College Campuses, 1967," accessed May 19, 2021, https://www.gilderlehrman.org/history-resources/spotlight-primary-source/ronald-reagan-unrest-college-campuses-1967; Aaron Bady and Mike Konczal, "From Master Plan to No Plan: The Slow Death of Public Higher Education," *Dissent Magazine*, 2012, https://www.dissentmagazine.org/article/from-master-plan-to-no-plan-the-slow-death-of-public-higher-education.
23. Devin Fergus, "My Students Pay Too Much for College. Blame Reagan," *Washington Post*, September 2, 2014, https://www.washingtonpost.com/posteverything/wp/2014/09/02/my-students-pay-too-much-for-college-blame-reagan/; Christopher Newfield, *Unmaking the Public University: The Forty-Year Assault on the Middle Class* (Cambridge, MA: Harvard University Press, 2011).
24. Louise Seamster and Raphaël Charron-Chénier, "Predatory Inclusion and Education Debt: Rethinking the Racial Wealth Gap," *Social Currents* 4, no. 3 (2017), https://doi.org/10.1177/2329496516686620.
25. Judith Scott-Clayton and Jing Li, "Black-White Disparity in Student Loan Debt More Than Triples After Graduation," *Brookings* (blog), October 20, 2016, https://www.brookings.edu/research/black-white-disparity-in-student-loan-debt-more-than-triples-after-graduation/.
26. Brandon A. Jackson and John R. Reynolds, "The Price of Opportunity: Race, Student Loan

Debt, and College Achievement," *Sociological Inquiry* 83, no. 3 (2013): 335–68, https://doi.org/10.1111/soin.12012.

27. Fenaba R. Addo, Jason N. Houle, and Daniel Simon, "Young, Black, and (Still) in the Red: Parental Wealth, Race, and Student Loan Debt," *Race and Social Problems* 8, no. 1 (2016): 64–76, https://doi.org/10.1007/s12552-016-9162-0.
28. Racial disparities in debt are adjusted for family structure in adolescence, urban residence, survey year, age at YAST survey, and gender.
29. Addo, Houle, and Simon, "Young, Black, and (Still) in the Red," 64–76.
30. Addo, Houle, and Simon, "Young, Black, and (Still) in the Red."
31. Judith Scott-Clayton, *The Looming Student Loan Default Crisis Is Worse Than We Thought* (Washington, DC: Brookings Institution, 11, 2018), https://www.brookings.edu/research/the-looming-student-loan-default-crisis-is-worse-than-we-thought/.
32. J. Fredericks Volkwein and Bruce P. Szelest, "Individual and Campus Characteristics Associated with Student Loan Default," *Research in Higher Education* 36, no. 1 (1995): 41–72, https://doi.org/10.1007/BF02207766; J. Fredericks Volkwein et al., "Factors Associated with Student Loan Default Among Different Racial and Ethnic Groups," *Journal of Higher Education* 69, no. 2 (1998): 206–37, https://doi.org/10.2307/2649206.
33. Jacob P. K. Gross et al., "What Matters in Student Loan Default: A Review of the Research Literature," *Journal of Student Financial Aid* 39, no. 1 (2009): 19–29.
34. US Department of Education, "College Scorecard Data," 2021, https://collegescorecard.ed.gov/data/.
35. Jason N. Houle and Fenaba R. Addo, "Racial Disparities in Student Debt and the Reproduction of the Fragile Black Middle Class," *Sociology of Race and Ethnicity* 5, no. 4 (2019): 562–77.
36. Scott-Clayton and Li, "Black-White Disparity in Student Loan Debt."
37. Glen H. Elder Jr., Monica Kirkpatrick Johnson, and Robert Crosnoe, "The Emergence and Development of Life Course Theory," in *Handbook of the Life Course*, ed. Jeylan T. Mortimer and Michael J. Shanahan, Handbooks of Sociology and Social Research (Boston, MA: Springer US, 2003), 3–19, https://doi.org/10.1007/978-0-306-48247-2_1; Glen H. Elder Jr., *Life Course Dynamics: Trajectories and Transitions, 1968–1980* (Ithaca, NY: Cornell University Press, 1985).
38. Houle and Addo, "Racial Disparities in Student Debt," 562–77.

Chapter 2

1. Fenaba Addo, Jason Houle, and Daniel Simon, "Young, Black, and (Still) in the Red: Parental Wealth, Race, and Student Loan Debt," *Race and Social Problems* 8, no. 1 (2016): 64–76.
2. Mary Pattillo, *Black Picket Fences: Privilege and Peril Among the Black Middle Class* (Chicago, IL: University of Chicago Press, 1999); William Darity, Fenaba R. Addo, and Imari Z. Smith, "A Subaltern Middle Class: The Case of the Missing 'Black Bourgeoisie' in America," *Contemporary Economic Policy* 39, no. 3 (2021): 494–502, https://doi.org/10.1111/coep.12476.
3. Jason N. Houle, "Disparities in Debt: Parents' Socioeconomic Status and Young Adult Student Loan Debt," *Sociology of Education* 87 (2014): 53–69.
4. Houle, "Disparities in Debt, " 53–69.
5. Camille Z. Charles, Vincent J. Roscigno, and Kimberly Torres, "Racial Inequality and College Attendance: The Mediating Role of Parental Investments," *Social Science Research* 36, no. 1 (2007): 329–52; Eric Grodsky and Melanie Jones, "Real and Imagined Barriers to College Entry: Perceptions of Cost," *Social Science Research* 36, no. 2 (2007): 745–66.
6. Houle, "Disparities in Debt," 53–69.

7. Darity, Addo, and Smith, "A Subaltern Middle Class," 494–502; George Wilson and Vincent Roscigno, "Race and Downward Mobility from Privileged Occupations: African American/White Dynamics Across the Early Work-Career," *Social Science Research* 39, no. 1 (2010): 67–77; Bart Landry and Kris Marsh, "The Evolution of the New Black Middle Class," *Annual Review of Sociology* 37 (2011): 373–94.
8. Fabian T. Pfeffer, Sheldon Danzinger, and Robert F. Schoeni, "Wealth Disparities Before and After the Great Recession," *ANNALS of the American Academy of Political and Social Science* 650, no. 1 (2013): 98–123.
9. Darrick Hamilton et al., *Umbrellas Don't Make It Rain: Why Studying and Working Hard Isn't Enough for Black Americans* (Oakland CA: Insight Center for Community Economic Development, 2015).
10. Su Jin Jez, "The Differential Impact of Wealth Versus Income in the College-Going Process," *Research in Higher Education* 55, no. 7 (2014): 710–34.
11. Addo, Houle, and Simon, "Young, Black, and (Still) in the Red," 64–76.
12. Yunju Nam et al., *Bootstraps Are for Black Kids: Race, Wealth, and the Impact of Intergenerational Transfers on Adult Outcomes* (Oakland, CA: Insight Center for Community Economic Development, 2015).
13. Alexandra Killewald, Fabian T. Pfeffer, and Jared N. Schachner, "Wealth Inequality and Accumulation," *Annual Review of Sociology* 43, no. 1 (2017): 379–404, https://doi.org/10.1146/annurev-soc-060116-053331.
14. Jacob William Faber and Ingrid Ellen, "Race and the Housing Cycle: Differences in Home Equity Trends Among Long-Term Homeowners," *Housing Policy Debate* 26, no. 3 (2016): 456–73; Lauren J. Krivo and Robert L. Kaufman, "Housing and Wealth Inequality: Racial-Ethnic Differences in Home Equity in the United States," *Demography* 41 (2004): 585–605.
15. Addo, Houle, and Simon, "Young, Black, and (Still) in the Red," 64–76.
16. Susan M. Dynarski and Judith E. Scott-Clayton, "The Cost of Complexity in Federal Student Aid: Lessons from Optimal Tax Theory and Behavioral Economics," *National Tax Journal* 59, no. 2 (2006): 319–56; Fenaba Addo, *Ensuring a More Equitable Future: Exploring and Measuring the Relationship Between Family Wealth, Education Debt, and Wealth Accumulation* (Chapel Hill: University of North Carolina at Chapel Hill, Postsecondary Value Commission, 2021), https://files.eric.ed.gov/fulltext/ED612727.pdf.
17. Houle, "Disparities in Debt," 53–69.
18. Rourke O'Brien, "Depleting Capital? Race, Wealth and Informal Financial Assistance," *Social Forces* 91, no. 2 (2012): 375–96.
19. Jasmine D. Hill, "Kin Support of the Black Middle Class: Negotiating Need, Norms, and Class Background," *Social Problems* 69, no. 1 (2020): 3–21, https://doi.org/10.1093/socpro/spaa039.
20. Donald E. Heller, "Merit Aid and College Access" (presented at the Symposium on the Consequences of Merit-Based Student Aid, University of Wisconsin–Madison, March 1, 2006), http://citeseerx.ist.psu.edu/viewdoc/download?doi=10.1.1.544.2863&rep=rep1&type=pdf.
21. Derek V. Price, "Merit Aid and Inequality: Evidence from Baccalaureate & Beyond," *Journal of Student Financial Aid* 31, no. 2 (2001): 5–18.
22. Andrew Kreighbaum, "Report Finds Parents of College Students Taking Out More Debt and Repaying at Slower Rates," *Inside Higher Ed*, November 29, 2018, https://www.insidehighered.com/news/2018/11/29/report-finds-parents-college-students-taking-out-more-debt-and-repaying-slower-rates.
23. Adam Looney and Vivien Lee, *Parents Are Borrowing More and More to Send Their Kids to College—and Many Are Struggling to Repay* (Washington, DC: Brookings Institution, 2018),

https://www.brookings.edu/research/parents-are-borrowing-more-and-more-to-send-their-kids-to-college-and-many-are-struggling-to-repay/.

24. Katrina M. Walsemann and Jennifer A. Ailshire, "Student Debt Spans Generations: Characteristics of Parents Who Borrow to Pay for Their Children's College Education," *Journals of Gerontology Series B* 72, no. 6 (2017): 1084–89, https://doi.org/10.1093/geronb/gbw150.
25. Rachel Fishman, "The Wealth Gap PLUS Debt," New America, May 15, 2018, http://newamerica.org/education-policy/reports/wealth-gap-plus-debt/.
26. Sara Goldrick-Rab, *Paying the Price: College Costs, Financial Aid, and the Betrayal of the American Dream* (Chicago, IL: University of Chicago Press, 2016).
27. Tara Siegel Bernard, "Fafsa Says How Much You Can Pay for College. It's Often Wrong," *New York Times*, November 15, 2019, https://www.nytimes.com/2019/11/15/your-money/fafsa-financial-aid-student-loans.html.
28. William Elliott and Terri Friedline, "'You Pay Your Share, We'll Pay Our Share': The College Cost Burden and the Role of Race, Income, and College Assets," *Economics of Education Review* 33 (2013): 134–53, https://doi.org/10.1016/j.econedurev.2012.10.001.
29. Elliott and Friedline, "'You Pay Your Share, We'll Pay Our Share,'" 134–53; Mark Colas, Sebastian Findeisen, and Dominik Sachs, "Optimal Need-Based Financial Aid," *Journal of Political Economy* 129, no. 2 (2020): 492–533, https://doi.org/10.1086/711952.
30. Bridget Terry Long and Erin Riley, "Financial Aid: A Broken Bridge to College Access?," *Harvard Educational Review* 77, no. 1 (2007): 39–63, https://doi.org/10.17763/haer.77.1.765h8777686r7357.
31. Dynarski and Scott-Clayton, "The Cost of Complexity in Federal Student Aid," 319–56; Susan Dynarski and Mark Wiederspan, "Student Aid Simplification: Looking Back and Looking Ahead" (working paper, Working Paper Series, National Bureau of Economic Research, Cambridge, MA, February 9, 2012), https://doi.org/10.3386/w17834.
32. Fernando Furquim et al., "Navigating the Financial Aid Process: Borrowing Outcomes Among First-Generation and Non-First-Generation Students," *ANNALS of the American Academy of Political and Social Science* 671, no. 1 (2017): 69–91, https://doi.org/10.1177/0002716217698119; Michael S. Kofoed, "To Apply or Not to Apply: FAFSA Completion and Financial Aid Gaps," *Research in Higher Education* 58, no. 1 (2017): 1–39, https://doi.org/10.1007/s11162-016-9418-y.
33. Dynarski and Wiederspan, "Student Aid Simplification."
34. Eric P. Bettinger et al., "The Role of Application Assistance and Information in College Decisions: Results from the H&R Block Fafsa Experiment," *Quarterly Journal of Economics* 127, no. 3 (2012): 1205–42.
35. Sara Goldrick-Rab, "Conditional Pell Dollars Miss Students Who Need Them Most," *Education Next* 14, no. 2 (2014): 59–64; Robert Kelchen, "Financial Need and Aid Volatility Among Students with Zero Expected Family Contribution," *Journal of Student Financial Aid* 44, no. 3 (2015): 179–201.
36. Furquim et al., "Navigating the Financial Aid Process," 69–91; Sara Goldrick-Rab et al., "Reducing Income Inequality in Educational Attainment: Experimental Evidence on the Impact of Financial Aid on College Completion," *American Journal of Sociology* 121, no. 6 (2016): 1762–1817, https://doi.org/10.1086/685442.

Chapter 3

1. Anne Johnson, Tobin Van Ostern, and Abraham White, "The Student Debt Crisis," Center for American Progress, October 25, 2012, https://www.americanprogress.org/issues/education-postsecondary/reports/2012/10/25/42905/the-student-debt-crisis/.

2. Fenaba Addo, Jason Houle, and Daniel Simon, "Young, Black, and (Still) in the Red: Parental Wealth, Race, and Student Loan Debt," *Race and Social Problems* 8, no. 1 (2016): 64–76; Jason N. Houle and Fenaba R. Addo, "Racial Disparities in Student Debt and the Reproduction of the Fragile Black Middle Class," *Sociology of Race and Ethnicity* 5, no. 4 (2019): 562–77, https://doi.org/10.1177/2332649218790989.
3. Sarah Brown, "Nearly Half of Undergraduates Are Students of Color. But Black Students Lag Behind," *Chronicle of Higher Education*, February 14, 2019, https://www.chronicle.com/article/nearly-half-of-undergraduates-are-students-of-color-but-black-students-lag-behind/.
4. Susannah Snider, "Spot a Freshman Financial Aid Offer That Won't Pay Senior Year Bills," *US News & World Report*, April 1, 2015, https://www.usnews.com/education/best-colleges/paying-for-college/articles/2015/04/01/watch-out-for-front-loaded-financial-aid-packages.
5. Janice McCabe and Brandon A. Jackson, "Pathways to Financing College: Race and Class in Students' Narratives of Paying for School," *Social Currents* 3, no. 4 (2016): 367–85, https://doi.org/10.1177/2329496516636404.
6. FinAid.org, "Tuition Inflation," accessed April 13, 2021, https://www.finaid.org/savings/tuition-inflation/.
7. Federal Student Aid: An Office of the US Department of Education, "Subsidized and Unsubsidized Loans," accessed April 13, 2021, https://studentaid.gov/understand-aid/types/loans/subsidized-unsubsidized.
8. Jason N. Houle, "Disparities in Debt: Parents' Socioeconomic Resources and Young Adult Student Loan Debt," *Sociology of Education* 87, no. 1 (2014): 53–69, https://doi.org/10.1177/0038040713512213.
9. Anthony P. Carnevale and Nicole Smith, *Balancing Work and Learning: Implications for Low-Income Students* (Washington, DC: Georgetown University Center on Education and the Workforce, 2018), https://cew.georgetown.edu/cew-reports/learnandearn/; Daniel Douglas and Paul Attewell, *Assessing The Impact of Student Work During College* (Piscataway, NJ: Rutgers Education and Employment Research Center, 2019), https://smlr.rutgers.edu/sites/smlr/files/Documents/Centers/EERC/eerc_working_students_012119.pdf.
10. Jill Barshay, "Working in College Interferes with Studies but Boosts Adult Earnings," The Hechinger Report, June 17, 2019, https://hechingerreport.org/the-paradox-of-working-while-in-college/; Sandy Baum, Martha Johnson, and Victoria Lee, "Understanding College Affordability," Urban Institute, February 6, 2018, http://collegeaffordability.urban.org/covering-expenses/working-during-college/; Jacqueline E. King, *Money Matters: The Impact of Race/Ethnicity and Gender on How Students Pay for College* (Washington, DC: American Council on Education, Fulfillment Services, 1999), https://eric.ed.gov/?id=ED443364.
11. Carnevale and Smith, *Balancing Work and Learning.*
12. Natasha Yurk Quadlin and Daniel Rudel, "Responsibility or Liability? Student Loan Debt and Time Use in College," *Social Forces* 94, no. 2 (2015): 589–614, https://doi.org/10.1093/sf/sov053.
13. Debra Branch McBrier and George Wilson, "Going Down?: Race and Downward Occupational Mobility for White-Collar Workers in the 1990s," *Work and Occupations* 31, no. 3 (2004): 283–322, https://doi.org/10.1177/0730888404266383; Franklin D. Wilson, Marta Tienda, and Lawrence Wu, "Race and Unemployment: Labor Market Experiences of Black and White Men, 1968–1988," *Work and Occupations* 22, no. 3 (1995): 245–70, https://doi.org/10.1177/0730888495022003002; Gregory Sharp, Ellen Whitehead, and Matthew Hall, "Tapped Out? Racial Disparities in Extrahousehold Kin Resources and the Loss of Homeownership," *Demography* 57, no. 5 (2020): 1903–28, https://doi.org/10.1007/s13524-020-00913-4.
14. Courtney D. Cogburn, "Culture, Race, and Health: Implications for Racial Inequities and Population Health," *Milbank Quarterly* 97, no. 3 (2019): 736–61, https://doi.org/10.1111/146

8-0009.12411; David R. Williams, Jourdyn A. Lawrence, and Brigette A. Davis, "Racism and Health: Evidence and Needed Research," *Annual Review of Public Health* 40, no. 1 (2019): 105–25, https://doi.org/10.1146/annurev-publhealth-040218-043750.

15. Debra Umberson and Mieke Beth Thomeer, "Family Matters: Research on Family Ties and Health, 2010 to 2020," *Journal of Marriage and Family* 82, no. 1 (2020): 404–19, https://doi.org/10.1111/jomf.12640.
16. Debra Umberson, "Black Deaths Matter: Race, Relationship Loss, and Effects on Survivors," *Journal of Health and Social Behavior* 58, no. 4 (2017): 405–20, https://doi.org/10.1177/0022146517739317.
17. Student Borrower Protection Center, *Private Student Lending* (Washington, DC: Student Borrower Protection Center, 2020), https://protectborrowers.org/private-student-loans/.
18. Rajeev Darolia and Dubravka Ritter, "Strategic Default Among Private Student Loan Debtors: Evidence from Bankruptcy Reform," *Education Finance and Policy* 15, no. 3 (2020): 487–517, https://doi.org/10.1162/edfp_a_00285; Student Borrower Protection Center, *Private Student Lending.*
19. Erin Dillon and Kevin Carey, "Drowning in Debt: The Emerging Student Loan Crisis," Education Sector, January 1, 2009, https://eric.ed.gov/?id=ED505892.
20. Student Borrower Protection Center, *Private Student Lending.*
21. Center for Responsible Lending, "Quicksand: Borrowers of Color & the Student Debt Crisis," July 22, 2019, https://www.responsiblelending.org/research-publication/quicksand-borrowers-color-student-debt-crisis; Federal Student Aid: An Office of the US Department of Education, "Federal Versus Private Loans," accessed April 13, 2021, https://studentaid.gov/understand-aid/types/loans/federal-vs-private.
22. Student Borrower Protection Center, *Educational Redlining* (Washington, DC: Student Borrower Protection Center, 2020), https://protectborrowers.org/educational-redlining-2/.
23. Danielle Douglas-Gabriel, "Senate Democrats Raise Concerns About Educational Redlining in Student Lending," *Washington Post*, July 31, 2020, https://www.washingtonpost.com/education/2020/07/30/senate-democrats-raise-concerns-about-educational-redlining-student-lending/.
24. Louise Seamster and Raphaël Charron-Chénier, "Predatory Inclusion and Education Debt: Rethinking the Racial Wealth Gap," *Social Currents* 4, no. 3 (2017), https://doi.org/10.1177/2329496516686620.
25. Richard Rothstein, *The Color of Law: A Forgotten History of How Our Government Segregated America* (London, England: W.W. Norton & Company, 2017); Keeanga-Yamahtta Taylor, *Race for Profit: How Banks and the Real Estate Industry Undermined Black Homeownership* (Chapel Hill, NC: University of North Carolina Press, 2019).
26. Marion Fourcade and Kieran Healy, "Classification Situations: Life-Chances in the Neoliberal Era," *Accounting, Organizations and Society* 38, no. 8 (2013): 559–72, https://doi.org/10.1016/j.aos.2013.11.002.
27. Richard Williams, Reynold Nesiba, and Eileen Diaz McConnell, "The Changing Face of Inequality in Home Mortgage Lending," *Social Problems* 52, no. 2 (2005): 181–208, https://doi.org/10.1525/sp.2005.52.2.181.
28. Institute of Education Sciences, US Department of Education, "Indicator 23: Postsecondary Graduation Rates," February 2019, https://nces.ed.gov/programs/raceindicators/indicator_red.asp.
29. Erica Blom and Tomas Monarrez, "Understanding Equity Gaps in College Graduation," Urban Institute, January 31, 2020, 1–47, https://www.urban.org/research/publication/understanding-equity-gaps-college-graduation.

30. Rajashri Chakrabarti et al., "Tuition, Debt, and Human Capital," *SSRN Electronic Journal* (2020): 56, https://doi.org/10.2139/ssrn.3532593.
31. Rachel E. Dwyer, Laura McCloud, and Randy Hodson, "Debt and Graduation from American Universities," *Social Forces* 90, no. 4 (2012): 1133–55, https://doi.org/10.1093/sf/sos072.
32. Dongbin Kim, "The Effect of Loans on Students' Degree Attainment: Differences by Student and Institutional Characteristics," *Harvard Educational Review* 77, no. 1 (2007): 64–100, https://doi.org/10.17763/haer.77.1.n14t69l0q8292784.
33. Johnson, Ostern, and White, "The Student Debt Crisis."
34. Rachel E. Dwyer, Laura McCloud, and Randy Hodson, "Youth Debt, Mastery, and Self-Esteem: Class-Stratified Effects of Indebtedness on Self-Concept," *Social Science Research* 40, no. 3 (2011): 727–41, https://doi.org/10.1016/j.ssresearch.2011.02.001.
35. Institute of Education Sciences, US Department of Education, *Time to Degree, The NCES Fast Facts Tool Provides Quick Answers to Many Education Questions* (Washington, DC: National Center for Education Statistics, 2019), https://nces.ed.gov/fastFacts/display.asp?id=569.
36. Sara Goldrick-Rab and Fabian T. Pfeffer, "Beyond Access: Explaining Socioeconomic Differences in College Transfer," *Sociology of Education* 82, no. 2 (2009): 101–25; Doug Shapiro et al., *Transfer and Mobility: A National View of Student Movement in Postsecondary Institutions, Fall 2011 Cohort. (Signature Report No. 15)* (Herndon, VA: National Student Clearinghouse Research Center, 2018), https://eric.ed.gov/?id=ED592100.
37. Houle and Addo, "Racial Disparities in Student Debt," 562–77.
38. Dick Startz, "When It Comes to Student Success, HBCUs Do More with Less," *Brookings* (blog), January 18, 2021, https://www.brookings.edu/blog/brown-center-chalkboard/2021/01/18/when-it-comes-to-student-success-hbcus-do-more-with-less/; Marybeth Gasman, "Comprehensive Funding Approaches for Historically Black Colleges and Universities," University of Pennsylvania Graduate School of Education and North Carolina Central University, 2010, https://repository.upenn.edu/gse_pubs/331.
39. Alberto Ortega and Omari H. Swinton, "Business Cycles and HBCU Appropriations," *Journal of Economics, Race, and Policy* 1 (2018): 176–95, https://doi.org/10.1007/s41996-018-0009-5.
40. Jen Mishiory, Mark Huelsman, and Suzanne Kahn, "How Student Debt and the Racial Wealth Gap Reinforce Each Other," The Century Foundation, September 9, 2019, https://tcf.org/content/report/bridging-progressive-policy-debates-student-debt-racial-wealth-gap-reinforce/.
41. Laura Hamilton and Kelly Nielsen, *Broke: The Racial Consequences of Underfunding Public Universities* (Chicago, IL: University of Chicago Press, 2021).
42. The Institute for College Access and Success, *Quick Facts About Student Debt* (Washington, DC: The Institute for College Access and Success, 2019), https://ticas.org/files/pub_files/qf_about_student_debt.pdf.
43. Columbia University, Teachers College, "By the Numbers: For-Profit Colleges," *Center for Analysis of Postsecondary Education and Employment* (blog), April 6, 2021, https://capseecenter.org/research/by-the-numbers/for-profit-college-infographic/; Erin Dunlop Velez et al., *Baccalaureate and Beyond (B&B:16/17): A First Look at the Employment and Educational Experiences of College Graduates, 1 Year Later* (Washington, DC: National Center for Education Statistics: US Department of Education, 2019), https://nces.ed.gov/pubs2019/2019241.pdf?utm_content=&utm_medium=email&utm_name=&utm_source=govdelivery&utm_term=.
44. Sandra Staklis, Vera Bersudskaya, and Laura Horn, *Students Attending For-Profit Postsecondary Institutions: Demographics, Enrollment Characteristics, and 6-Year Outcomes*, Web Tables

(Washington, DC: National Center for Education Statistics: US Department of Education, 2011), https://eric.ed.gov/?id=ED581716.

45. Tressie McMillan Cottom, *Lower Ed: The Troubling Rise of For-Profit Colleges in the New Economy* (New York, NY: New York Press, 2017).
46. Cottom, *Lower Ed*; Suzanne Mettler, *Degrees of Inequality: How the Politics of Higher Education Sabotaged the American Dream* (New York, NY: Basic Books, 2014).
47. Rachel E. Dwyer, Jason Houle, and Erica Phillips, "Opportunity for Sale: State Disinvestment in Higher Education and the Rise of For-Profit College Enrollments" (presented at Meetings of the American Sociological Association, Philadelphia, PA, 2018).
48. Sara Goldrick-Rab and Jason N. Houle, "Student Debt Accountability and Its Unintended Racial Consequences," in *Accountability and Opportunity in Higher Education: The Civil Rights Dimension*, ed. Gary Orfield and Nick Hillman (Cambridge, MA: Harvard Education Press, 2018), 151–75; Addo, Houle, and Simon, "Young, Black, and (Still) in the Red: Parental Wealth, Race, and Student Loan Debt," 64–76.
49. Richard Fausset, "Georgia State, Leading U.S. in Black Graduates, Is Engine of Social Mobility," *New York Times*, May 15, 2018, https://www.nytimes.com/2018/05/15/us/georgia-state-african-americans.html.
50. Raj Chetty et al., "Mobility Report Cards: The Role of Colleges in Intergenerational Mobility" (working paper, Working Paper Series, National Bureau of Economic Research, Cambridge, MA, July 24, 2017), https://doi.org/10.3386/w23618.
51. McCabe and Jackson, "Pathways to Financing College," 367–85.
52. Anthony Abraham Jack, *The Privileged Poor: How Elite Colleges Are Failing Disadvantaged Students* (Cambridge, MA: Harvard University Press, 2019).

Chapter 4

1. Judith Scott-Clayton, *The Looming Student Loan Default Crisis Is Worse Than We Thought* (Washington, DC: Brookings Institution, 2018), https://www.brookings.edu/research/the-looming-student-loan-default-crisis-is-worse-than-we-thought/.
2. Morgan Taylor et al., *Race and Ethnicity in Higher Education: 2020 Supplement* (Washington, DC: American Council on Education, 2020), http://1xfsu31b52d33idlp13twtos-wpengine.netdna-ssl.com/wp-content/uploads/2020/11/REHE-2020-final.pdf.
3. Laura Sullivan et al., *Stalling Dreams: How Student Debt Is Disrupting Life Chances and Widening the Racial Wealth Gap* (Waltham, MA: Institute on Assets and Social Policy, Brandeis University, 2019), https://heller.brandeis.edu/iere/pdfs/racial-wealth-equity/racial-wealth-gap/stallingdreams-how-student-debt-is-disrupting-lifechances.pdf.
4. Taylor et al., *Race and Ethnicity in Higher Education.*
5. Taylor et al., *Race and Ethnicity in Higher Education.*
6. Lance J. Lochner and Alexander Monge-Naranjo, "Default and Repayment Among Baccalaureate Degree Earners" (working paper, Working Paper Series, National Bureau of Economic Research, Cambridge, MA, February 2014).
7. Susan Dynarski, "An Economist's Perspective on Student Loans in the United States," CESifo Working Paper Series (Munich: Ludwig-Maximilians University, 2015), http://papers.ssrn.com/sol3/papers.cfm?abstract_id=2694441.
8. S. Michael Gaddis, "Discrimination in the Credential Society: An Audit Study of Race and College Selectivity in the Labor Market," *Social Forces* 93 (2015): 1451–79.
9. Patrick Mason, "Persistent Discrimination: Racial Disparity in the United States, 1967–1988," *American Economic Review* 90, no. 2 (2000): 312–16.

10. Daniel Schneider, "Wealth and the Marital Divide," *American Journal of Sociology* 117, no. 2 (2011): 627–67, https://doi.org/10.1086/661594.
11. Jeffrey Dew, "Two Sides of the Same Coin? The Differing Roles of Assets and Consumer Debt in Marriage," *Journal of Family and Economic Issues* 28, no. 1 (2007): 89–104, https://doi.org/10.1007/s10834-006-9051-6; Jeffrey Dew and Joseph Price, "Beyond Employment and Income: The Association Between Young Adults' Finances and Marital Timing," *Journal of Family and Economic Issues* 32, no. 3 (2011): 424–36, https://doi.org/10.1007/s10834-010-9214-3.
12. Jacob P. Gross et al., "What Matters in Student Loan Default: A Review of the Research Literature," *Journal of Student Financial Aid* 39, no. 1 (2009): 19–29.
13. Elizabeth C. Martin and Rachel E. Dwyer, "Financial Stress, Race, and Student Debt During the Great Recession," *Social Currents* 8, no. 5 (2021): 424–45, https://doi.org/10.1177/23294965211026692.
14. Student Borrower Protection Center, *Private Student Lending* (Washington, DC: Student Borrow Protection Center, 2020), https://protectborrowers.org/wp-content/uploads/2020/04/PSL-Report_042020.pdf.
15. Congressional Budget Office, "Income-Driven Repayment Plans for Student Loans: Budgetary Costs and Policy Options," February 2020, https://www.cbo.gov/publication/56277.
16. Taylor et al., *Race and Ethnicity in Higher Education*.
17. Nicholas W. Hillman and Jacob P. K. Gross, *Can Income-Driven Repayment Policies Be Efficient, Effective, and Equitable?* (Washington, DC: Lumina Foundation, 2014), http://www.luminafoundation.org/files/publications/ideas_summit/Can_Income-Driven_Repayment_Policies_Be_Efficient_Effective_and_Equitable.pdf.
18. Persis Yu, *Relief for Borrowers in Income-Driven Repayment* (Washington, DC: Student Borrower Protection Center, 2020), https://protectborrowers.org/wp-content/uploads/2021/02/Delivering-on-Debt-Relief-Final.pdf#page=74.
19. Katherine Welbeck, *Race: Examining Legal Remedies for Disparate Student Debt Outcomes* (Washington, DC: Student Borrower Protection Center, 2020), https://protectborrowers.org/wp-content/uploads/2020/12/CCFL-QR-74-1-Welbeck-article-rev-1-1.pdf.
20. Consumer Financial Protection Bureau, *Student Loan Servicing: Analysis of Public Input and Recommendations for Reform* (Washington, DC: Consumer Financial Protection Bureau, 2105), https://files.consumerfinance.gov/f/201509_cfpb_student-loan-servicing-report.pdf.
21. Ben Kaufman, "New Data Show Borrowers of Color and Low-Income Borrowers Are Missing Out on Key Protections, Raising Significant Fair Lending Concerns," Student Borrower Protection Center, November 2, 2020, https://protectborrowers.org/new-data-show-borrowers-of-color-and-low-income-borrowers-are-missing-out-on-key-protections-raising-significant-fair-lending-concerns/; Welbeck, *Race: Examining Legal Remedies for Disparate Student Debt Outcomes*.
22. Kaufman, "New Data Show Borrowers of Color and Low-Income Borrowers Are Missing Out."
23. US Department of Education, "Income-Driven Plans Questions and Answers | Federal Student Aid," accessed June 28, 2021, https://studentaid.gov/manage-loans/repayment/plans/income-driven/questions.
24. Tara Siegel Bernard, "The Should-Be Solution to the Student-Debt Problem," *New York Times*, October 13, 2019, sec. Your Money, https://www.nytimes.com/2019/10/13/your-money/student-loans-income-repayment.html.
25. "Salary Paycheck Calculator – Calculate Net Income," ADP, April 5, 2016, https://www.adp.com/resources/tools/calculators/salary-paycheck-calculator.aspx.
26. Student Loan Planner, "Income-Based Repayment Calculator," *Student Loan Planner* (blog), January 21, 2021, https://www.studentloanplanner.com/income-based-repayment-calculator/.

27. Meredith Kolodner, "Does Income-Based Loan Repayment Drive Borrowers of Color into Debt?," The Hechinger Report, 2021, https://hechingerreport.org/do-income-based-repayment-plans-drive-young-borrowers-of-color-deeper-into-debt/.
28. Marshall Steinbaum, *The Student Debt Crisis Is a Crisis of Non-Repayment* (New York: Jain Family Institute, 2020), https://www.jainfamilyinstitute.org/assets/msd4-2020-student-debt-crisis-is-a-crisis-of-non-repayment.pdf.
29. Andrew Keshner, "Education Department Explains Why Only 1% of People Who Applied for Public-Loan Forgiveness Were Accepted," MarketWatch, September 22, 2019, https://www.marketwatch.com/story/education-dept-admits-much-criticized-loan-forgiveness-program-has-obstacles-for-borrowers-2019-09-20.

Chapter 5

1. Tammy La Gorce, "In Love and Out of Debt," *New York Times*, October 16, 2020, sec. Fashion, https://www.nytimes.com/2020/10/16/fashion/weddings/in-love-and-out-of-debt.html.
2. Dignity and Debt Network, "Digging Out with Dignity: Solving the Student Loan Crisis and Honoring Meaning at the Margins," Dignity and Debt, accessed June 24, 2021, https://www.dignityanddebt.org/.
3. Louis Hyman, *Debtor Nation: The History of America in Red Ink (Politics and Society in Twentieth-Century America)* (Princeton, NJ: Princeton University Press, 2011).
4. David Graeber, *Debt: The First 5,000 Years* (New York, NY: Melville House, 2012).
5. Kate Ashford, "College Students Using Loans for Spring Break, Alcohol, Drugs," *Forbes*, March 29, 2017, https://www.forbes.com/sites/kateashford/2017/03/29/loans-spring-break/?sh=5cb913dc6db6.
6. Amy Ruining Sun and Jason N. Houle, "Trajectories of Unsecured Debt Across the Life Course and Mental Health at Midlife," *Society and Mental Health* 10, no. 1 (2020): 61–79.
7. Elizabeth Sweet et al., "The High Price of Debt: Household Financial Debt and Its Impact on Mental and Physical Health," *Social Science & Medicine* 91 (2013): 94–100; Katrina M. Walsemann, Jennifer A. Ailshire, and Gilbert C. Gee, "Student Loans and Racial Disparities in Self-Reported Sleep Duration: Evidence from a Nationally Representative Sample of US Young Adults," *Journal of Epidemiology & Community Health* 70 (2016): 42–48; Rachel E. Dwyer, Laura McCloud, and Randy Hodson, "Youth Debt, Mastery, and Self-Esteem: Class-Stratified Effects of Indebtedness on Self-Concept," *Social Science Research* 40, no. 3 (2011): 727–41.
8. Alisia G. T. T. Tran et al., "At What Costs? Student Loan Debt, Debt Stress, and Racially/Ethnically Diverse College Students' Perceived Health," *Cultural Diversity and Ethnic Minority Psychology* 24, no. 4 (2018): 459–69, https://doi.org/10.1037/cdp0000207.
9. Walsemann, Ailshire, and Gee, "Student Loans and Racial Disparities in Self-Reported Sleep Duration, " 42–48.
10. Patricia Drentea, "Age, Debt and Anxiety," *Journal of Health and Social Behavior* 41 (2000): 437–50; Patricia Drentea and John R. Reynolds, "Where Does Debt Fit in the Stress Process Model?," *Society and Mental Health* 5, no. 1 (2015): 16–32.
11. Katheryn Hancock, "A Certainty of Hopelessness: Debt, Depression, and the Discharge of Student Loans Under the Bankruptcy Code," *Law and Psychology Review* 33 (2009): 151–66.
12. Dennis Hogan and Nan Marie Astone, "The Transition to Adulthood," *Annual Review of Sociology* 12 (1986): 109–30.
13. Frank F. Furstenberg, "On a New Schedule: Transitions to Adulthood and Family Change," *Future of Children* 20, no. 1 (2010): 67–87.
14. Jason N. Houle, "A Generation Indebted: Young Adult Debt Across Three Cohorts," *Social Problems* 61 (2014): 448–65; Reid Cramer et al., *The Emerging Millennial Wealth Gap* (Wash-

ington, DC: New America Foundation, 2019), https://d1y8sb8igg2f8e.cloudfront.net/documents/The_Emerging_Millennial_Wealth_Gap_4y0UuVQ.pdf.

15. Cody Warner and Jason N. Houle, "Precocious Life Course Transitions, Exits from, and Returns to the Parental Home," *Advances in Life Course Research* 35 (2018): 1–10, https://doi.org/10.1016/j.alcr.2017.11.001.
16. Lei Lei and Scott J. South, "Racial and Ethnic Differences in Leaving and Returning to the Parental Home: The Role of Life Course Transitions, Socioeconomic Resources, and Family Connectivity," *Demographic Research* 34 (2016): 109–42.
17. Scott J. South and Lei Lei, "Failures-to-Launch and Boomerang Kids: Contemporary Determinants of Leaving and Returning to the Parental Home," *Social Forces* 94, no. 2 (2015): 863–90; Warner and Houle, "Precocious Life Course Transitions, " 1–10.
18. Jason N. Houle and Cody Warner, "Into the Red and Back to the Nest? Student Debt, College Completion, and Returning to the Parental Home Among Young Adults," *Sociology of Education* 90 (2017): 89–108.
19. Fenaba R. Addo, "Debt, Cohabitation, and Marriage in Young Adulthood," *Demography* 51, no. 5 (2014): 1677–1701.
20. Sharon Sassler, "The Process of Entering into Cohabiting Unions," *Journal of Marriage and Family* 66, no. 2 (2004): 491–505, https://doi.org/10.1111/j.1741-3737.2004.00033.x.
21. Addo, "Debt, Cohabitation, and Marriage in Young Adulthood," 1677–1701.
22. Abby Stivers and Elizabeth Popp Berman, "Parents, Partners, Plans, and Promises: The Relational Work of Student Loan Borrowing," *Socius* 6 (2020): 2378023120915003, https://doi.org/10.1177/2378023120915003.
23. Fenaba R. Addo and Xing Zhang, "Debt Concordance and Relationship Quality: A Couple-Level Analysis," *Journal of Family and Economic Issues* 41, no. 3 (2020): 405–23, https://doi.org/10.1007/s10834-020-09687-8.
24. Trevor Smith, "How Unpaid Internships Reinforce the Racial Wealth Gap," The American Prospect, February 4, 2019, https://prospect.org/api/content/5f06d425-531c-5618-b015-ea4b8c0da520/; S. Michael Gaddis, "Discrimination in the Credential Society: An Audit Study of Race and College Selectivity in the Labor Market," *Social Forces* 93 (2015): 1451–79.
25. Jesse Rothstein and Cecilia Elena Rouse, "Constrained After College: Student Loans and Early-Career Occupational Choices," *Journal of Public Economics* 95, no. 1 (2011): 149–63, https://doi.org/10.1016/j.jpubeco.2010.09.015; Alexandra Minicozzi, "The Short Term Effect of Educational Debt on Job Decisions," *Economics of Education Review* 24, no. 4 (2005): 417–30, https://doi.org/10.1016/j.econedurev.2004.05.008.
26. Lindsay J. DePalma, "The Passion Paradigm: Professional Adherence to and Consequences of the Ideology of 'Do What You Love,'" *Sociological Forum* 36, no. 1 (2021): 134–58, https://doi.org/10.1111/socf.12665; Aliya Hamid Rao and Megan Tobias Neely, "What's Love Got to Do with It? Passion and Inequality in White-Collar Work," *Sociology Compass* 13, no. 12 (2019): e12744, https://doi.org/10.1111/soc4.12744.
27. Anna Helhoski, "How to Choose a College Major with Loan Debt in Mind," *NerdWallet*, October 15, 2020, https://www.nerdwallet.com/article/loans/student-loans/how-to-choose-a-college-major-with-loan-debt-in-mind.
28. Natasha Quadlin, "Funding Sources, Family Income, and Fields of Study in College," *Social Forces* 96, no. 1 (2017): 91–120, https://doi.org/10.1093/sf/sox042.
29. Lorelle L. Espinosa et al., *Race and Ethnicity in Higher Education: A Status Report* (Washington, DC: American Council on Education, 2019), https://1xfsu31b52d33idlp13twtos-wpengine.netdna-ssl.com/wp-content/uploads/2019/02/REHE-Chapter-4-SA.pdf.

30. Rachel Fishman, "Graduate Students: The Low-Hanging Enrollment Fruit," *New America*, October 20, 2020, http://newamerica.org/education-policy/edcentral/graduate-student-enrollment/.
31. Hironao Okahana, Enyu Zhou, and Janet Gao, *Graduate Enrollment and Degrees: 2009 to 2019* (Washington, DC: Council of Graduate Schools, 2020), https://cgsnet.org/publication-pdf/6486/CGS_GED19_Report_final2.pdf.
32. Julie R. Posselt and Eric Grodsky, "Graduate Education and Social Stratification," *Annual Review of Sociology* 43 (2017): 353–78.
33. Jon Marcus, "Graduate Programs Have Become a Cash Cow for Struggling Colleges. What Does That Mean for Students?," *PBS NewsHour*, September 18, 2017, https://www.pbs.org/newshour/education/graduate-programs-become-cash-cow-struggling-colleges-mean-students.
34. Karen L. Webber and Rachel Burns, "Increases in Graduate Student Debt in the US: 2000 to 2016," *Research in Higher Education*, 62 (2021): 709–32, https://doi.org/10.1007/s11162-020-09611-x.
35. "NCES Trendstats," NPSAS: 1996–2016 Graduate Student Loans by Race/Ethnicity, National Center for Education Statistics, 2021, https://nces.ed.gov/datalab/trendstats/trendsoutput.aspx?ts_x=bkbcbhec.
36. Jaymes Pyne and Eric Grodsky, "Inequality and Opportunity in a Perfect Storm of Graduate Student Debt," *Sociology of Education* 93, no. 1 (2020): 20–39, https://doi.org/10.1177/0038040719876245; Judith Scott-Clayton, "Information Constraints and Financial Aid Policy" (working paper, Working Paper Series, National Bureau of Economic Research, Cambridge, MA, 2012), http://www.nber.org/papers/w17811.
37. Robert Kelchen, "Examining Trends in Graduate Student Debt by Race and Ethnicity," *Robert Kelchen* (blog), May 15, 2018, https://robertkelchen.com/2018/05/15/examining-trends-in-graduate-student-debt-by-race-and-ethnicity/.
38. Robert Kelchen, "What Explains Racial Gaps in Large Graduate Student Debt Burdens?," *Robert Kelchen* (blog), May 18, 2018, https://robertkelchen.com/2018/05/17/what-explains-racial-gaps-in-large-graduate-student-debt-burdens/.
39. Pyne and Grodsky, "Inequality and Opportunity," 20–39.
40. Elise Gould, *State of Working America Wages 2019: A Story of Slow, Uneven, and Unequal Wage Growth over the Last 40 Years* (Washington, DC: Economic Policy Institute, 2020), https://www.epi.org/publication/swa-wages-2019/.
41. Darrick Hamilton et al., *Umbrellas Don't Make It Rain: Why Studying and Working Hard Isn't Enough for Black Americans* (Oakland CA: Insight Center for Community Economic Development, 2015), https://socialequity.duke.edu/wp-content/uploads/2019/10/Umbrellas_Dont_Make_It_Rain_Final.pdf.

Chapter 6

1. William R. Emmons and Bryan J. Noeth, "Why Didn't Higher Education Protect Hispanic and Black Wealth?," in *The Balance: Perspectives on Household Balance Sheets* (St. Louis, MO: Federal Reserve Bank of St. Louis, 2015).
2. Daniel Cooper and J. Christina Wang, "Student Loan Debt and Economic Outcomes. Current Policy Perspective No. 14-7," *Federal Reserve Bank of Boston*, 2014; Min Zhan, Xiaoling Xiang, and William Elliott, "Education Loans and Wealth Building Among Young Adults," *Children and Youth Services Review* 66, (2016): 67–75.
3. Zhan, Xiang, and Elliott, "Education Loans and Wealth Building," 67–75.

4. Christian A. L. Hilber and Yingchun Liu, "Explaining the Black–White Homeownership Gap: The Role of Own Wealth, Parental Externalities and Locational Preferences," *Journal of Housing Economics* 17, no. 2 (2008): 152–74, https://doi.org/10.1016/j.jhe.2008.02.001.
5. Wilhelmina A. Leigh and Danielle Huff, *African Americans and Homeownership: The Subprime Lending Experience, 1995 to 2007* (Washington, DC: The Joint Center for Political and Economic Studies, 2007).
6. Andre Perry, Jonathan Rothwell, and David Harshbarger, "The Devaluation of Assets in Black Neighborhoods," *Brookings* (blog), November 27, 2018, https://www.brookings.edu/research/devaluation-of-assets-in-black-neighborhoods/.
7. Meta Brown and Sydnee Caldwell, "Young Student Loan Borrowers Retreat from Housing and Auto Markets," *Federal Reserve Bank of New York*, 2013, 175–213; William Elliott, Michal Grinstein-Weiss, and IlSung Nam, "Is Student Debt Compromising Homeownership as a Wealth-Building Tool?" (working paper, Center for Social Development, Washington University in St. Louis, 2013); Jason N. Houle and Lawrence Berger, "Is Student Loan Debt Discouraging Homeownership Among Young Adults?," *Social Service Review* 89, no. 4 (2015): 589–621, https://doi.org/10.1086/684587; Jodi C. Letkiewicz and Stuart J. Heckman, "Homeownership Among Young Americans: A Look at Student Loan Debt and Behavioral Factors," *Journal of Consumer Affairs* 52, no. 1 (2018): 88–114; Alvaro A. Mezza et al., *On the Effect of Student Loans on Access to Homeownership* (Washington, DC: Divisions of Research & Statistics and Monetary Affairs, Federal Reserve Board, 2015).
8. Robert Hiltonsmith, *At What Cost? How Student Debt Reduces Lifetime Wealth* (New York: Demos, August, 2013).
9. Marion Fourcade and Kieran Healy, "Classification Situations: Life-Chances in the Neoliberal Era," *Accounting, Organizations, and Society* 38, no. 8 (2013): 559–72.
10. Ashlyn Aiko Nelson, "Credit Scores, Race, and Residential Sorting," *Journal of Policy Analysis and Management* 29, no. 1 (2010): 39–68; Rourke L. O'Brien and Barbara Kiviat, "Disparate Impact? Race, Sex, and Credit Reports in Hiring," *Socius* 4 (2018): 2378023118770069.
11. Dora Gicheva and Derek Thompson, "The Effects of Student Loans on Long-Term Household Financial Stability," in *Student Loans and the Dynamics of Debt*, ed. Brad Hershbein and Kevin Hollenbeck (Kalamazoo, MI: W. E. Upjohn Institute for Employment Research, 2015), 287–316.
12. Jason N. Houle and Lawrence Berger, "Children with Disabilities and Trajectories of Parents' Unsecured Debt Across the Life Course," *Social Science Research* 64 (2017): 184–96; Patryk Babiarz, Richard Widdows, and Tansel Yilmazer, "Borrowing to Cope with Adverse Health Events: Liquidity Constraints, Insurance Coverage, and Unsecured Debt," *Health Economics* 22, no. 10 (2013): 1177–98; Teresa A. Sullivan, Elizabeth Warren, and Jay Lawrence Westbrook, *The Fragile Middle Class: Americans in Debt* (New Haven, CT: Yale University Press, 2000).
13. Melvin L. Oliver and Thomas Shapiro, *Black Wealth, White Wealth: A New Perspective on Racial Inequality* (New York: Routledge, 2006); Richard Rothstein, *The Color of Law: A Forgotten History of How Our Government Segregated America* (London, England: W. W. Norton & Company, 2017); William A. Darity Jr. and A. Kirsten Mullen, *From Here to Equality: Reparations for Black Americans in the Twenty-First Century* (Chapel Hill, NC: University of North Carolina Press, 2020), https://uncpress.org/book/9781469654973/from-here-to-equality/.
14. Jason Houle and Fenaba Addo, "Racial Disparities in Student Debt and the Reproduction of the Fragile Black Middle Class," *Sociology of Race and Ethnicity* 5 (2019): 562–77.
15. Tatjana Meschede et al., "'Family Achievements?': How a College Degree Accumulates Wealth for Whites and Not for Blacks," *Federal Reserve Bank of St. Louis Review*, 99, no. 1 (2017): 121–37.

16. Meschede et al., "'Family Achievements?,'" 121–37.
17. Fenaba R. Addo, Jason N. Houle, and Daniel Simon, "Young, Black, and (Still) in the Red: Parental Wealth, Race, and Student Loan Debt," *Race and Social Problems* 8, no. 1 (2016): 64–76.
18. Darrick Hamilton and William A. Darity, "The Political Economy of Education, Financial Literacy, and the Racial Wealth Gap," *Review* 99, no. 1 (2017): 59–76; William Darity Jr., Fenaba R. Addo, and Imari Z. Smith, "A Subaltern Middle Class: The Case of the Missing 'Black Bourgeoisie' in America," *Contemporary Economic Policy* 39, no. 3 (2021): 494–502, https://doi.org/10.1111/coep.12476.
19. Mary Pattillo, *Black Picket Fences: Privilege and Peril Among the Black Middle Class* (Chicago, IL: University of Chicago Press, 1999).
20. Michael Hout, "Social and Economic Returns to College Education in the United States," *Annual Review of Sociology* 38, no. 1 (2012): 379–400, https://doi.org/10.1146/annurev.soc.012809.102503.
21. Anthony P. Carnevale, Stephen J. Rose, and Ban Cheah, *The College Payoff: Education, Occupations, Lifetime Earnings* (Washington, DC: Georgetown University Center on Education and the Workforce, 2011).
22. Darity, Addo, and Smith, "A Subaltern Middle Class," 494–502.
23. Fabian T. Pfeffer and Alexandra Killewald, "Intergenerational Wealth Mobility and Racial Inequality," *Socius* 5 (2019): 2378023119831799.
24. Fenaba R. Addo, "Middle Class Attainment in Young Adulthood: Higher Education and Wealth Inequality" (presentation at the Southern Economic Association Conference, Ft. Lauderdale, FL, 2019).
25. Claudia Buchmann and Thomas A. Diprete, "The Growing Female Advantage in College Completion: The Role of Parental Resources and Academic Achievement," *American Sociological Review* 71, no. 4 (2006): 515–41; Jhumpa Bhattacharya, Anne Price, and Fenaba R. Addo, *Clipped Wings: Closing the Wealth Gap for Millennial Women* (Chicago, IL: The Insight Center, 2019).
26. Louise Seamster and Raphaël Charron-Chénier, "Predatory Inclusion and Education Debt: Rethinking the Racial Wealth Gap," *Social Currents* 4, no. 3 (2017): 199–207.
27. Raj Chetty et al., "Race and Economic Opportunity in the United States: An Intergenerational Perspective" (working paper no. 24441, National Bureau of Economic Research, Cambridge, MA, 2018).
28. Bart Landry and Kris Marsh, "The Evolution of the New Black Middle Class," *Annual Review of Sociology* 37 (2011): 373–94; George Wilson, "Racialized Life-Chance Opportunities Across the Class Structure: The Case of African Americans," *ANNALS of the American Academy of Political and Social Science* 609, no. 1 (2007): 215–32.

Chapter 7

1. "Billionaire Robert F. Smith Pays Debt of Graduates; 135th Commencement at Morehouse College," May 19, 2019, Morehouse College, YouTube, 35:55, https://www.youtube.com/watch?v=-P1CcRphVnM&ab_channel=MorehouseCollege.
2. Sophie Alexander, "Billionaire Created a Perfect Experiment by Erasing $34 Million in Student Debt," *Bloomberg*, July 24, 2020, https://www.bloomberg.com/news/articles/2020-07-24/a-34-million-student-debt-wipe-out-sets-up-a-perfect-economic-experiment.
3. Howard Waitzkin, "John D. Stoeckle and the Upstream Vision of Social Determinants in Public Health," *American Journal of Public Health* 106, no. 2 (2016): 234–36, https://doi.org/10.2105/AJPH.2015.302936.

4. Dignity and Debt Network, "Digging Out with Dignity: Solving the Student Loan Crisis and Honoring Meaning at the Margins," *Dignity and Debt*, accessed June 24, 2021, https://www.dignityanddebt.org/.
5. Annie Nova, "Pressure Mounts for Biden to Forgive Student Debt," *CNBC*, April 13, 2021, https://www.cnbc.com/2021/04/13/pressure-mounts-for-biden-to-forgive-student-debt-.html; Luke Herrine, "The Law and Political Economy of a Student Debt Jubilee," *Buffalo Law Review* 68, no. 2 (2020): 281.
6. Fenaba Addo and Ashley Harrington, "Op-Ed: Black Student Loan Borrowers 'Need Cancellation, and They Need It Now,'" *Yahoo!Finance*, January 17, 2021, https://finance.yahoo.com/news/oped-black-student-loan-need-cancellation-and-they-need-it-now-132132244.html.
7. Marco Di Maggio, Ankit Kalda, and Vincent Yao, "Second Chance: Life Without Student Debt" (working paper, Working Paper Series, National Bureau of Economic Research, Cambridge, MA, May 2019), https://doi.org/10.3386/w25810.
8. Scott Fullwiler et al., *The Macroeconomic Effects of Student Debt Cancellation* (Annandale-on-Hudson, NY: The Levy Economic Institute of Bard College, 2018), http://www.levyinstitute.org/pubs/rpr_2_6.pdf; Berrak Bahadir and Dora Gicheva, *The Effect of Student Debt on Consumption: A State-Level Analysis* (Washington, DC: FDIC, 2019), https://www.fdic.gov/news/events/consumersymposium/2019/documents/papers/bahadir-paper.pdf; "Unburdened: How Canceling Student Debt Can Boost Growth, Equity, and Innovation," Roosevelt Institute, January 27, 2021, https://rooseveltinstitute.org/publications/unburdened-how-canceling-student-debt-can-boost-growth-equity-and-innovation/.
9. Cory Turner, "Why Public Service Loan Forgiveness Is So Unforgiving," NPR.org, October 27, 2018, https://www.npr.org/2018/10/17/653853227/the-student-loan-whistleblower.
10. "Improving the Public Service Loan Forgiveness Program," 100 Day Docket: Student Defense, National Student Legal Defense Network, September 2020, https://www.defendstudents.org/news/body/docket/100-Day-Docket-Improving-PSLF.pdf; Kevin Carey, "It's Easy to Forget, but a Program to Forgive Student Loans Already Exists," *New York Times*, July 24, 2019, sec. The Upshot, https://www.nytimes.com/2019/07/24/upshot/student-debt-forgiveness-already-happening.html.
11. Adam Minsky, "Democrats Introduce Bill to Discharge Private Student Loans for Borrowers and Cosigners Due to Disability," *Forbes*, April 20, 2021, https://www.forbes.com/sites/adamminsky/2021/04/20/democrats-introduce-bill-to-discharge-private-student-loans-for-borrowers-and-cosigners-due-to-disability/?sh=43355181141d.
12. Robert Kelchen, "What Explains Racial Gaps in Large Graduate Student Debt Burdens?," *Robert Kelchen* (blog), May 18, 2018, https://robertkelchen.com/2018/05/17/what-explains-racial-gaps-in-large-graduate-student-debt-burdens/.
13. Kery Murakami, "Large Debate Looms over Canceling Parents' Debt for Student Loans," *Inside Higher Ed*, January 28, 2021, https://www.insidehighered.com/news/2021/01/28/large-debate-looms-over-canceling-parents-debt-student-loans.
14. Katrina M. Walsemann and Jennifer A. Ailshire, "Student Debt Spans Generations: Characteristics of Parents Who Borrow to Pay for Their Children's College Education," *Journals of Gerontology Series B* 72, no. 6 (2017): 1084–89, https://doi.org/10.1093/geronb/gbw150.
15. Abigail Johnson Hess, "The U.S. Already Has Student Debt Forgiveness—but Barely Anyone Gets It," *CNBC*, March 23, 2021, https://www.cnbc.com/2021/03/23/the-us-already-has-student-debt-forgivenessbut-barely-anyone-gets-it.html.
16. Matthew Chingos and Donald Marron, "Is Student Loan Forgiveness an Effective Form of Economic Stimulus?," Urban Institute, July 28, 2020, https://www.urban.org/urban-wire/student-loan-forgiveness-effective-form-economic-stimulus; Sandy Baum, "Mass Debt

Forgiveness Is Not a Progressive Idea," *Education Next* (blog), October 20, 2020, https://www.educationnext.org/mass-debt-forgiveness-not-progressive-idea-fallacy-of-forgiveness-forum/; David Leonhardt, "Eliminating All Student Debt Isn't Progressive," *New York Times*, November 18, 2018, sec. Opinion, https://www.nytimes.com/2018/11/18/opinion/student-debt-forgiveness-college-democrats.html.

17. Dignity and Debt Network, "Digging Out with Dignity."
18. Addo and Harrington, "Op-Ed: Black Student Loan Borrowers 'Need Cancellation.'"
19. Charlie Eaton et al., "Student Debt Cancellation IS Progressive: Correcting Empirical and Conceptual Errors," Roosevelt Institute, June 8, 2021, https://rooseveltinstitute.org/publications/student-debt-cancellation-is-progressive/.
20. Raphaël Charron-Chénier et al., Expert Letter to Senator Elizabeth Warren, April 18, 2019, Brandeis University, https://elizabethwarren.com/wp-content/uploads/2019/04/Experts-Letter-to-Senator-Warren-.pdf.
21. Andre M. Perry Marshall Steinbaum, and Carl Romer, "Student Loans, the Racial Wealth Divide, and Why We Need Full Student Debt Cancellation," *Brookings* (blog), June 23, 2021, https://www.brookings.edu/research/student-loans-the-racial-wealth-divide-and-why-we-need-full-student-debt-cancellation/.
22. Raphaël Charron-Chénier et al., "Student Debt Forgiveness Options: Implications for Policy and Racial Equity," Roosevelt Institute, August 14, 2020, https://rooseveltinstitute.org/publications/student-debt-forgiveness-options-implications-for-policy-and-racial-equity/.
23. Jason N. Houle and Fenaba R. Addo, "Racial Disparities in Student Debt and the Reproduction of the Fragile Black Middle Class," *Sociology of Race and Ethnicity* 5, no. 4 (2019): 562–77.
24. Mark Huelsman et al., "Less Debt, More Equity: Lowering Student Debt While Closing the Black-White Wealth Gap," *Demos*, November 24, 2015, https://www.demos.org/research/less-debt-more-equity-lowering-student-debt-while-closing-black-white-wealth-gap.
25. Naomi Zewde and Darrick Hamilton, "What Canceling Student Debt Would Do for the Racial Wealth Gap," *New York Times*, February 1, 2021, sec. Opinion, https://www.nytimes.com/2021/02/01/opinion/student-debt-cancellation-biden.html.
26. Megan Leonhardt, "We Asked More Than 500 Congress Members About Student Loan Forgiveness—Here's What We Found," *CNBC*, April 22, 2021, https://www.cnbc.com/2021/04/22/student-loan-forgiveness-where-members-of-congress-stand.html.
27. Sylvain Catherine and Constantine Yannelis, "The Distributional Effects of Student Loan Forgiveness" (working paper, Working Paper Series, National Bureau of Economic Research, Cambridge, MA, December 2020), https://doi.org/10.3386/w28175.
28. "Tax Consequences of Student Loan Discharges for Borrowers in Income-Driven Repayment Plans," The Institute for College Access & Success, July 15, 2020, https://ticas.org/affordability-2/tax-consequences-of-student-loan-discharges-for-borrowers-in-income-driven-repayment-plans/.
29. Dorothy A Brown, *The Whiteness of Wealth: How the Tax System Impoverishes Black Americans—and How We Can Fix It* (New York, NY: Penguin Random House, 2021).
30. James C. Cox, Daniel Kreisman, and Susan Dynarski, "Designed to Fail: Effects of the Default Option and Information Complexity on Student Loan Repayment," *Journal of Public Economics* 192 (2020): 104298, https://doi.org/10.1016/j.jpubeco.2020.104298; Bruce Chapman and Lorraine Dearden, "Conceptual and Empirical Issues for Alternative Student Loan Designs: The Significance of Loan Repayment Burdens for the United States," *ANNALS of the American Academy of Political and Social Science* 671, no. 1 (2017): 249–68, https://doi.org/10.1177/0002716217703969.
31. Cox, Kreisman, and Dynarski, "Designed to Fail."

32. Julia Barnard et al., *Road to Relief: Supporting Federal Student Loan Borrowers During the COVID-19 Crisis and Beyond* (Washington, DC: Center for Responsible Lending, 2020), https://www.responsiblelending.org/research-publication/road-relief-supporting-federal-student-loan-borrowers-during-covid-19-crisis.
33. Richard Fossey and Robert C. Cloud, "Income-Driven Repayment Plans for Distressed Student-Loan Debtors: Not a Silver Bullet for Easing the Student Loan Crisis," *Teachers College Record*, February 6, 2017, https://www.tcrecord.org/Content.asp?ContentId=21816; Marshall Steinbaum, *The Student Debt Crisis Is a Crisis of Non-Repayment* (New York: Jain Family Institute, 2020), https://www.jainfamilyinstitute.org/assets/msd4-2020-student-debt-crisis-is-a-crisis-of-non-repayment.pdf.
34. Susan Dynarski and Mark Wiederspan, "Student Aid Simplification: Looking Back and Looking Ahead" (working paper, Working Paper Series, National Bureau of Economic Research, Cambridge, MA, February 9, 2012), https://doi.org/10.3386/w17834.
35. Alberto Guzman-Alvarez and Lindsay C. Page, "FAFSA Verification: An Undue Burden for Students and Public Colleges," *Brookings* (blog), June 7, 2021, https://www.brookings.edu/blog/brown-center-chalkboard/2021/06/07/fafsa-verification-an-undue-burden-for-students-and-public-colleges/.
36. Spiros Protopsaltis and Sharon Parrott, "Pell Grants—A Key Tool for Expanding College Access and Economic Opportunity—Need Strengthening, Not Cuts," Center on Budget and Policy Priorities, 2017, https://www.cbpp.org/research/federal-budget/pell-grants-a-key-tool-for-expanding-college-access-and-economic.
37. Olivia Sanchez, "Pell Changes Could Mean More Eligible Students, More Money, More Programs," The Hechinger Report, April 23, 2021, https://hechingerreport.org/pell-changes-could-mean-more-eligible-students-more-money-more-programs/.
38. Protopsaltis and Parrott, "Pell Grants—a Key Tool for Expanding College Access."
39. Eddy Conroy et al., *The Real Price of College: How Using the Negative Expected Family Contribution Can Better Support Students* (Philadelphia, PA: The Hope Center, April 2021), https://hope4college.com/wp-content/uploads/2021/05/NegativeEFC_PolicyMemo.pdf.
40. Sara Goldrick-Rab, *Paying the Price: College Costs, Financial Aid, and the Betrayal of the American Dream* (Chicago, IL: University of Chicago Press, 2016); Laura Hamilton and Kelly Nielsen, *Broke: The Racial Consequences of Underfunding Public Universities* (Chicago, IL: University of Chicago Press, 2021).
41. Dominique J. Baker, "State-Federal Partnerships May Be the Key to Reducing Black Student Debt," *The Education Trust* (blog), 2020, https://edtrust.org/resource/state-federal-partnerships-may-be-the-key-to-reducing-black-student-debt/.
42. Adam Harris, "The Steep Cost of Decades of Discrimination," *The Atlantic*, May 10, 2021, https://www.theatlantic.com/politics/archive/2021/05/bidens-unprecedented-funding-black-colleges/618846/.
43. David L. Kirp, "Why Stanford Should Clone Itself," *New York Times*, April 6, 2021, sec. Opinion, https://www.nytimes.com/2021/04/06/opinion/stanford-admissions-campus.html.
44. Sara Goldrick-Rab, "Should College Education Be Free?," *Wall Street Journal*, March 20, 2018, https://www.wsj.com/articles/should-college-education-be-free-1521558856.
45. Douglas N. Harris, "Is Free College a Good Idea? Increasingly, Evidence Says Yes," *Brookings* (blog), May 10, 2021, https://www.brookings.edu/blog/brown-center-chalkboard/2021/05/10/is-free-college-a-good-idea-increasingly-evidence-says-yes/.
46. Sara Goldrick-Rab and Nancy Kendall, *F2CO: Redefining College Affordability* (Washington, DC: Lumina Foundation, 2014), http://www.luminafoundation.org/files/publications/ideas_summit/Redefining_College_Affordability.pdf.

47. Goldrick-Rab and Kendall, *F2CO*.
48. Laura W. Perna and Elaine W. Leigh, "Understanding the Promise: A Typology of State and Local College Promise Programs," *Educational Researcher* 47, no. 3 (2018): 155–80.
49. Harris, "Is Free College a Good Idea?"
50. Sara Goldrick-Rab et al., "Reducing Income Inequality in Educational Attainment: Experimental Evidence on the Impact of Financial Aid on College Completion," *American Journal of Sociology* 121, no. 6 (May 1, 2016): 1762–1817, https://doi.org/10.1086/685442; Rajashri Chakrabarti, William Nober, and Wilbert van der Klaauw, "Is Free College the Solution to Student Debt Woes? Studying the Heterogeneous Impacts of Merit Aid Programs," *Liberty Street Economics* (blog), October 10, 2019, https://libertystreeteconomics.newyorkfed.org/2019/10/is-free-college-the-solution-to-student-debt-woes.html.
51. Douglas N Harris et al., "The Promise of Free College (and Its Potential Pitfalls)," *Brookings* (blog), September 20, 2018, https://www.brookings.edu/research/the-promise-of-free-college-and-its-potential-pitfalls/.
52. Michael Hout, "Social and Economic Returns to College Education in the United States," *Annual Review of Sociology* 38 (2012): 379–400.
53. Sean Illing, "The Case for Canceling Student Debt—All of It," *Vox*, May 13, 2021, https://www.vox.com/policy-and-politics/22383450/student-debt-forgiveness-biden-astra-taylor.
54. Rachel E. Dwyer, Jason N. Houle, and Erica Philips, "Opportunity for Sale: State Disinvestment in Higher Education and the Rise of For-Profit College Enrollments" (Annual Meetings of the American Sociological Association, Philadelphia, PA, 2018).
55. Stephen Hayes and Andrea Lowe, "Holding For-Profit Schools Accountable for Civil Rights Violations," Student Borrower Protection Center, December 4, 2020, https://protectborrowers.org/holding-for-profit-schools-accountable-for-civil-rights-violations/.
56. Danielle Douglas-Gabriel, "Student Debt Is Hitting African Americans the Hardest. These Experts Have a Plan to Fix It," *Washington Post*, September 20, 2019, https://www.washingtonpost.com/local/education/student-debt-is-hitting-african-americans-the-hardest-these-experts-have-a-plan-to-fix-it/2019/09/20/5f786e48-d0fb-11e9-b29b-a528dc82154a_story.html.
57. Darrick Hamilton and William Darity, "Can 'Baby Bonds' Eliminate the Racial Wealth Gap in Putative Post-Racial America?," *Review of Black Political Economy* 37, no. 3–4 (2010): 207–16, https://doi.org/10.1007/s12114-010-9063-1.
58. Darrick Hamilton, "How 'Baby Bonds' Could Help Close the Wealth Gap," September 2018, TED Talk, 12:28, https://www.ted.com/talks/darrick_hamilton_how_baby_bonds_could_help_close_the_wealth_gap/.
59. Naomi Zewde, "Universal Baby Bonds Reduce Black-White Wealth Inequality, Progressively Raise Net Worth of All Young Adults," *Review of Black Political Economy* 47, no. 1 (2020): 3–19, https://doi.org/10.1177/0034644619885321.
60. "Growing Momentum for 'Baby Bonds' as Booker, Pressley Re-Introduce Landmark Legislation to Combat the Growing Racial Wealth Gap," U.S. Senator Cory Booker of New Jersey, February 4, 2021, https://www.booker.senate.gov/news/press/growing-momentum-for-baby-bonds-as-booker-pressley-re-introduce-landmark-legislation-to-combat-the-growing-racial-wealth-gap.
61. Hamilton and Darity, "Can 'Baby Bonds' Eliminate the Racial Wealth Gap?," 207–16.
62. William Darity Jr., Fenaba R. Addo, and Imari Z. Smith, "A Subaltern Middle Class: The Case of the Missing 'Black Bourgeoisie' in America," *Contemporary Economic Policy* 39, no. 3 (2021): 494–502, https://doi.org/10.1111/coep.12476.
63. Sheila Jackson Lee, "H.R. 40—117th Congress (2021–2022): Commission to Study and Develop

Reparation Proposals for African Americans Act," legislation, April 14, 2021, 2021/2022, https://www.congress.gov/bill/117th-congress/house-bill/40.

64. "2020 Poll on Reparations," Democracy in Color, 2020, https://democracyincolor.com/2020reppoll.
65. Marc Dixon and Andrew W. Martin, "We Can't Win This on Our Own: Unions, Firms, and Mobilization of External Allies in Labor Disputes," *American Sociological Review* 77, no. 6 (2012): 946–69, https://doi.org/10.1177/0003122412460649.

Afterword

1. Whitney N. Laster Pirtle, "Racial Capitalism: A Fundamental Cause of Novel Coronavirus (COVID-19) Pandemic Inequities in the United States," *Health Education & Behavior* 47, no. 4 (2020): 504–8, https://doi.org/10.1177/1090198120922942.
2. Ana Hernandez Kent and Lowell R. Ricketts, "Disparities by Race, Ethnicity and Education Underlie Millennials' Comeback in Wealth," Federal Reserve Bank of St. Louis, April 2021, https://www.stlouisfed.org/on-the-economy/2021/april/disparities-race-ethnicity-education-millennials-comeback-wealth.
3. Deepa Shivaram, "HBCUs Erasing Student Debt with Federal Funds Brings Hope for Students and Schools," *NPR*, August 14, 2021, sec. Education, https://www.npr.org/2021/08/14/1027401478/hbcu-student-debt-federal-funds-wealth-gap.
4. Andrew Skerritt, "FAMU Spends Over $16M to Pay Off Student Outstanding Balances," *FAMU Forward* (blog), July 31, 2021, http://www.famunews.com/2021/07/famu-spends-over-16m-to-pay-off-student-outstanding-balances/.
5. Emily Stewart, "What the Covid-19 Relief Bill Does for Student Loan Forgiveness, Explained," *Vox*, March 8, 2021, https://www.vox.com/policy-and-politics/2021/3/8/22319784/student-loan-debt-stimulus-bill.

Appendix

1. Bureau of Labor Statistics, *National Longitudinal Studies Handbook* (Washington, DC: US Department of Labor, 2005).
2. Meta Brown et al., "Do We Know What We Owe? A Comparison of Borrower- and Lender-Reported Consumer Data," FRBNY Economic Policy Review (New York: Federal Reserve Bank of New York, 2015), https://www.newyorkfed.org/medialibrary/media/research/epr/2015/EPR_2015_comparisons_brown.pdf.
3. Jason N. Houle, "Disparities in Debt: Parents' Socioeconomic Status and Young Adult Student Loan Debt," *Sociology of Education* 87 (2014): 53–69.
4. Houle, "Disparities in Debt," 53–69; Jason N. Houle, "A Generation Indebted: Young Adult Debt Across Three Cohorts," *Social Problems* 61 (2014): 448–65; Jason N. Houle and Fenaba R. Addo, "Racial Disparities in Student Debt and the Reproduction of the Fragile Black Middle Class," *Sociology of Race and Ethnicity* 5, no. 4 (2019): 562–77; Jason N. Houle and Cody Warner, "Into the Red and Back to the Nest? Student Debt, College Completion, and Returning to the Parental Home Among Young Adults," *Sociology of Education* 90 (2017): 89–108; Fenaba R. Addo, "Debt, Cohabitation, and Marriage in Young Adulthood," *Demography* 51, no. 5 (2014): 1677–1701; Fenaba R. Addo, Jason N. Houle, and Daniel Simon, "Young, Black, and (Still) in the Red: Parental Wealth, Race, and Student Loan Debt," *Race and Social Problems* 8, no. 1 (2016): 64–76; Fenaba R. Addo, Jason N. Houle, and Sharon Sassler, "The Changing Nature of the Association Between Student Loan Debt and Marital Behavior in Young Adulthood," *Journal of Family and Economic Issues* 40, no. 1 (2019): 86–101, https://doi.org/10.1007/s10834-018-9591-6.

5. Mario Luis Small, "How to Conduct a Mixed Methods Study: Recent Trends in a Rapidly Growing Literature," *Annual Review of Sociology* 37, no. 1 (2011): 57–86, https://doi.org/10.1146/annurev.soc.012809.102657.
6. Judith Scott-Clayton, *The Looming Student Loan Default Crisis Is Worse Than We Thought* (Washington, DC: Brookings Institution, 2018), https://www.brookings.edu/research/the-looming-student-loan-default-crisis-is-worse-than-we-thought/; Judith Scott-Clayton and Jing Li, *Black-White Disparity in Student Loan Debt More Than Triples After Graduation*, vol. 2, Evidence Speaks Reports (Washington, DC: Brookings Institution, 2016).
7. Fenaba R. Addo et al., *Changing the Narrative on Student Borrowers of Color* (Washington, DC: Lumina Foundation, 2021), https://www.luminafoundation.org/resource/borrowers-of-color/.
8. Sara Goldrick-Rab, *Paying the Price: College Costs, Financial Aid, and the Betrayal of the American Dream* (Chicago, IL: University of Chicago Press, 2016); Tressie McMillan Cottom, *Lower Ed: The Troubling Rise of For-Profit Colleges in the New Economy* (New York, NY: The New Press, 2017).

ACKNOWLEDGMENTS

It truly took a village to write this book, and we are grateful for the support, guidance, and advice we received along the way. First and foremost, this book would not have been possible without the generosity of our interviewees, who so willingly shared their (often painful) stories and gave us a few hours of their precious time. We hope that we have done justice to their experiences.

No project can be a success without money and time. The Rockefeller Center at Dartmouth College and the Institute for Research on Poverty at the University of Wisconsin–Madison provided generous grant support that gave us the financial resources necessary to launch our qualitative data collection. We also thank Jayne Fargnoli and Harvard Education Press for supporting this project through COVID-related delays and gave us the time needed to complete this book.

We are thankful for our incredible student research assistants at Dartmouth College and UW–Madison who worked tirelessly behind the scenes. Antonio Byrd managed participant recruitment, conducted many of the early interviews, and was critical in getting our qualitative data collection off the ground. Gustavo De Almeida Silva, now a PhD student at Brown University, is one of those rare students who seemed like a colleague even as an undergraduate. Gustavo was integral to the development of our interview guide. Many other students summarized interview transcripts, coded and cleaned data, and read countless chapter drafts over the years: Katell Ane, Cameron Guage, Kristabel Konta, Daniel Lin, Samrit Mathur, Kailas Sane, Alexander Soong, and Camille Wiggins were all vital members of our research team.

This project would not have been possible without the support of our colleagues at Dartmouth, Wisconsin, Duke, and UNC–Chapel Hill who provided feedback on chapter drafts and helped us sharpen the focus of this project; they include John Campbell, Marc Dixon, George Edmondson,

Janice McCabe, Kim Rogers, Jessica Su, and Emily Walton. We feel lucky to be in such supportive academic departments. Fenaba often wrote in community and wanted to acknowledge Ruth, Bianca, Angela, Tod, Tiffany, WRAP, The Breakfast Club, Terri, and Wylin for their fellowship, support, guidance, and countless poms.

We started writing and researching student debt over a decade ago—first independently when we wrote our dissertations, and later together when we met and shared an office suite as Robert Wood Johnson Foundation Health and Society scholars at UW–Madison. We are grateful to our mentors and advisors who believed in and supported our work before many in our discipline saw value in it: Amy Blackstone, Francine Blau, J. Michael Collins, William "Sandy" Darity, Michelle Frisco, Daniel Lichter, Molly Martin, John Mullahy, Steph Robert, and Sharon Sassler. We would not be where we are today without the continued support of these people.

We feel lucky to be part of an incredible, vibrant intellectual community of scholars who care deeply about debt and inequality. Some of these scholars are our frequent coauthors—including Lonnie Berger, Rachel Dwyer, Sara Goldrick-Rab, Sharon Sassler, Dan Simon, Amy Ruining Sun, and Cody Warner—whose work is featured in this book. Others have helped us sharpen our thinking on student debt through conversations, comments on manuscripts, or just by being brilliant people, including Dominique Baker, Charlie Eaton, Seth Frotman, Eric Grodsky, Darrick Hamilton, Laura Hamilton, Ashley Harrington, Robert Kelchen, Louise Seamster, and Fred Wherry. Our participation in Fred Wherry's *Dignity and Debt* network and the Lumina Foundation's *Borrowers of Color Working Group* has left a lasting impact on us and changed the course of this book project for the better. Jeff Himpele, a member of the *Dignity and Debt* network, graciously donated his time and talents to us, and designed several of the figures used in this book.

Finally, none of this would have been possible without the unwavering support of our families. Jason thanks Jo for sharing in all the successes and frustrations of this project over the years; and for always being game to lend a critical eye to the work—even when she would rather be thinking about the regulatory environment of organic food and farming. Fenaba thanks Senay (my biggest fan), Nia (my sunshine), her mom, Valerie, sister, Afua, the Monks, and Tekie-Negusse family for unwavering support, and the ancestors on whom I stand.

ABOUT THE AUTHORS

Jason N. Houle is an associate professor of sociology at Dartmouth College in Hanover, New Hampshire. Jason was born and raised in the western mountains of rural Maine and graduated with a BA in sociology from the University of Maine in Orono. He received his PhD in sociology and demography at the Pennsylvania State University in 2011 and was a Robert Wood Johnson Foundation Health and Society Scholar at the University of Wisconsin–Madison from 2011 to 2013. His scholarly interests center on two main areas: the persistence of social inequality across generations and the social determinants of health and mental health. To that end, the bulk of his published work focuses on the causes and consequences of rising indebtedness in the US. He lives in Wilder, Vermont, with his partner Jo and their dog, Moose.

Fenaba R. Addo is an associate professor of public policy at the University of North Carolina–Chapel Hill. Widely published in academic journals and policy outlets, her work on racial disparities in student debt, older Black women and wealth, and the Millennial racial wealth gap reflects her interests in bridging social demography with economic inequality, and sheds light on the ways that societal inequalities stem from historical legacies of racial exclusion and discrimination, and how they get reproduced over time. She received her PhD in policy analysis and management from Cornell University and holds a BS in economics from Duke University. Born and raised in Brooklyn, New York, she loves so many things but especially enjoys travel, food and wine, hip-hop and R&B, and the arts.

INDEX

Abrams, Stacey, 13, 14, 15, 22, 123
accrued interest, 68, 70, 71, 77, 82, 144
accumulation crisis, 2, 3
  See also debt accumulation
adulthood, transition to, 91–92, 108
advocacy groups, 140–141
Affordable Budget-Conscious (ABC) plan, 131–132
Ailshire, Jennifer, 89
American Dream, 110, 140
American Families plan, 136, 137
American Rescue Plan, 135, 145
America Opportunity Accounts Act, 139
Arbery, Ahmaud, 140, 143
Asian American borrowers, 3, 154
asset accumulation, 112–115
auto loan debt, 4

baby bonds, 138–139
bait and switch pricing, 46–47
Baker, Dominque, 134, 135
bankruptcy, 90, 115
Biden, Joe, 126, 127, 129, 134, 135, 136
Black Americans
  COVID-19 pandemic and, 143–145
  education gospel in, 18–19
Black borrowers
  average loan debt of, 2, 69–70
  debt crisis for, 3–4, 15, 25–26
  debt repayment by, 11–12, 16, 24–28, 67–83, 85–106
  discrimination against, 54
  in IDR plans, 79–83
  loan default by, 2, 9–10, 25, 67–68, 72, 74–78
Black college graduates
  See also Black borrowers
  graduate school and, 101
  in labor market, 73
  in middle class, 120
  return to parental home by, 92–95
Black families
  college contributions by, 34–35
  extended families, 37
  median net wealth of, 33–34, 118–119
  wealth gap for, 7–8, 10–12, 27–36, 59, 104, 108–109, 115–119, 129, 138–141
Black Lives Matter, 141
Black men, 120–121
Black middle class, 4, 10
  college costs and, 29–30
  fragility of, 11, 30, 33, 50, 118, 122, 124
  higher education and, 117–122
  home ownership and, 109–112
  reproduction of, 107–122
  as subaltern, 120, 122
  wealth inequalities and, 31–36
Black Millennials, 121
Black parents, loans taken out by, 38–40
Black students
  See also Black borrowers
  college enrollment by, 8, 19, 20
  debt accumulation by, 11, 13–17, 19–24, 27, 30–32
  debt crisis for, 124–125
  degree attainment by, 18
  dropout rates for, 45, 55
  family hardships and, 49–52
  in graduate school, 101–106

Black students *(Cont.)*
  at HBCUs, 59
  at for-profit institutions, 60
  race and, 9–10
  socioeconomic background of, 31
  working during college by, 48, 133
Black women, 120–121
Bonilla-Silva, Eduardo, 14, 15
Booker, Cory, 139
boomeranging, 92–95
branch campuses, 8, 59, 134, 135
Brown, Dorothy, 130

capital
  cultural, 31, 63
  social, 36, 63
capital assets, 112, 119
careers, 91, 98–101
  See also employment; jobs
Carey, Kevin, 53
Cefalu, Andrew, 1
Cefalu, Melissa, 1
Cemper, Tanner, 85
certificate programs, 102
Chakrabarti, Rajashri, 55
Charron-Chénier, Raphaël, 21, 54, 129
Chetty, Raj, 62
civil rights movement, 21
cohabitation, 96
college affordability, 132–138
college completion, 22
  crisis, 3
  gender disparity in, 121
college costs
  increases in, 6–7, 29, 45, 47, 58, 133–134
  "net costs," 40
college degree
  economic value of, 3, 119
  as engine of upward mobility, 117–122, 124
  failure to complete, 3
  importance of getting, 17–19, 136
  lifetime earnings and, 119
  racial disparities in benefits of, 10, 12
  time to complete, 57–58
college dropouts, 9, 45–46, 48, 54–58
college enrollment, 8
  growth in, 19, 20
  growth of, 4
college graduates
  See also Black college graduates; white college graduates
  repayment ability of, 9–10
college persistence, 54–58
college prep resources, 37
College Promise programs, 137
colleges and universities, 57
  See also higher education
  branch campuses, 8, 59, 135
  elite institutions, 8, 37–38, 60–63
  financial aid packages from, 41, 58, 60–64, 102
  historically Black, 54, 59, 134–135, 144
  private, 7, 8, 16, 135
  for-profit, 21, 22, 58–60, 126, 138, 155
  public, 6–7, 58–60
  regional, 134, 135
  transferring, 57
  two-year institutions, 7, 54, 58–59, 136, 155
  underfunded, 8, 9, 22, 27, 59, 133, 135, 144
college years
  challenges during, 46
  debt accumulation during, 45–65
  working during, 47–49, 133
community colleges, 7, 155
  See also two-year institutions
  cost increases at, 7
  free access to, 136
completion rates, 3
Consolidated Appropriations Act of 2021, 134
consumer debt, 114–115
Consumer Financial Protection Bureau (CFPB), 80
Conyers, John, 140
Coronavirus Aid, Relief, and Economic Security (CARES) Act, 144
cost of living, 6, 7
Cottom, Tressie McMillan, 18, 60, 85, 125, 155
COVID-19 pandemic, 143–145
Cox, James, 131
credit access, 54, 112–115

credit card debt, 4, 53, 114–115
credit score, 68, 107, 113–114
cultural capital, 31, 63
cultural inferiority, 15
cultural values, 97

Darity, William, 12, 119, 138–140
dating market, 97
dead-end jobs, 98, 99, 101
debt, sinful connotations of, 86–87
debt accumulation
by Black students, 11, 13–17, 27, 30–32
during college years, 45–65
familial wealth and, 34
from graduate school, 101–106
racial disparities in, 2–4, 9–12, 19–24, 27, 31, 60, 68, 104
social inequality and, 8
through interest and fees, 26, 68, 70, 71, 77, 82, 144
Debt Collective, 140
debt collectors, 68
debt forgiveness, 53, 81–82, 99, 123–124, 126–130, 141, 145
debt repayment
accrued interest and, 67, 68, 70, 71, 82, 144
anxiety about, 65, 76, 85–86, 88–91
Black borrowers and, 11–12, 16, 24–28, 85–106
challenges of, 67–83, 113–114
difficulty with, 4–5
in early repayment period, 69–74
grace period before, 69
hidden costs of, 85–106
income-driven, 11, 24–25, 53, 78–83, 130–132, 145
loan defaults and, 74–78
opportunity costs of, 108–109
personal responsibility narrative of, 85, 86–88
of private loans, 53–54
racial disparities in, 24–28, 80
social inequality and, 8–9
sticker shock over, 70–71
suspension of, during pandemic, 143–144
by white borrowers, 27, 85

defaults. See loan defaults
deferment. See loan deferment
deficit narratives, 100, 125
Deming, David, 134
Democratic Party, 141
depression, 90
Dillon, Erin, 53
Di Maggio, Marco, 126
Direct Loan program, 69
discrimination, 9, 10, 11, 12, 14, 18, 20, 46, 50
housing market, 111
labor market, 18, 73
in private loan market, 54
divorce, 114
double standards, 13, 14, 15
down payments, 110–111
downstream policies, 125, 126–132, 144
downward mobility, 33, 120
Drentea, Patricia, 89
Dwyer, Rachel, 56, 65, 74
Dynarski, Susan, 43–44, 72, 131

Eaton, Charlie, 129
Economic Bill of Rights, 139
economic inequality, 3–4, 7–8
education gospel, 18–19, 86, 101–106, 124, 136
elite institutions, 8, 37–38, 60–63
Elliott, William, 41, 109
emergency savings, 33, 112, 114
employment
See also careers; jobs
after college, 67, 70, 72–73
during college years, 47–49, 133
racial disparities in, 18, 73
entry-level positions, 72
Equality of Opportunity Project, 62
expected family contribution (EFC), 40–41, 45, 134
extended families, 37

FAFSA. See Free Application for Federal Student Aid (FAFSA)
familial wealth, 110–111
family contributions
toward college costs, 45, 49
toward loan repayment, 73–74

family dynamics, 93
family formation, 95–98
family incomes, 7–8
family members
  financial hardships for, 49–52
  financial support for, 72, 74, 75, 83, 93–94, 109–110
federal loans, 52, 69, 77, 78–83
fees, 26
financial aid, 7, 16–17, 20
  bait and switch tactics in, 46–47
  from colleges, 38, 41, 58, 60–64, 102
  errors in, 47
  failure of, 40–44
  fixing, 133–134
  for graduate school, 102–103
  loans as, 30–31
  middle-income squeeze and, 36
  navigating system of, 42–44, 63–65, 133
  need-based, 36, 41, 42, 58, 144
  parental wealth and, 35–36
  unmet need and, 41
financial anxiety, 65, 76, 85–86, 88–91, 126
financial assets, 119
financial assistance, toward loan repayment, 73–74
financial decision-making, 5–6, 22, 24
financial emergencies, 75
financial help, from extended family, 37
financial literacy, 74, 85, 87, 125
financial security, 33, 73, 91–92, 103, 110, 115, 118
financial strain, from student loans, 74–75
financial stress, 85–86, 88–91
first-generation students, 9, 14, 15, 20, 29
  family responsibilities of, 83
  financial resources for, 63–64
  working during college by, 48
fiscal irresponsibility, 5–6, 13, 22, 24
Fishman, Rachel, 39
flagship universities, 8
Florida A&M University, 144
Floyd, George, 140, 143
forbearance. See loan forbearance
for-profit colleges, 21, 22, 58–60, 126, 138, 155
four-year college graduates. See college graduates
Foxx, Virginia, 5, 6, 125
Free Application for Federal Student Aid (FAFSA), 30, 35–36, 40–42, 44, 133, 134
free college, 136–138, 141
Freedmen's Bureau, 123
Friedline, Terri, 41

Gee, Gilbert, 89
gender disparity, 120–121
generational inequalities, 9, 11, 14, 115–116
Georgia State University, 62, 135
Goldberg, Michelle, 14
Goldrick-Rab, Sara, 41, 134, 136, 155
Goldstein, Adam, 129
"good debt," 24
grace period, 69
graduate school, 101–106, 128
grandparents, financial help by, 37
grants, 30, 40, 43, 61
Great Recession, 11, 111, 119
Grodsky, Eric, 105
Gross, Jacob, 25

Halpin, Tiela, 1
Hamilton, Darrick, 12, 128, 138, 139
Hamilton, Laura, 129, 134
Harshbarger, David, 111
HBCUs. See Historically Black Colleges and Universities (HBCUs)
higher education
  appropriations for, 6, 7, 20–21, 136–137, 144
  Black women in, 120–121
  failures of, 124–125
  funding cuts for, 21, 46, 58–60, 134–135
  importance of, 17–19
  landscape of, 8
  paying for, 29–32, 36–40
  reinvesting in public, 134–135, 138
  rising cost of, 6–7, 29, 45, 47, 58, 133–134
  upward mobility and, 11, 12, 18, 19, 107–108, 117–122, 124, 141
high-interest loans, 114–115
Hiltonsmith, Robert, 113

Historically Black Colleges and Universities (HBCUs), 54, 59, 134–135, 144
Hodson, Randy, 56
home equity, 35, 111, 119
homeownership, 35, 107, 109–112, 117, 123
Hope Center, 140
hopelessness, 88–91
household income, 35–36
housing market discrimination, 111

illness, 114
Income-Based Repayment (IBR), 78
Income Contingent Repayment (ICR), 78–79
income-driven repayment (IDR), 11, 24–25, 53, 78–83, 130–132, 145
information asymmetries, 76–77
interest
  accrued, 68, 70, 71, 77, 82, 144
  on loans, 26, 67
interest rates
  credit score and, 113
  on private loans, 52, 53, 54, 78
  on unsecured debt, 114–115
intergenerational inequalities, 9, 11, 14, 115–116
intergenerational wealth, 30, 117–122
internships, 48, 98–99

Jack, Anthony, 63
Jackson, Brandon, 21, 46, 63
Jim Crow policies, 117, 154
job discrimination, 73
job loss, 114
jobs
  See also careers
  during college years, 47–49, 133
  dead-end, 98, 99, 101
  entry-level, 72
  loan forgiveness and, 99
  part-time, 48–49
  working multiple, 98
job searches, 92

Kalda, Ankit, 126
Kelchen, Robert, 104
Kelley, Liz, 1
Kemp, Brian, 13, 14, 15, 125
Kreisman, Daniel, 131

labor market, 9, 72–73
  college degree and, 119
  entering, 91–92
  racial disparities in, 18
Latinx borrowers, 3, 154
Lee, Sheila Jackson, 140
Lee, Vivien, 39
Lewis, John, 140
Li, Jing, 21, 26–27
lifetime earnings, 119
limitations of study, 154–155
living expenses, 136
loan balances, 68
loan consolidation, 82
loan defaults, 2, 24–25, 74–78
  by Black borrowers, 67–68, 72
  by college graduates, 9
  impact on credit history, 113–114
  increase in, 4–5
  racial disparities in, 2, 25–26
  rates of, 25
  standard repayment plan and, 81
  by white borrowers, 2, 4, 25
loan deferment, 16, 67, 71, 77, 78
loan forbearance, 67, 68, 77, 143–144
loan forgiveness. See debt forgiveness
loan payments, 3, 24, 26, 72, 75–78, 81–82, 90, 109, 113
loan repayment. See debt repayment
loans. See student loans
loan servicers, 68, 69, 71, 72, 74, 75–78, 80, 82, 89, 150
Looney, Adam, 39
lower middle class, 33
low-income students, 137
  dropout rates for, 56
  working during college by, 48

majors, choice of, 100
Marable, Manning, 138
market-based economies, 91
marriage, 95–98
married households, 73
Martin, Elizabeth, 74

master's degree programs, 101–103, 105
McCabe, Janice, 46, 63
McCloud, Laura, 56
media coverage, of student debt, 1–2, 6
Mellon Mays Program, 62
mental strain, of debt, 68–69, 88–91
merit aid, 38, 41
Messner, Hayley, 85
Meyers, Jodi, 1
Michigan One University campaign, 135
middle class, 11, 33–36
  See also Black middle class
  higher education and attainment of, 117–122, 124
  home ownership and, 110–111
  wealth-based measures of, 119–121
midstream solutions, 132–138
Mills, C. Wright, 6
minimum wage, 7
minority-serving institutions (MSIs), 8, 134, 144
mortgage debt, 4
mortgage qualification, 110, 113

National Collegiate, 126
National Consumer Law Center, 140
National Longitudinal Study of Youth, 1997 Cohort (NLSY97), 22, 147–148
Native American borrowers, 154
Navient, 76
need-based aid, 41, 42, 58, 144
need-blind admissions, 60
negative amortization, 71, 82
net worth, 108, 109, 117, 118
New Deal, 123
nonpayment, 74–78
nontraditional students, 155

One University campaign, 135
opportunity costs, 43, 108–109

parental debt, 38–40, 128, 155
parental home, returning to, 92–95
parental wealth, student debt and, 34–36
Parent Loan for Undergraduate Student (PLUS) loans, 16, 38–40, 128, 155
parents
  college-educated, 31
  cultural capital of, 63
  job loss by, 49
  loans by, 36–37
  wealth and income of, 9, 11, 34–36
part-time jobs, 48–49
passion principle, 99
Pay As You Earn (PAYE), 79
payment plans, 69, 71, 72, 131
  See also income-driven repayment
Pell Grants, 30, 40, 61, 133–134
Perry, Andre, 111
personal relationships, 95–98
personal responsibility, 64, 85, 86–88
PLUS loans. See Parent Loan for Undergraduate Student (PLUS) loans
police violence, 140, 143
Popp Berman, Elizabeth, 96–97
postinterview surveys, 150–153
practical majors, 100
predatory inclusion, 21, 28, 54
predatory institutions, 9, 22, 58–60
Pressley, Ayanna, 68
private colleges, 7, 8, 16, 135
private loans, 46, 52–54
  accrued interest on, 67, 68, 144
  forbearance of, 144
  forgiveness of, 128
  interest rates on, 78
  lack of protections in, 78
professionals, student debt of, 1–2, 14
property values, 111
psychological anguish, 88–91
Public Service Loan Forgiveness (PSLF), 82, 126, 127, 145
public universities
  cost increases at, 6–7
  defunding of, 58–60
pull factors, in returning home, 93–94
push factors, in returning home, 92–94
Pyne, James, 105

Quadlin, Natasha, 48, 100
qualitative data, 148–154
quantitative data, 147–148, 153

race, student debt and, 2–4, 9–12
racial discrimination. See discrimination
racial disparities, 7, 10, 13–14
cultural justifications for, 15
in debt accumulation, 2–4, 9–12, 19–24, 27, 31, 60, 68, 104, 125
in debt at graduation, 26–27
in debt post-graduation, 26–27
in debt repayment, 24–28, 80
in default rates, 25–26
in graduate school debt, 104
in labor market, 18, 73
reproduction of, 125
structural conditions for, 15
racialization
definition of, 14
of higher education defunding, 58–60
of student debt, 13–28, 89, 94–95, 108, 109, 117, 121–122, 124
racial justice, 140
racial segregation, 117
racial wealth gap, 7–8, 10–12, 14, 27–36, 59, 104, 108–109, 115–119, 129, 138–141
racism
in post-civil rights era, 15
structural, 20–21
systemic, 3, 10, 115–116, 123, 125, 138–141, 154
racist stereotypes, 21
Reagan, Ronald, 21
redlining practices, 115–116, 123
regional public colleges, 134, 135
regret, 86–88, 110
relational work, 96–97
rent, 15, 24, 37, 47, 51, 52, 69, 70, 75–76, 80–81, 91, 93, 114–115
reparations for slavery, 138, 139–140
repayment. See debt repayment
repayment crisis, 2–3
residential independence, 92–95
residential segregation, 54, 111
retirement savings, 39–40, 112–113
Revised Pay As Your Earn (REPAYE), 79
Reynolds, John, 21
Robinson, Larry, 144
Rothwell, Jonathan, 111
Rudel, Daniel, 48

Sallie Mae, 53, 76, 77–78
Sanders, Bernie, 126, 136
savings, 107
emergency, 114
for future, 108–109, 112
retirement, 112–113
scholarships, 36, 38, 41, 45, 47, 57, 61, 102, 137
Scott-Clayton, Judith, 2, 4, 21, 25, 26–27
Seamster, Louise, 15, 21, 54, 129
segregation, 54, 111, 117
self-blame, 86–88
self-worth, 86
shame, 86
Shapiro, Thomas, 129
six-figure debts, 104
slavery, 115, 123, 154
slavery reparations, 138, 139–140
sleep problems, 89
Smith, Robert F., 123–124, 144
social capital, 36, 37, 63
social class, 9
social inequality, 8–9
social mobility, 11, 12, 18, 19, 62, 107–108, 117–122, 124, 141
socioeconomic background, of Black students, 31
Spizzirri, Amanda, 1
Standard Repayment Plan, 69, 71, 72, 81, 131
state appropriations, 134–135, 137
Steinbaum, Marshall, 82
sticker shock, 70–71
stigma
of debtors, 6
of student debt, 97
Stivers, Abby, 96–97
stress, from student debt, 65, 68–69, 76, 88–91
structural racism, 20–21
Student Aid Index, 134
student body, diversity of, 46
Student Borrower Protection Center, 140

student debt
  See also debt accumulation; debt repayment; student loans
  aggregate outstanding, 4, 5
  anxiety about, 65, 76, 88–91, 126
  asset accumulation and, 112–115
  average amount of, 1
  Black middle class and, 107–122
  burden of, 25–26
  career plans and, 98–101
  consequences of failing to pay, 68–69
  on credit cards, 53
  as crisis, 2–3
  default rates on, 4, 9–10
  family formation and, 95–98
  forgiveness of, 53, 81–82, 99, 123–124, 126–130, 141, 145
  from graduate school, 101–106, 128
  media coverage of, 1–2, 6
  mental strain of, 68–69, 88–91
  misrepresentation of, 1–2
  parental wealth and, 34–36
  racial disparities in, 2–4, 9–12, 14, 19–24, 26–27, 31, 60, 68, 104, 125
  racialization of, 13–28, 89, 94–95, 108, 109, 117, 121–122, 124
  racial wealth gap and, 115–117
  returning to parental home and, 92–95
  roots of rising, 4–12
  six-figure, 104
  stigma of, 87, 97
  student employment and, 48
  toll of, on college persistence, 54–58
student debt crisis, 1, 3, 10–11, 28, 39, 121, 123
  for Black students, 124–125
  downstream solutions to, 125, 126–132, 144
  loan forgiveness and, 123–124
  midstream solutions f or, 132–138
  upstream solutions to, 125, 138–141
student employment, 47–49
student loan crisis, 82
student loans
  See also student debt
  accrued interest on, 68, 70, 71, 77, 82, 144
  average amount of, 69–70
  combinations of, 72
  complex system of, 71–72, 76–77, 79–80
  defaulting on, 2, 4–5, 9, 24–26, 67–68, 72, 74–78, 113–114
  discharge of, in bankruptcy, 90
  federal, 52, 69, 77, 78–83
  as financial aid, 16–17, 30–31
  lack of transparency about, 71
  limits on, 47, 52
  private, 46, 52–54, 67, 68, 78, 128, 144
  subsidized, 72
  unsubsidized, 72
student protests, 21
students of color, 8
  See also Black students
  financial supports for, 62
subprime borrowers, 54
subsidized loans, 72
Sullivan, Laura, 129
systemic racism, 3, 10, 115–116, 123, 125, 138–141, 154

tax breaks, 134
tax burden, of loan forgiveness, 130, 145
Taylor, Astra, 138
Taylor, Breonna, 140, 143
time pressure, 97–98
transfer credits, 57
transition to adulthood, 91–92, 108
transparency, lack of, 71
Trump, Donald, 15
tuition, increases in, 6, 45, 47
tuition-based system, 21
two-year college graduates, loan defaults by, 9
two-year institutions, 54, 155
  free access to, 136
  funding cuts for, 58–59
  rising cost of, 7
Type 2 errors, 128
Type I errors, 128

Umberson, Debra, 50
underemployment, 68, 73
underfunded institutions, 8, 9, 22, 27, 59, 60, 133, 135, 144
undergraduates, racial diversity of, 46

unemployment, 68, 73
unemployment rates, 9
universities. See colleges and universities
University of California system, 21
unsubsidized loans, 72
Upstart, 54
upstream policies, 125, 138–141
upward mobility, 11, 12, 18, 19, 62, 107–108, 117–122, 124, 141

Vietnam War protests, 21

wages, 9, 105, 119
Walsemann, Katrina, 89
Warner, Cody, 94
Warren, Elizabeth, 126, 127, 129
wealth accumulation, 108–109, 113, 121
wealth inequalities, 7–8, 10, 11
  intergenerational, 14, 115–116
  racial, 7–8, 11–12, 14, 27–36, 59, 104, 108–109, 115–119, 129, 138–141
  student debt and, 115–117
Wells Fargo, 54
white borrowers, 3
  debt repayment by, 27, 85
  default rates of, 25
white college graduates
  debt repayment by, 27
  in labor market, 73
  loan defaults by, 2, 4, 25
  in middle class, 120
white families
  college contributions by, 34
  home equity of, 35
  median net wealth of, 33, 34, 118–119
  wealth gap and, 8
white students, 9
  debt accumulation by, 20, 22
  merit aid for, 38, 41
white young adults
  home ownership and, 110–111
  residential independence of, 94–95
work-life balance, 90, 98
work-study, 48

Xiang, Xiaoling, 109

Yao, Vincent, 126
young adults, 91–95, 110–111
  See also Black college graduates
Yu, Persis, 128

Zewde, Naomi, 139
Zhan, Min, 109
Zola, Irving, 125